STUDIES IN
ACCOUNTING HISTORY

STUDIES IN ACCOUNTING HISTORY

TRADITION AND INNOVATION FOR THE TWENTY-FIRST CENTURY

Edited by Atsuo Tsuji and Paul Garner

Published under the Auspices of the Accounting History Association of Japan
Contributions in Economics and Economic History, Number 163

GREENWOOD PRESS
Westport, Connecticut • London

657.09
S933

Library of Congress Cataloging-in-Publication Data

Studies in accounting history : tradition and innovation for the
   twenty-first century / edited by Atsuo Tsuji and Paul Garner.
       p.   cm.—(Contributions in economics and economic history,
   ISSN 0084–9235 ; no. 163)
      Includes index.
      ISBN 0–313–29489–5 (alk. paper)
      1. Accounting—History—20th century.   I. Tsuji, Atsuo.
   II. Garner, Paul.   III. Series.
   HF5611.S78   1995
   657'.09—dc20   94–47429

British Library Cataloguing in Publication Data is available.

Library of Congress Catalog Card Number: 94–47429
ISBN: 0–313–29489–5
ISSN: 0084–9235

First published in 1995

Greenwood Press, 88 Post Road West, Westport, CT 06881
An imprint of Greenwood Publishing Group, Inc.

Printed in the United States of America

The paper used in this book complies with the
Permanent Paper Standard issued by the National
Information Standards Organization (Z39.48–1984).

10 9 8 7 6 5 4 3 2 1

Contents

Preface

Atsuo Tsuji

It is a great honor to publish here the selected papers contributed to the Sixth World Congress of Accounting Historians, which was held at Kyoto, Japan, in 1992. Approximately fifty colleagues, including keynote speakers, applied for presentation. Applicants' countries amounted to fifteen, including Europe, East Europe, North America, and Asian Pacific countries. Intending to publish the book as a record of the Congress, I, as the convenor of that Congress, have undertaken to compile these fifty articles in cooperation with Professor Paul Garner.

The job of selecting the papers, reduced to thirteen pieces, was particularly hard, and it brought us many difficulties, because all works presented, including the keynote speech, were of an unprecedented high quality. Considering both regional factors and treated themes, we have selected the thirteen papers contained in this book. We regret to say that we were not able to include many other excellent gems.

On the title of this book, I have talked the matter over with Professor Garner, and consequently the title, *Studies in Accounting History: Tradition and Innovation for the Twenty-first Century*, has been adopted. Frankly speaking, this title was the main theme of the Kyoto Congress. Citing from my convenor's message to colleagues that was presented to the Congress, I would like to comment on some implications.

The world situation has changed enormously since our last Congress was held in Sydney 1988. Such changes have occurred not only in political and socioeconomic but also academic fields, seeking for reformation or reorganization of a ''new order'' from a global view point.

In accounting fields, including accounting history, such movements are not yet clear. One notable tendency, however, is that some of our colleagues are trying to enlarge accounting fields as part of our social environment.

In relation to these so-called ''new waves,'' the reinvestigation and reexamination of the significance of historical analysis or accounting history will be an unavoidable theme for us. I recall an excellent maxim advocated by the prominent Chinese philosopher Confucius, who lived before Christ, ''Examine old things carefully and comprehend new things progressively!'' (which is found in the *Analects of Confucius*). The theme of the Sixth Congress, ''Tradition and Innovation,'' originates in this aphorism, and we hope the Congress will be able to effectively attain the theme.

We also have cause to be grateful for the warm support, both emotionally and physically, received from so many people. We are all indebted not only to the members of the Accounting History Association of Japan, but also the Science Council of Japan, the Japan Accounting Association, and the Japan Institute of Certified Public Accountants. These last three organizations kindly accepted our request to be co-sponsors of the Congress. Furthermore, we would like to express gratitude to the leading auditing corporations in Japan for their donations.

In addition, thanks are due to the colleagues and acquaintances who understand the purpose of this meeting and consequently made generous personal donations. Particular thanks are due to Professors Yoshihiro Hirabayashi and Hiroshi Okano, Graduate School of Business, Osaka City University, and all the members of the Preparatory Committee for their tireless dedication in the preparation for the Congress. Without the ardent support of these people we would not have been able to convene the Congress, let alone achieve fruitful results.

Preface

Paul Garner

I am grateful to Professor Emeritus Atsuo Tsuji of Osaka City University for his proposal that I join with him as co-editor of this timely and much needed new volume, *Studies in Accounting History*, based on selected papers from the Sixth World Congress of Accounting Historians, conducted with great dedication and skill by the hosts in Kyoto in August 1992. We are also grateful to the Greenwood Publishing Group, Inc., and the Yushodo Shoken Company for their agreeing to publish the book and market it widely throughout the English speaking world.

After it was decided in 1989 to hold the Sixth Congress in Japan, the Planning Committee from Osaka City University immediately began to work to organize an exceptionally fine endeavor in their neighboring city which is so famous, Kyoto. This Committee, consisting of Professor Tsuji, Professor Hirabayashi, Professor Okano, and assisted by Professor Emeritus Shirai, began its efforts some three years before the actual event. During those years, and in connection with other occasions for visiting Japan, I met annually with the Committee three times for the purpose of assisting in any way desired the arrangements and speakers for the August 1992 event. During those days in Osaka I was impressed with the dedication and attention and skill of the Planning Committee. Nothing was left undone in making the proposed congress an event that would live long in the memories of the participants, and also contribute to the coverage of accounting history topics which had not been previously researched in depth by other authorities.

As early as 1924, the importance of studying the historical aspects of accountancy was emphasized by the late Professor Henry R. Hatfield in a classic article in *The Journal of Accountancy* (April, 1924) in which he points out that accountancy has a respectable intellectual history dating from 1494 when Friar Luca Pacioli published the first printed textbook on the subject. This author, a friend of Leonardo de Vinci, wrote other books on mathematics, and his 1494 volume on accounting soon had impact on all the countries of Europe.

When the several hundred delegates from many countries assembled in Kyoto at the famed Mikado Conference Hotel, they were pleasantly surprised to find in the registration material three sizable printed volumes of all of the papers to be presented by the numerous authors who had been invited to present their research findings to the assembled audiences.

Since I have had the privilege, for which I am most grateful, of being involved in accounting history matters for almost seven decades, I can reflect on the topics treated by the authors of these papers. They show an unusually wide range of research and investigation, far beyond any of the five preceding World Congresses, even though the other World Congresses presented many excellent results of scholarly research.

These papers herein deal with developments in the long history of accountancy in three continents, and with a unique large range of sub-areas of this development. Most of the papers reflect research on aspects of accounting in past centuries which are new discoveries, so to speak, and concerning which little printed material had previously been written.

The co-editors selected a large majority of the Congress papers for inclusion in this volume, but regretfully the limited size of this volume in pages precluded the inclusion of all of the papers. However, the co-editors have the original volumes presented at the registration and will furnish copies of the few remaining papers to any scholar who wishes to have a presentation.

In my opinion, this selection of items treated by the various authors at the Sixth World Congress is indicative of the growth of accounting history research and publication in the several countries represented by the authors. This growth has been most heartwarming to myself and many other observers in the past half century. When accounting history topics began to be almost universal in their exploration, very few individuals would have predicted the successes that are now attained in the many countries of the world. The inauguration of the Academy of Accounting Historians more than twenty years ago, now consisting of hundreds of members in many countries, and the successes of regional and countrywide history organizations, such as Japan, Great Britain, and elsewhere, have combined to give emphasis to the importance of accounting history in society at large. A modest number of universities and colleges now have courses in their curricula dealing with accounting history and in addition accounting history is brought into more traditional accounting courses on an annual basis to the point that tens of thousands of younger students are exposed to accounting traditions during their formal study years. There are also now available for scholarly historical research output several journals of quality which are more and more being referred to in accounting and management literature.

While accounting history has a long and meritorious development with many classic books and articles to its credit, the amount of literature now available in these closing days of the 20th century should have many gaps closed in the 21st century.

In summary, the current status of accounting history is still full of challenge of additional attention by both seasoned and beginning scholars in the many countries of the world. There is no reason why the discipline cannot be further enlarged in the next century, since accounting history research and reporting in articles and books have no limit.

In conclusion, as one of the co-editors of this volume, I would like to express my thanks again to the hosts, the planning group, and the authors of papers of the Sixth World Congress in Kyoto for the success of their endeavor, and also the hope that the publication of this volume will be useful as well as an instrument to further promote accounting history attention in all of its aspects in the decades ahead.

1

Accounting History and Public Policy

Gary John Previts

HISTORY AND POLICY

When I first corresponded with Professors Hirabayashi and Okano about the title of this paper, I proposed to address the subject entitled ''Accounting History: A Lens for the Study of Public Policy and Capital Markets in the United States.'' The topic remains appropriate, but for convenience I will employ a shorter title, ''Accounting History and Public Policy.'' By this I mean principally, of course, the public policy that relates to financial accounting, reporting, and disclosure involving the accounting profession and the CPA professional. It will be necessary, at times, to mention also that tax policy has been a factor in the development of accountancy, but that study and other related investigations, such as case law and public policy, is best left to other scholars and historians.

World events in recent years have placed before us as historians a series of analytical challenges to study and to better understand the place that our discipline has within the cascade of events that have tumbled human institutions and governments in rapid succession, for if historians are ''prophets who look to the past,'' we have much to foretell.

At our last Congress in Sydney, we heard plenary historical papers from Professors Johnson of the United States, Someya of Japan, Jaruga of Poland, Daoyang of China, and Chambers of Australia. The variety of the authorship and themes was an example of the global attention being given to our discipline and its emerging role as a factor in the global system of enterprise. Today I rise to address you on the subject of accounting history and public policy. As an accountant trained in economic history, and one self-trained in the history of accounting thought and institutions, I acknowledge that my interpretations may not be in full accord with those of the community of scholars who are political scientists. Indeed, their views are sought and welcomed. But I do not intend to make a virtue of my impotence in their field or depreciate the value to be derived from whatever benefit may reside in my remarks. I accept that all historians must declare that their history is interpretation and limited, as is all interpretation.

Ranke's declaration in 1824 that the function of history was not to judge but "merely to show what actually occurred" fails to impress me (Ratner: 1950, 135). Rather, to me, "The essential idea is that each culture and period needs to be studied both in terms of the particular qualities, elements and patterns that characterize it at any given time of observation, and in terms of the processes whereby they came into being, and continue to function or operate." This view of the function of historical interpretation would begin to satisfy Dewey; I believe it will more than challenge us for the time being and to come (Ratner: 1950, 143).

But enough of my "apology." All of my work is a product of my limitations, which are several. I take comfort therefore in an historian's creed, attributed by Professor Schlesinger to the great Dutch historian Peter Geyl, which is: "History is indeed an argument without end" (*Wall Street Journal:* May 11, 1988, 18).

So let us debate "How do we best develop and use the lessons of accounting history to assist in the development of public policy?"

A PERSPECTIVE ON TODAY'S HISTORICAL AGENDA

For Francis Fukuyama, however, there may be no value in such a debate. In his view we have reached the "End of History" (*Chronicle of Higher Education:* October 25, 1989, A48). The finale of Soviet communism and the seemingly relentless movement toward an ultimate form of social democratic government with market economic mechanisms, he argues, has ended the march of history with a final pattern of sovereignty, the liberal democracy.

For others, also historians, including my friend Professor Roberts, there is a view that historical perspective, in a detached noncurrent sense, may also be a proposition of the past. He articulates a view that change is so rapid and knowledge is changing so swiftly as to make it inconceivable to consider the "past" as a separate state of study, that there is only the "changing present." This is a curiously attractive notion, what I would call "proactive history," and it deserves more attention and should be developed in more detail. It does support a need to redefine the meaning of history toward a state in which it is used purposefully as an instrument of contemporary relevance, a necessary vehicle for efficient human development.

As a pragmatist I cannot share Fukuyama's conclusion about the end of history. The limits of history suggested by Professor Roberts evoke another series of thoughts but are not the focus of my remarks, at least in this address.

Yet of course, I am concerned about the world of today. This world does have many similarities, but differences, important ones as to the balance or mix of the economies of our world, exist too. There are, for example, at least four major types of economic systems that operate today. These systems represent (1) those free market trading societies found in principal English-speaking countries; (2) the mixed economies of major European countries in which government-directed enterprises coexist with privately owned enterprises with varying degrees of labor representation; (3) the state-supported market economies wherein families of corporations act in effective cooperation, as in Japan; and (4) those economies, including China, that retain a system of enterprise organization typical of centrally planned economies that have folded under the mandate of communism.

In today's post–Cold War era, new forms of global economic trading alliances must be crafted to permit such systems to adapt to serve the needs of their peoples and to respect their strengths and differences and to contribute to the overall prosperity of a world whose population wishes to retain some form of its national identity while seeking to improve its well-being. No one model of the four mentioned is likely to convert the others to its complete image and likeness, and yet we will, if only because of the principles of economic comparative advantages, be compelled to compete with one another while we must also trade with one another.

If successful resolution of differences over trade and investment are to be based on understanding, particularly among nations with different forms of market-based systems, accounting historians must contribute to the knowledge of how and why public policy differences exist in these economies. This can be done by studying the evolution of the public policy that relates accounting standards to corporate operations, investing and reporting.

What can the accounting historian do to aid this quest? In response, I would advise that we be concerned about the clarity, if not the relevance, of our observations, and I would paraphrase Fitzgerald, who observed: "[T]he world we will have tomorrow is not likely to come about purely by chance . . . history suggests that the circumstances of the present are the result of the events of the past. . . . That is to say, today's destinations are the result of yesterday's directions" (*Braniff Magazine:* July 1989, 17). What are these directions? In Western Europe, in the wake of the decline of Soviet communism, popular newspapers register indecision and disorientation as to whether a public policy is "left" or "right" in charting a new system. In New York City the Mayor appears on the floor of the New York Stock Exchange (NYSE) to commence celebrations marking the NYSE's 200th year—dating back to the meeting under the buttonwood tree in lower Manhattan. In Asia the 1992 opening of Seoul's stock exchange to foreign investors found Japan, Britain and the United States present to participate significantly during this debut (*Wall Street Journal*: January 6, 1992, C16).

In more than thirty locations in developing nations in East Asia, Latin America, and elsewhere in the world, stock markets operate with a capitalization of more than $500 billion (*Wall Street Journal*: November 7, 1991, A16).

U.S. investment abroad in plants, ventures, and acquisitions, according to reports by the Conference Board, reached new levels by 1991. At the end of 1989, U.S. direct foreign investment at current value was estimated to be more than $800 billion (*Deloitte & Touche Review:* September 23, 1991, 4–5).

Most especially since the 1960s, U.S. corporations also have been acquired by investors from every major capital market country and by acquiring operations in other world markets as well (Chandler: 1990, 621–28). The purpose of this review is to establish the global interdependence of capital market systems and further the theory that we must be prepared to think continually in such interdependent global terms. To many this should come as no surprise. To others the notion of acknowledging ''interdependence'' is troublesome, threatening the ideas of national sovereignty and cultural heritage. So there is danger in dismissing such a premise as ''trivial''—for such visions when taken as obvious are easily overlooked.

As for accounting historians, much remains to be done before we can contribute an understanding of our separate national accounting histories into a more comprehensive portrayal. This broader expression must be forthcoming and can provide a ''proactive'' prologue to assist in forming an agenda for developing a global public policy premise as to the role of accountancy and financial reporting.

This post-Cold War age in which we enter will be a swifter age, an age of TRANSFORMATION, not merely of change. America was transformed from a solely rural agricultural society into one dominated by industrial urban activity, with enormous attendant social changes. It is now changing from a society dominated by national industrial urban work and education habits into one that must be less parochial and more global. It is the age of a GLOBAL INVESTMENT society in which mass production, mass consumption, mass investment, mass technology, and mass communication technologies have been leveraged even further into instantaneous capabilities that overcome time and space in ways never before experienced in human history. Accounting historians who do not carefully consider a vision of such proportion may well contribute to the body of historical data, but when they interpret their details, the results will be lacking.

THE UNITED STATES AND ITS HISTORICAL CONTEXT

American investment brings with it expectations and experiences, biases and value systems that reflect the centuries-long operations of American businesses under a system of government and property rights that are peculiar or distinctive, just as the heritage of other capital market economies is unique. While it may be true that, more than ever before, U.S. investors and managers are sensitive to the cultural differences among neighbor markets, the habits of operation that have developed are those of domestic experience and will manifest themselves, just as those habits that are entirely Japanese will also be manifested in operations by companies such as Honda in locations such as Marysville, Ohio—near my own residence.

In the complex fabric of these cross-cultural exchanges of investment, the historian in general and the accounting historian in particular can contribute to increased understanding by revealing histories relevant to the development of accounting thought and practice.

In particular, from the most enhanced perspective, accounting historians can and must attempt to consider the cultural significance of accounts in their society over periods of time, over eras of economic change. This essay is an attempt to do that to provide an historical explanation of the significance of accounting in the United States so that other accountants and historians may consider it and hopefully will undertake competing explanations or related efforts over time.

Accounting historians, including Zeff (1984) and more recently Miranti (1990), have addressed facets of historical issues that have affected public policy in the United States. But a general outline of such matters has been lacking. This paper serves to begin such an outline of events with 1791, the period of the U.S. Constitution, through the market collapse of 1987. Such a history divides itself into several parts. I have noted two principal eras. The first is that of laissez-faire capitalism from the mercantile capitalism identified with the time of the Constitution and Bill of Rights through the origins of the industrial corporate progressive period of regulation.

The second part is that popularly identified by Chandler (1977) as managerial capitalism, which includes those public policies of socialization of credit, such as deposit insurance and securities regulation. Most recently, capitalism has come into another form of managerial influence relating to the management of investment fund portfolios, most importantly those of pension funds.

Each of these periods is viewed in anticipation of global markets and a variety of forms of capitalism emerging in major industrial free-enterprise economies. The historical explication of this outline is dynamic and will absorb the contributions of any who might be enticed to follow its call.

THE POLITICAL BASIS OF THE AMERICAN REPUBLIC[1]

Peter Drucker points out that "in 1700, one of the founding fathers of modern political thought, the Englishman James Harrington, explained in his *Oceana* that the 'Glorious Revolution' of 1688 in England was inevitable because economic power, which had moved into the hands of the landed gentry, was no longer in alignment with political power, which had remained in the hands of the King and of great nobles."

" 'Power,' Harrington said, paraphrasing Aristotle, 'follows property.' Political power has to be in alignment with economic power and vice versa" (Drucker: 1980, 189).

When the Boston Tea Party took place as a protest against King George and the English Parliament's Stamp Tax, at issue was a principle, that of "taxation without representation." The revolutionaries undertook a symbolic act of violence in order to provide the strongest signals about the expropriation of private property by government through taxation levies without consent of the governed.

The recognition of the high importance of ownership of private productive property as the cornerstone of colonial and mercantile capitalism underlies what would become the basis of the revolution against British mercantile policy.

Following this revolution, the founders of the United States added to the Constitution the Bill of Rights, the first ten amendments which are the fundamental guarantees which protect the rights of individuals. The original constitution itself was a political compromise among the fractious colonies and did not focus on protecting the rights of citizens, most importantly the right to protect individual property from use or appropriation without "representation."[2] The property right, therefore, as the right to representation, was also woven into the formative character of the American system. Alexander Hamilton, the principal architect of the Federalist arguments to forge a central government to direct a nation of United States, recognized fully the need for balance between wealth (economic power as represented by propertied individuals) and franchise (political power as held by the masses who could vote in greater numbers to achieve representation).

The struggle to achieve alignment between wealth, or economic power as constituted by control over property and political power, as operating in the right to be represented, was being woven into the fiber of the political character of Americans who would participate in the formation of the United States. The working out of the arrangements can be separated into three stages, each in turn undergoing phases en route to the next, as constant change in demographics, education, technology, and fundamental societal values derive the basis for amending the alignment established by Hamilton, referred to by Drucker as being between economic power (wealth/private property) and political power (franchise/representative voting).

CAPITAL MARKETS IN THE UNITED STATES

From under the buttonwood tree near Wall Street in 1792 to the unseen electronic networks of "stock around the clock" trading in 1992, the notion of the individual citizen's right to accumulate and trade private property has been the foundation of popular public capital formation. Accountancy as a discipline (and accounting as the technical practice of this discipline) exists to document, measure, and report the transactions related to the capital being traded.

The role of public policy in this system is to ensure that the "system" operates fairly in the public interest. Accounting practice and the profession of accountancy have been instruments of public policy since the passage of the first CPA law in New York in 1896. Early CPAs, beginning with Robert Montgomery, George O. May, and Arthur Carter, and continuing with those who have followed them, increasingly have advised the federal government in matters from the definition of taxable income to public policy to corporate disclosure and auditing in the wake of the stock market crash of 1929 (Previts and Merino: 1979). Today, professional organizations representing accountants such as the American Institute of CPAs, the Financial Executives Institute, and the Institute of Management Accountants testify and lobby in behalf of a wide array of issues from litigation exposure to tax and disclosure policy and internal control requirements.

To prescribe and/or evaluate the role of accountancy and the effectiveness with which accountants participate in this system of alignment requires further explication of the evolution of business entities and the manner in which they have sought capital and accounted for it in the two centuries since the first meeting under the buttonwood tree. Why is an understanding of this role of any import? If there is lack of relevant and reliable financial information and timely communication between those who own property and invest their rights in this property and those who use or control it, then the system is less able to operate.

THREE STAGES OF CAPITAL MARKETS AND ACCOUNTANCY IN THE UNITED STATES

Proprietary Enterprise: The Invisible Hand

This laissez-faire period extends from the time of the completion of the U.S. Constitution and the passage of the Bill of Rights to the origin of the period of progressive politics at the start of the 20th century. Perhaps the most enduring stereotype of American capitalism is the figure of J.P. Morgan, an individual who from his birth in 1837 to his death in 1913 bespoke the personal power of money in corporate industrial development from railroads to steel. Others might choose John Jacob Astor (1763–1848) or the Vanderbilts—Cornelius, "The Commodore" (1794–1877) or William "Billy" (1821–1885) or John D. Rockefeller (1839–1937), whose name itself became synonymous with "wealth." Astor preceded Morgan, the Vanderbilts, and Rockefeller and was more a mercantile prince than one whose fortunes were related to the industrial development of the country. But the point is that they all were contemporaries in the exploitation of laissez-faire capitalism in the United States. Their success as entrepreneurs, as individuals, was as beneficiaries of the system that survived because of the ability of individuals to succeed in their exploitation of their right to own and control private productive property. That system was put in place by Hamilton and the founding fathers and strengthened by the decisions of John Marshall's Supreme Court. Private property and the proprietor were favored as the instruments of development—and their capital would soon shift from the proprietorship and partnership form to corporate as this form of entity became socially accepted and popularly suited to the accumulation of capital during the first decades of the nineteenth century. By the 1840s financial information about New England railroad corporations, a prime example of the emerging popular engine of entrepreneurial enterprise, was to be found in business publications of the 1840s. An extract from the 1853 volume of *Hunt's Merchants' Magazine* shows a published tabulation of financial results for three dozen such railroads, as had become commonplace (see Table 1.1). Notice that the determination of net income is the prominent resulting column. This evidence strongly supports the existence at the time of a sufficiently sophisticated cadre of accountants in the employ of the investors and operators of these entities who, acting in the interest of investment return considerations, had developed a common measurement and reporting system.

By the 1880s the need for "Compulsory Book-keeping" was espoused in the pages of *The Book-Keeper,* published in New York. The notion was that there should "be enacted laws requiring all persons engaged in business or conducting commercial operations with the general public . . . to keep or cause to be kept an authentic and properly adjusted set of accounts" (November 22, 1881, 120). Speculators and the growing class of professionals who traded on Wall Street, such as Henry Clews, were aware of the potential power of such financial publicity as a means to curb abuses. But the public will and the political means were ineffectual in achieving it despite the frequent financial panics that laid low the economy in 1837 and again in 1873 and 1893.

Early, preclassical accountants would not be successful in influencing the law and public policy in this area. But their influence on public policy would result in the CPA movement, beginning with the passage of the law of 1896 in the state of New York. This signaled the initial rite of a professional movement embracing public policy (Miranti: 1990). By 1896 the industrial securities market had already survived a major re-capitalization, directed by J. P. Morgan, which occurred in the late 1880s, when railroad corporations were bankrupted or had accepted preferred stock in exchange for bonds in response to the failure of railroad companies (Navin and Sears: 1955). Proprietary entities and the early corporation were vehicles of an individual's economic power in pursuing a public policy attuned to the manifest destiny of settling an entire continent that would become a nation composed not of just thirteen states but several dozen. Permitting individuals to direct this development allowed all the self-interest forces to abuse the public interest. But the term "public interest" was not part of the political language needed to develop the vast continent of the United States.

A prominent example of the public policy of this period is found in the manner of disposition of the entire territory of the Louisiana Purchase. Acquired from Napoleon with public funds at the start of the 19th century to become public domain, this vast territory would, by the end of the next century, become predominantly private property owned by thousands of individuals and indus-

Table 1.1
Operations of the Railways of Massachusetts, 1852

COMPILED FOR THE MERCHANTS' MAGAZINE BY DAVID M. BARFOUR, ESQ., OF BOSTON FROM THE ANNUAL REPORTS TO THE LEGISLATURE.

In the following table, "Interest" and "Amount paid other Companies in tolls" for passengers and freight, are not considered as running expenses, and are therefore deducted from the total of expenses; and the "Amount paid other Companies in tolls," and the amount received for "interest" are deducted from the total receipts.

Names of railways	Length in miles: Of main roads	Of branches	Double track & sidings	Cost	Receipts: From Passengers	From freight and gravel	From mails, &c.	Total	Expenses: Of road-bed	Of motive power	Miscellaneous	Total	Net Income	Net income p.c. on cost
Worcester	45	24	59	$4,845,967	424,714	314,943	19,162	$758,819	$69,153	$71,386	$269,201	$409,740	$349,079	7.20
Western	155		62	9,953,759	615,481	685,063	39,329	1,339,873	158,988	122,598	375,092	656,678	683,195	6.86
Providence and Worcester	43		13	1,731,498	129,044	118,566	6,081	253,691	13,783	14,956	85,437	114,176	139,515	8.06
Worcester and Nashua	46		5	1,321,946	88,435	67,212	6,462	162,109	11,982	12,581	59,266	83,829	78,280	5.92
Fitchburg and Worcester	14		1	312,229	16,212	12,900	2,291	31,403	3,167	2,302	12,993	18,462	12,941	4.14
Connecticut River	50	2	8	1,801,946	124,788	93,237	10,980	229,005	25,408	22,459	95,287	143,154	85,851	4.76
Pittsfield and North Adams	19		1	443,678	17,532	21,963	900	40,395	5,028	2,277	10,782	18,087	22,308	5.03
Berkshire	21			600,000				42,000				560	41,440	7.00
Stockbridge and Pittsfield	22			448,700				31,409					31,409	7.00
West Stockbridge	3		1	41,516				1,827				22	1,805	4.35
Providence	41	12	23	3,546,204	256,423	155,029	18,032	429,484	40,280	34,717	141,862	216,859	212,625	6.00
Taunton Branch	11	1	1	307,136	46,648	27,985	1,591	76,224	9,138	9,498	33,188	51,824	24,400	7.94
New Bedford	20	1	1	520,476	73,544	31,914	2,456	107,914	13,842	10,689	39,592	64,123	43,791	8.41
Norfolk County	26		1	1,245,928	28,992	20,557	907	50,516	423	5,122	21,555	27,100	23,416	1.88
Stoughton Branch	4			93,433	6,371	5,534	115	12,020				4,102	7,918	8.46
Lowell	26		40	1,995,249	157,170	222,004	8,934	388,108	54,216	45,257	155,820	255,293	132,815	6.66
Nashua	15		17	651,215	48,901	73,201	9,768	131,870	12,912	18,747	49,373	81,032	50,838	7.81
Lawrence	12		2	346,063	28,446	8,495	4,838	41,779	3,093	2,824	12,404	18,321	23,458	6.78
Salem and Lowell	17		2	362,672	20,640	33,054		53,694	27,479	19,769		47,248	6,446	1.78
Stony Brook	13			265,813				13,536					13,536	5.09
Boston and Maine	74	9	46	4,092,927	422,868	220,595	15,538	659,001	88,208	43,960	191,138	323,306	335,695	8.20
South Reading Branch	8	1	1	236,227	15,326	7,949	7,073	30,348				22,111	8,237	3.49
Fitchburg	51	17	66	3,633,674	253,371	311,778	9,425	574,574	65,758	52,980	216,849	335,587	238,987	6.58
Vermont and Massachusetts	69	8	5	3,451,629	74,205	99,607	44,867	218,679	35,229	24,128	73,155	132,512	86,167	2.50
Harvard Branch	7			25,701				5,853				6,831		
Lexington and West Cambridge				237,328				7,480				450	7,030	2.96
Peterboro' and Shirley				263,540				16,102				2,150	13,952	5.29
Eastern	55	20	21	3,621,874	384,798	69,974	44,201	488,973	33,883	39,785	145,329	218,997	269,976	7.45
Essex	20	1	3	609,007	21,082	10,076	5,560	36,718	6,320	3,959	24,258	34,537	2,181	0.36
Newburyport	15		1	255,614	14,283	4,036		18,319	205	1,343	11,758	13,306	5,013	2.00
Old Colony	37	8	17	2,293,535	209,122	93,496	6,184	308,802	39,118	24,114	132,069	196,301	112,501	4.95
Dorchester and Milton	3			124,718				7,630				42	7,588	6.00
South Shore	11			428,831				24,680					24,680	6.00
Fall River	42	1	5	1,050,000	132,907	88,556	7,476	228,939	27,014	25,391	77,451	129,856	99,083	9.44
Cape Cod Branch	28	1	2	633,907	40,487	18,685	1,571	60,744	6,218	6,071	18,398	30,687	30,056	4.74
Grand Junction	6		3	1,282,073		3,000		3,000	857		16,270	17,127		
Total	1044	106	407	53,076,013	3,641,790	2,819,409	273,801	6,885,517	751,702	597,144	2,288,296	3,674,410	3211107	Av. 6.05

Source: Hunt's Merchants' Magazine, May 1853, p. 638. Reproduced from the original by David A. Ozog, 1993. In reproducing this table, several footing and cross-footing errors were discovered on the original. This table shows the numbers as they appeared in *Hunt's Merchants' Magazine* in May 1853.

trial, transportation, communication, and financial corporations. This political "transaction" suggested the extent to which private forces undertook development with the aid of a public policy that freely provided public domain—in the form of real estate—for transformation into private productive property, the cornerstone of the American capitalistic system.

Accounting per se during the laissez-faire era served the proprietor, especially the arch-proprietor and investor, Morgan. One of his most trusted associates was Charles H. Dabney, under whom Morgan served his apprenticeship. Chandler and Tedlow note that Dabney was "an expert accountant." Later Morgan characterized these days in a letter to his father as follows: "I am never satisfied unless I either do everything myself or personally superintend everything done even to an entry in the books" (Chandler and Tedlow: 1985, 285–86).

The era experienced many prominent accounting theorists who recognized each other's work (Previts and Sheldahl: 1988). Among the seminal contributors was Thomas Jones, who American historians acknowledge pioneered the acceptance of the distinction between nominal and real accounts and the preparation of financial statements as the "end product" of the accounting process (Chatfield: 1974). Important contributions were also made by Silas Packard, the senior author of the 1878 edition of Bryant and Stratton's Counting House Book-Keeping chapter, which is among the earliest important attempts to establish through accounting textbooks a basic understanding of the relationship between the accounting function and "Wealth and Its Measurement."[3]

The integration of the factory ledger into the financial double entry recording process is also an achievement of this time. Paul Garner (1954) has said that this feat may be equal in importance to the discovery of double entry itself. Regretfully, we do not know much more about the precise origins of this accomplishment than we know about the precise origins of double entry per se. Also in the 1880s Charles Sprague, who would later author the important book *The Philosophy of Accounts* (1907), published his initial series of papers on the "Algebra of Accounts" in *The Book-Keeper* explicating the accounting equation that would facilitate and expand the notions of "proprietary" accounting.[4]

THE IMPACT OF ACCOUNTING IN THE LAISSEZ-FAIRE ERA

The cultural significance of accounts, to adopt D.R. Scott's phrase, during this period may be said to have been limited to its utility as an entrepreneurial instrument. It was common to characterize the chief figures of the period using accounting-related terms and to distinguish events in those terms. Some examples come to mind: John D. Rockefeller, who also had an ability for accounts, was characterized by later critics as a "bloodless Baptist book-keeper," a melodic if damning expression giving testimony to his inherent character and that of the process of accounting.

When Cyrus Field (the American inventor) was attempting to secure British investors for an oceanic telegraph cable, he was challenged by skeptics who said, "Suppose you make the attempt but lose your cable on the ocean bottom? What will you do?" "Charge it to profit and loss and go to work to lay another," Field replied (Previts and Merino: 1979, 66).

The American laissez-faire era was one often characterized by the use of such bookkeeping terms. The expressions "in the red," or "in the black," were used to mean in turn, "experiencing a loss" or "something to the gain." These were popular idioms that derived from the practice of entering losses in red ink and entering profits in black ink—ink being permanent and the color rendering a signal.

An historical interpretation of the relationship of accounting and public policy during this period suggests that accounting was a functional activity directed to serve the self-interest of the proprietary business and that no public interest or professional role had been cast. Individual accountants served individuals with proprietary goals. Reports became commonplace products of the accounting process, enabling diverse individual partners beyond the daily operations of business entity itself to obtain information about the longer-term character of enterprise performance and worth. With the advent of the income tax during the Civil War in the 1860s, an opportunity for further influence over the execution of policy for funding government arose, but income taxation would not become a permanent instrument of fiscal policy until after the start of the twentieth century. The role of accounting and public policy during that era will be distinguished from this time of laissez-faire, so we will have an opportunity to consider it in the discussion of that period. Accounting was proprietary-direct because self-interest was consistent with the public policy of laissez-faire. The first stirrings of accountancy as a public interest profession, however, do appear toward the end of the laissez-faire era.

An important public policy development involving accountancy's prelude to professionalism is "the CPA Movement," which culminated in the passage of CPA laws in major states by 1910 and in most all states by the mid-1920s (Wilkinson: 1928). As a progressive political movement appears, the formation of a new accounting profession, licensed to protect the public interest, is to be a part of the economic and political balance to a "bottom line society" and the coming of age of accountancy.

Corporate Enterprise: The Visible Hand

This new era of government/market interface was predicated upon an earlier legislative event, the Sherman Act, which recognized the responsibility of the federal government to regulate interstate commerce. Trust-busting legislation such as the Clayton Act made illegal the interlocking of positions on competing corporate boards of directors. The passage of federal income tax legislation in 1913 would eventually become an important basis for professional accounting activity, although it might not have been foreseen as that from the outset. The advent of regulatory legislation, the Federal Reserve System, and the federal income tax laws provided the accounting practitioner and those who had established the CPA Movement with their economic sphere (Previts and Merino: 1979, 135–36). It remained to be seen how the public and the profession would develop in response to these new domains of activity.

Just as the railroad boom and the corporate entity marked the origins of industrial capitalism within the laissez-faire era, so the consolidation of industries and the trust movement, as typified by the formation of the United States Steel Company (USS) in 1903, signaled its drawing to a close. The formation of USS (which incidentally today operates as USS Kobe Steel) was the ultimate activity of J. P. Morgan's career as the unofficial "Central Bank" of the United States. Shortly after his death, this central banking function was restored as part of the public policy function of the federal government with the formation of the Federal Reserve System. The role of the individual as the central player in the markets for goods and investments of the economy was now subsumed into the activities of the central government and into the hands of the rising class of professional managers as explained by Chandler in his award-winning volume, *The Visible Hand.* Acknowledgement of Professor Chandler's valuable contribution to framing the study of the U.S. business experience can best be done by suggesting that any accounting historian who is not familiar with the study lacks an appreciation of an important competing explanation in a vibrant market for historical explanation. To assert and demonstrate that the rise of a professional managerial class in a corporate society represents a key to understanding the power over the process of allocating resources is an important, if not brilliant, deduction. To assert the theme that the visibility of the professional manager in the corporate business organization replaced Adam Smith's "invisible hand" of the market to distribute a society's resources is a most useful depiction for historical explanation (Chandler: 1977).

As the visible hand of professional managers swept through the corporate commonwealth, the investment community was similarly undergoing change. The individual proprietor as the principal investor was supplanted by the individual as member of the general public who became involved in investing beyond local and regional entities through the formation of national trading markets and exchanges that provided high volume and liquidity as protections and attractions. Individuals would always find a buyer (liquidity) because of the volume transacted at the exchange. With such public capital markets came new and untold risks as well: bear pooling, stock manipulations, and the operation of the "greater fool theory." One could almost always expect to find someone less well informed on whom to foist a poor investment, or so the thinking went until the market crash of 1929. As events unfolded, it became evident that buying on "tips" or "hunches" was not unlike picking a racehorse the same way. The New Deal government of Franklin Roosevelt proposed that there be legislation and public policy to protect the public interest, and with the passage of the federal Securities Laws of the 1930s, national reforms were in place.

Their passage is commonly identified as being a catalyst for the growth of the public accounting profession and in particular the auditing function. And well it may be, for the Securities Laws were clearly a major change in the social contract and a clear signal about the need to protect the public interest.

However, state legislation, the so-called "blue sky" laws, had been in place for many years. They had been ineffectual because of the ability of promoters to use interstate schemes to move beyond a single state's jurisdiction.

And lest the issue be misperceived, remember that at the turn of the century, there were fewer than 1,000 CPAs in the United States. In contrast, in 1992, AICPA membership numbered more than 300,000, an increase from 9,500 at the end of World War II. Early attempts by members of the organized profession to affect public policy and related agenda may be described as self-serving, although both had clear public service and public interest aspects. One attempt relates to the involvement of leading accountants of the time, such as Col. Robert Montgomery, in assisting in defining the legislative notion of taxable income. The other attempt involves the efforts of the partners of the firm of Price Waterhouse to assist the Federal Reserve Board in designing a set of uniform account and report forms. These were important precedents for accountants' participation in banking reforms and availed a response to the increasing socialization of credit and the as yet unforeseen regulation of the securities markets.

The young profession was shocked in 1914 when the Federal Trade Commission (FTC) Chairman, Edward Healy, proposed procedures and a fee schedule for the audits of corporations to be prescribed by the government (Previts and Merino: 1979, 148). In 1925 Alexander Banks, president of the competing national CPA association, the American Society, warned that an attempt of Professor W. Z. Ripley of Harvard to rekindle Healy's proposal for FTC audits was ill conceived. Banks argued that auditing was "a job for public accountants." Banks contended: "How to give full information to those who are entitled to it, and at the same time withhold details from those not entitled to it, is a problem which we accountants have been pondering for years" (Banks: 1925, 177–79).

Another means to assess the role of accounting activities on public policy is to consider the evolution of case law involving the accountant's duties. The development of this case law element is not undertaken here, but one may wish to consider Chapter Six in Previts and Merino (1979) and subsequent related chapter material.

The form of managerial capitalism ascribed to the economic activity preceding World War II is the one to which accountants addressed much of their theory development and reporting literature. It formed the basis for the separation of management and ownership theme of Berle and Means in the 1930s. The collapse of the stock market and the awarding of the public franchise of auditing to a divided CPA profession (the American Society was associated with "native-born" CPAs, the American Institute with those with English affiliations) was a boon that accelerated the growth of the CPA population well into the

1960s. And as the income tax process became further a part of every person's economic activity, so too did the matters of tax compliance, planning, and preparation. Both areas represent an expression of the more complete involvement of a central and regulatory form of government over the fiscal life of the economy as a response to the perceived weaknesses of the capital markets and later out of the necessity for a planned economic response to the activities of the war effort.

As to the former, the role of the profession in the regulation of the securities markets, Galambos notes that: Central to the regulatory strategy [the SEC] leaders chose was the use of the accounting profession as a neutral third party to assure the accuracy of the financial information needed from business. By using independent accountants, the SEC avoided the need for a large public bureaucracy. In trading some part of its traditional standing as the employee of business for the status of a detached third party, the accounting profession enhanced its prestige and also created new jobs for its members. The investing public was the big winner. It gained more reliable data about potential investments and could compare opportunities more accurately (Galambos and Pratt: 1988, 104).

As to the latter, by the 1950s an accord had been achieved with the legal profession to address the bar's objection that accountants had undertaken the "unauthorized practice of law" by involving themselves in tax work.

The ranks of the accounting profession mushroomed as the number of public companies under the audit requirements of the securities laws was expanded by the 1964 federal laws to include all publicly traded companies whose securities were traded in the over-the-counter markets as well as in the major exchanges.

With the financing of the postwar economy and the increased complexity of a permanently ordained federal income tax on individuals and corporations, the profession's future seemed secure in the domain of a public policy related to regulation and redistribution through taxation and socialized credit, such as deposit insurance. Since the 1970s CPAs have also been involved in legislative initiatives related to governmental operations such as the Single Audit Act of the 1980s and, more recently, the federal Chief Accountants Act, which reflects a measure of both self-interest and public interest (Previts and Brown: 1992).

In the 1970s the public accountancy profession's interest in expanding the scope of its work into the market for advisory services was challenged in the public forum on the basis of the concern over conflict of interest. A thinly veiled political attack on the profession directed for the benefit of management consulting firms who feared the threat of Big Eight competition, was published in the Congressional staff study entitled "The Accounting Establishment." Using several forays into the structure of the CPA profession and the recently initiated standard setting process as a tactic, the study exposed weaknesses in CPA structure and governance. For the first time the profession itself had to "go public" as did the companies it professed to serve. Attendant restructuring of the profession, including the formation of the division of CPA firms within the AICPA resulted, and a temporary proxy disclosure requirement relating to non-attest services offered to public company audit clients was withdrawn after a few ineffectual years. In this new period of public attention, the AICPA has worked in cooperation with other professional organizations to form study commissions, more notably the Commission on Auditors' Responsibilities (Cohen Commission) in the 1970s and the Commission on Fraudulent Financial Reporting (Treadway Commission) in the 1980s. These groups absorbed some of the political shock waves from Congressional inquiries and provided and promoted legislative and public policy recommendations to address the concerns raised. The success of these efforts has not been widely considered by historians to date.

Accounting professional organizations also became involved in the federal legislation identified as the Foreign Corrupt Practices Act (FCPA) adopted in late 1970s. The FCPA established penalties for payments made by U.S. public companies to foreign officials to influence contracts. The technical internal control provisions were influenced by extant professional accounting literature and standards, and therefore were considered by some as a testimony to the influence of the profession over the legislative process. But again, the input was not agenda setting but more self-serving and reactive to an item established by others, yet affecting the domain of accounting and reporting. Furthermore, by not including a provision in the law as to the qualifications of individuals who would establish the internal controls specified in the legislation, the profession failed to serve the public interest.[5] Subsequently, there has been some success in developing broader professional influence over such standards to ensure that they operate effectively and are undertaken and/or reviewed by competent individuals.

A more serious public policy issue related to the economic structure of the public accounting profession in recent decades has come from the Federal Trade Commission's recognition that organized professions have the ability to limit competition and entrance to the ranks of practice. The accounting profession is not the single target; medicine, law, and dentistry have also been cited. CPAs, however, seemed ill at ease in dealing with their vocation in the agenda of public policy. More recently, the FTC has reached an accord that permits the CPA to continue to enforce certain important "professional" standards, such as banning commissions and limiting contingent fees. But, again, the profession has reacted defensively to an agenda established by others and has been induced to employ "price competition" as a basis of fundamental franchise attest service, with potentially dire litigation consequences. Price competition for a professional service, which is fundamentally judgmental and qualitative and not tied to a physical commodity, strengthens the posture of the lowest bidder and encourages diminished investment in the human skills to serve such a low value line of endeavor.

For public practice units to be further placed in litigation peril as a result of a public policy of price competition for a professional judgmental service is a form of double economic jeopardy from which the public practice unit may not survive. If survival is achieved, the diminished attractiveness of the profession to those who are the best and the brightest seems clear.

The end of the decade of the 1980s found the U.S. accounting profession once again at odds with itself. Its principal professional organization, the AICPA, composed of 300,000 members, most of whom are engaged in corporate practice rather than public accounting, is seeking a new strategic direction. Small unit and major public accounting unit firms are at odds over litigation costs, regulatory costs, and the standards overload that smaller units profess occurs at the behest of protecting major firm partnership economic interests. The relevance and content of financial reports attracts criticism from most quarters, even though the participants in the process are recognized to be acting in good faith and beyond reproach.

The accounting debates that raged over proprietary and entity theory were appropriate given the shift to a corporate commonwealth and the fact that stock ownership in public corporations had become a nominal versus an operating right. Paton and Littleton's 1940 monograph became the ultimate source of guidance for the period. It stressed income determination as the golden text and acknowledged that ''interpretation'' was inherent in the intrinsic framework of accounting. This source went unchallenged as the conceptual benchmark for more than a quarter of a century and is a formidable influence today, especially for those supporting income as the principal product of the reporting process.

But the accountant's work and world began to be confronted by the phenomenon that Peter Drucker, writing in 1976, termed ''Pension Fund Socialism,'' the ability of workers to own the means of production and to control the economy by the cumulative investment power of their diversified pension portfolios. Whether or not Drucker's contention is valid is a potential argument without end. But the consequence of the rise of portfolio investment and the effect on financial accounting theory continues to challenge us today. This theory and the related premises about information tied to market efficiency, agency, and moral hazard dominated the academic accounting literature through the late 1980s.

A major public policy crisis relating to pension fund policy occurred in the 1970s and resulted in passage of what is called the ''second social security act,'' the Employee Retirement Income Security Act (ERISA). This law sought to ensure that such public company pension plans were properly funded and further ''socialized'' the process by creating the Pension Benefit Guarantee Corporation (PBGC) to underwrite shortfalls. With the surge of the stock market during the 1980s, most companies found their plans to be overfunded rather than at risk. The issue in the 1990s appears to be otherwise. The Bush Administration's 1993 budget proposals sought to change the PBGC's accounting system from accrual to cash accounting in order to reduce the budget deficit effect, anticipated to be about $8 billion. Accountants who became involved during the establishment of this policy matter were able to contribute to the technical aspects of ERISA and assist in measurement and compliance matters. In short, accountants were supportive in a technical way; they did not initiate the agenda, nor were they proactive in creating the legislative concepts in a major way. Not until the formation of the Financial Accounting Standards Board (FASB) in 1973 was a major accounting profession vehicle put in place with the capacity to influence public policy significantly and to affect the balance between economic and political power in the United States. No comprehensive analysis of the FASB's efforts within this public policy frame has yet been completed by historians. The value of such an effort is suggested by those who assert that the limitations of accounting history begin with an irrelevance induced by a technical topical focus. To evaluate the performance of the FASB as an instrument of public policy—and to some extent to trace back to the SEC's Accounting Series Release No. 4 the effects of such performance to include the Committee on Accounting Procedure and the Accounting Principles Board—is important. Both Chatov (1975) and Merino and Coe (1978) provide useful examples. And the recent critical historical literature—even if apparently skewed away from being historical work, serving more as a basis for neo-orthodoxies of political science—is becoming recognized for its contribution to this neglected area of historical endeavor, accounting history and public policy. Today, the organized accounting profession is represented by a variety of competing groups including the AICPA, the Institute of Management Accountants, the Institute of Internal Auditors, and the Financial Executives Institute. Each seeks to influence public policy, usually as it relates to its own domain of reporting and disclosure and usually to protect its own interest, true to trade association instinct and habit. Indeed, what seems to have been poorly understood in all of this, especially by CPAs, is that their charter or social contract requires them to serve the public interest. But the post-World War II generation of public accountants, trained and licensed in increasingly record numbers, were attracted to the profession because of the perceived prestige and security available to those aspiring to a professional status. The university programs that obliged this promising stream of students failed, as did the faculty for the most part, to establish a sense or culture, to instill a treatment effect beyond the technical CPA exam competence level. Particularly during the 1970s when the "teaching of values" in programs was a suspected impropriety, a burgeoning generation of CPAs was turned into practice lacking adequate exposure to the professional's compass value, a commitment to the public interest. Indeed (lest we abuse our academic selves too much) not until 1986, nearly a century after its formation, did the AICPA make explicit its own commitment to serve the public interest by means of amending its Mission Statement.[6]

THE INVESTOR FUND MARKETPLACE

It would be timid, would it not, to have laid forth so many elements about the history of accounting and the practices of the (mostly public) accounting profession and related public policy and then not to provide some assessment or interpretation? So let us attempt a perspective on (public/CPA) accountancy (a profession in the legal sense and, one might argue, since 1986 a self-admitted profession) and public policy, particularly since the latter involves financial accounting and reporting during the era of managerial capitalism. Although tax policy has become a subject of professional accounting interest, it is not the principal focus of this analysis.[7] The perspective is undertaken with an understanding that the background contains three intellectual legacies. One, the residual proprietary view, wherein Sprague's dogma, set forth in the equation and algebra of his proprietary times, established *the* transaction accounting model that carries forward to today, with all of its proprietary biases and baggage. The second legacy is grounded by the Paton and Littleton (1940) monograph, in both academe and practice. Its theory was responsive to the corporate commonwealth that the United States had become in both political and economic terms. The income determination process and the nominal individual investor were the focus of attention for its financial accounting and statement preparation efforts as consistent with the public policy of the New Deal and its progressive political traditional. With the advent of the funded pension plan, most prominently that of General Motors in the mid-1950s, and the subsequent rise of pension investment portfolios, the attention has shifted from an economy driven by the "visible hand" of the professional corporate manager to one guided as well by the visible hand of the professional portfolio/investment fund manager. Indeed, it is an economic and political system of capital directed and "controlled" by the visible hands of both communities of professional managers—corporate managers who oversee, buy, and sell a portfolio of operating companies in pursuit of long-term return, and a community of professional money managers who oversee portfolios seeking a short-term return that outperforms the market averages. In this reporting arena, accounting standards and public policy, out of habit, seem directed to address return on investment (ROI) signals and to resolve the needs of this new economy of the visible hands by tinkering with the model employed for decades to serve the needs of individual investors in a market directed by managerial capitalism of the visible hand alone (Davis: 1950).[8] A public disclosure policy designed to address only the information needs of the "nominal" individual investor under a system of managerial capitalism would seem to fall short of the needs of the individual investor-beneficiary (not an owner in an operating or controlling sense) within portfolio/investor fund capitalism. The magnitude of the investment funds' influence can be appreciated when it is understood that these funds control $2.2 trillion, according to 1990 estimates, and "represent the largest source of investment money in the U.S. . . ." (*Wall Street Journal*: March 22 1990, A16) (see Figure 1.1).

To the extent that accounting disclosure policy and public regulatory policy continue to be driven by the model of Berle and Means and managerial capitalism alone, they are ill suited to protect the public interest. Effective exercise of individual property rights suggests the information needs of the ultimate investor who retains the legal ownership of the investment property. If the information is not timely and relevant, the individual is disconnected from control

Figure 1.1
Distribution of Corporate Equity Ownership: Individuals versus Institutions

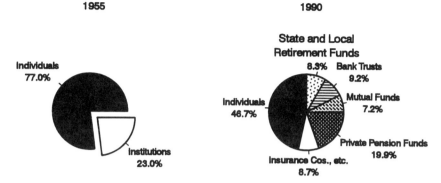

While the number of individual shareholders has shown strong growth, the share of their total equity
  ownership has fallen substantially in the last two generations. The total assets of pension plans
  has risen from $17.5 billion in 1950 to nearly $2.5 trillion in 1990.
Source: Testimony of Richard C. Breeden before Senate Banking Subcommittee 1991 as reported
  in "Trends in U.S. Capital Markets," *Deloitte & Touche Review* (November 4, 1991), pp. 4–
  5.

and is practically impotent. Being thus disengaged, the ultimate owners of pension funds cannot act in a timely or effective fashion to protect their property.
They may be unable to perceive when an investment manager is acting in their
best interests, or when they have benefited from changes in the market because
their investments are swiftly traded and widely diversified in a massive portfolio
of which their unit shares represent hyperfractional amounts (*Economist:* May
5, 1990). In fact, the argument has been made that the beneficiaries of the boom
of investment values in the 1980s were the very pension holders who decried
the waste and greed of Wall Street (Emmott: 1991).

THE OCTOBER 1987 MARKET: A PROGRAMMED
PORTFOLIO PLUNGE

At an October 1988 academic conference sponsored by Arthur Andersen &
Co., David Ruder, then Chairman of the Securities and Exchange Commission,
characterized the 1987 market plunge as a "Rush for the 'exits' by institutional
investors!" A more fitting one-line description of this incident may not be possible. It certainly places the investment fund managers at center stage in the
drama where, in fact, society should find them. Furthermore, other financial
failures of the 1980s evidence the inability of money managers, politicians, and
accountants and related public policy to demonstrate a unifying perception of
policy for the twin form of capitalism related in this address. This is apropos
given the political rhetoric of the moment that the U.S. first address investment

as a priority and restrain its consumption (Zuckerman: January 20, 1992, 68). As a result of waste, fraud, and mismanagement of investment resources, poorly conceived projects were funded and not properly controlled or evaluated, in part because of the lack of perception but also because of the unavailability of the skill and ability of many groups of stakeholders, not only investment managers. Furthermore, it can be argued that accountants were poorly trained to perform and report in this emerging economic structure because of the lack of educational preparation. Law, public policy, and regulatory administrative policy were not such as to be sensitive to measures because of the lack of proper information and reports. In other eras in the history of capital markets, a catastrophe of such proportion as that signaled by the market crash of 1987 would be overcome by the sheer ability of an economy to achieve long-term growth by enhanced productivity and by creating and satisfying new markets for goods, products, or services previously unavailable or undiscovered. Without such derived market demand to improve the quality of life and without the ability to convert rapidly and to measure the productivity of such rapid and risky shifts, global capital market systems are at risk. This peril is accented by the recent changes in Eastern Europe and the Persian Gulf, where economic power and political power are likely to change the mix of world economies in terms of military balance, energy supplies, and the production of consumer goods. Lately Professor Chandler has identified among the "recent changes in the growth, management, and financing of the modern industrial enterprise, six [which] have no precedents" (Chandler: 1990, 621). These six changes suggest the presence of a "market for corporations" that are bought and sold as unit properties, complete with operating management intact. This wholesaling of corporations as commodities betrays the global nature of competition among "nation-like" companies based in major capital market countries including the United States, Japan, Germany, and Britain. Companies now consist of countless operating corporations diversified beyond the ability of top management to oversee in any day-to-day sense. Chandler adds that the "buying and selling of corporations [is now] . . . an established business . . ." (Chandler: 1990, 624). The activity of today's portfolio-operating corporations on a global scale reinforces the need to "re-engineer" the investment-reporting process.

WORLD-CLASS REPORTING AND GLOBAL INTERDEPENDENT CAPITAL FORMATION

It may be weak tea to suggest that global reporting through a form of voluntary consensus may be the first step toward a new and anticipatory form of reporting. Yet a start has been underway since the formation of the International Accounting Standards Committee in 1976. Even though we may not yet have achieved resolution of the needs of the individual portfolio investment holder, that issue is not lost in moving also into consideration of the global issue, for the reporting constituencies are related. If global investors, also members of

Figure 1.2
Core Reporting Model

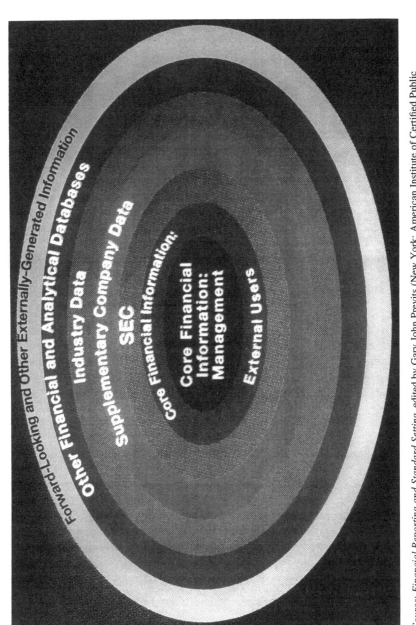

Source: Financial Reporting and Standard Setting, edited by Gary John Previts (New York: American Institute of Certified Public Accountants, Inc., © 1992), p. 63. Reprinted with permission.

investment funds, are well served, individual investors are also likely to be served by a pluralistic model of reporting as it evolves. While a picture is not always worth a thousand words, perhaps in this instance an illustration of the Core Reporting Model (see Figure 1.2) initiated in discussions at the AICPA Wharton School Conference in 1990 can be used to express this core model premise.

Each constitutent will be served by a different type of report with a core of information supplied to all (Previts: 1992, 63). Such a pluralistic approach to financial reporting would require so mu   to change that some consider the proposal unlikely. Yet at stake is the ability of the individual who underlies the investment process to relate to the structures of the globally interdependent investor-fund economy. Without such an ability and the knowledge so related, there can be no trust, no confidence, no incentive to risk and to invest, at least at the scale and with the consent considered appropriate in any society respecting self-determination by its citizenry. True enough, tax policies and other fiscal incentives in monetary policies can be set out like "bait" to attract and divert investors, but the likelihood that such investment will be longer term and founded on a commitment of understanding is hardly likely. The propensity to spend and consume may well outweigh the incentive to save and invest in such a "bait and switch" setting. The grassroots populace of industrialized and developing nations' individual investors is the ultimate capital source in a global enterprise economy. Such a process operates best when both knowledge of and trust in the system exist. Seeking a social policy that ensures an informed investing public whose members are familiar with their options and their role as beneficiaries of their investments in swiftly traded portfolios of global bonds and equities will suffice. In order to provide rapid and relevant information for such an objective, the technology of the CRT screen and the concept of the core model, as envisioned by Shaun F. O'Malley of Price Waterhouse and depicted in the Wharton papers, provide a promising potential and vision in combination. To achieve a public policy that will assist in encouraging such real-time and pluralistic disclosure may exhaust our abilities. But the cost of such an effort is not high when one considers the cost should the development of new disclosures be left to chance or, worse, should the individual investor in this new portfolio form of capitalism be neglected—for while the cost of education is high, the cost of ignorance is devastating.

CONCLUSIONS

The domain of professional accounting in the United States now extends to several aspects of public policy.[9] Although the initial CPA legislation was a franchise for attesting services, subsequent involvement activity in the practice of taxation, governmental, and nonprofit accounting and self-regulation through quality review have placed the profession in the center of public policy, not only in terms of self-interest but also because of a considered commitment to the public interest, as evidenced in the 1986 amendment to the AICPA's Mission Statement. It is to be expected that in the United States a change in the "social contract" or the charter for the accounting profession will be forthcoming in legislation expected to reflect the change in scope of service and the structure of the capital market. The existing national 'social contract,' as shaped by law, has been in place most prominently since the passage of the first securities laws in the era of the New Deal, prior to World War II. The U.S. capital market structure continues to change dramatically and as a new social contract for accountancy is shaped, a better understanding of accounting and public policy over time is needed. As mentioned, historians, including Zeff (1984), Merino and Coe (1978), and Miranti (1990), and critical academics, such as Briloff (1966), Committee (1983), and Chatov (1975), have considered U.S. public policy from historical perspectives. Yet the area has not been singled out for systematic, consistent, and comparative study by U.S. accounting historians, nor is it generally considered a topic for such inquiry (Previts, Parker, and Coffman: 1990). And lest we omit an even greater need, namely the necessity for similar efforts in all market settings, we would be remiss in our exhortation about the matter. For while studies in countries including Britain, Japan, Germany, Australia, and most major nations occur as a part of a related historical study there does not seem, as yet, to be a concerted historical effort, to foster comparative history in this public policy area (Willmott: 1991). As with most developments, such an initiative beginning even modestly is to be welcomed, and our Academy looks forward to learning more about the activities of historians so that a comprehensive bibliography may be undertaken to serve continuing efforts to study accounting history and public policy. Now that accounting history has "arrived," it is appropriate to accept the challenge and responsibility of developing insights, particularly those bearing on public policy, sharing them with a wider audience.

NOTES

1. All citizens of the Americas, North and South, as well as those in the West Indies, blanch at the term American being used by a resident of the United States in such a captive sense. Canadians are, in my experience, particularly sensitive. To all I ask indulgence and use the term merely as a convenient substitute for "Americans residing in the United States."

2. This insistence for democratic representation ensures the eventual failure of any attempt by the United States to continue colonizing adventures, such as those following the Spanish American War in the Philippines. Once a nation espouses democratic principles, it must accommodate the sovereign state under its care to exercise powers of self-determination, or else it destroys the basis of its own authority. This point was emphasized by Secretary of State Dean Rusk in commenting on Western democratic policies and the basis for the Viet Nam War.

3. I wish to express my gratitude to Professor Vangermeersh for the gift of a copy of

this book provided to me in December 1991. Without his diligent forensic efforts, an important link to the state of accounting during this period might have been overlooked.

4. The relationships of these authors and their prominent contemporaries were the subject of a paper presented at the 1988 World Congress of Historians, authored by myself and Professor Sheldahl and entitled "From Rote to Reason: The Development of American Accounting Thought from 1830 to 1880."

5. It is not easy to pass up such a tempting area for comment. Those who consider the impact of taxation on fiscal policy know that it drives many of the investment decisions in our society. Beginning with the more modern issue of the investment tax credit, including all other forms of tax incentives, and considering the implications of the use of tax-deductible interest-bearing debt on the entire leveraged buyout and merger frenzy of the early 1980s, one can suggest a host of correlating areas to engage accountants in the analysis of tax policy. Nevertheless, tax scholars and, hopefully, tax history scholars have the initiative here. In a related public policy area, the passage of the Single Audit Act in the early 1980s, and most recently the federal Chief Financial Officers Act, suggests that the initiatives of professional accounting lobbyists and other groups seeking greater accountability in the public sector are meeting with some success. Our focus is principally on the investor financial reporting and disclosure aspects of public policy.

6. A more self-serving suggestion would be to require persons with professional qualifications—CPA, CMA, CIA—to be employed in principal financial officer functions. This specification was not pursued. As a practical matter, however, the Institute of Internal Auditor's study conducted by Mautz and Colson in the early 1980s detected a major shift in salaries and personnel from mid-level public accounting positions to internal auditing functions in major public companies. The effect of the legislation was to place many more CPAs in such companies as staff auditors.

7. The mission statement states: "The mission of the AICPA is to act on behalf of its members and provide necessary support to assure that CPAs serve the public interest in performing quality professional services." The statement continues: "To achieve its mission, the AICPA: . . . 8. Unites CPAs—whether in public practice, industry, education or government—in their efforts to serve the public interest" (*The CPA Letter,* September 29, 1986, 1).

8. This analysis of the factors describing ROI (return on investment) was first brought to my attention in a letter to me from Professor A. D. Chandler dated May 10, 1974.

9. As recently as 1989, the American Institute of CPAs, for example, began publishing a bimonthly volume, *Digest of Washington Issues,* which addresses all of the legislative and political concerns and initiatives being addressed by the AICPA.

REFERENCES

American Institute of Certified Public Accountants, Financial Reporting and Standard Setting, Gary John Previts, editor (New York: AICPA, 1991).

Banks, Alexander S., "Informing Stockholders: A Job for Public Accountants in preference to the Federal Trade Commission" (November 4, 1925), reprinted in *Research in Accounting Regulation* (1987): pp. 177–79.

Berle, A. A., Jr., and G. C. Means, *The Modern Corporation and Private Property* (New York: Macmillan, 1932).

The Brady Commission Report of The Presidential Task Force on Market Mechanisms, (January 1988).

Bricker, Robert James, and Gary John Previts, "Changing the Orientation of Accounting: A Study of Property Rights and the Need to Respecify the Accounting Equation," Paper presented at the 75th Anniversary Annual Meeting of the American Accounting Association, Nashville, Tenn. (August, 1991).

Briloff, Abraham, "Old Myths and New Realities," *Accounting Review* (July, 1966).

Chandler, Alfred D., *The Visible Hand: The Managerial Revolution in American Business* (Cambridge, Mass.: Belknap, 1977).

Chandler, Alfred D., *Scale and Scope: The Dynamics of Industrial Capitalism* (Cambridge, Mass.: Belknap, 1990).

Chandler, Alfred D., and Richard Tedlow, *The Coming of Managerial Capitalism* (Homewood, Ill.: Irwin 1985).

Chatfield, Michael, *A History of Accounting Thought* (Hinsdale, Ill.: Dryden Press, 1974).

Chatov, Robert, *Corporate Financial Reporting* (New York: The Free Press, 1975).

Committee, Bruce, *Structuring a Public Accounting Audit Independence Theory from a Document Study of U.S. Congressional Testimony,* Ph.D. dissertation, University of Alabama (1983).

Davis, T. C., "How the du Pont Organization Appraises Its Performance," in *American Management Association*, Financial Management Series, no. 94 (1950):7.

Deloitte & Touche, "Growth in U.S. Investments Abroad," *Deloitte & Touche Review* (September 23, 1991): pp. 4–5.

Deloitte & Touche, "Trends in U.S. Capital Markets," *Deloitte & Touche Review* (November 4, 1991): pp. 5–6.

Drucker, Peter F., *The Unseen Revolution* (New York: Harper & Row, 1976).

Drucker, Peter F., *Managing in Turbulent Times* (New York: Harper & Row, 1980).

Emmott, Bill, Editor, "Capitalism: In Triumph, in Flux," A Survey of Capitalism: Punters or Proprietors? *The Economist* (May 5, 1990): pp. 5–20.

Emmott, Bill, Editor, "Gamblers, Masters and Slaves," An International Finance Survey, *The Economist* (April 27, 1991).

Fitzgerald, Ernest A., *Braniff Magazine* (July, 1989): p. 17.

Galambos, Louis G, and Joseph Pratt, *The Rise of the Corporate Commonwealth: United States Business and Public Policy in the 20th Century* (New York: Basic Books, 1988).

Garner, Paul, *The Evolution of Cost Accounting to 1925* (Tuscaloosa: The University of Alabama Press, 1954).

Hopkins, Selden R., and Charles E. Sprague, "Demand for Compulsory Book-Keeping," *The Book-Keeper* (November 22, 1881): pp. 120–21.

Kaye, Harvey J., "The Concept of the 'End of History' Constitutes a Challenge to the Liberal Consensus in Scholarship and in Public Life," *Chronicle of Higher Education* (October 25, 1989): p. A48.

Martin, Albro, "Uneasy Partners: Government-Business Relations in Twentieth Century American History," *Prologue* (Summer 1979): pp. 91–105.

Melloan, George, "Reading the Tea Leaves on Corporate Privatization,' " *Wall Street Journal* (September 19, 1989): p. A31.

Merino, Barbara D., and Teddy L. Coe, "Uniformity in Accounting: A Historical Perspective," *Journal of Accountancy* (August, 1978): pp. 62–69.

Mi, Kim Soo, "Foreign Investors' Debut in Seoul's Market Tops Expectations, Dominates Volume and Strategy," *Wall Street Journal* (January 6, 1992): p. C16.

Miranti, Paul J., Jr., *Accountancy Comes of Age: The Development of an American Pro-*
  fession, 1886–1940 (Chapel Hill: University of North Carolina Press, 1990).
Navin, Thomas R., and Marian V. Sears, "The Rise of a Market for Industrial Securities,
  1887–1902," *Business History Review* (1955): pp. 105–38.
Paton, William A, and A. C. Littleton, *An Introduction to Corporate Accounting Stan-*
  dards (Sarasota, Fla.: American Accounting Association, 1940).
Parker, R.H., *The Development of the Accountancy Profession in Britain to the Early*
  Twentieth Century, Monograph Five (Atlanta: The Academy of Accounting His-
  torians, 1986).
Phillips, Susan M., and J. Richard Zecher, *The SEC and the Public Interest* (Cambridge
  Mass.: MIT Press, 1981).
Previts, Gary John, "The SEC and Its Chief Accountants: Historical Impressions" *Jour-*
  nal of Accountancy (August, 1978): pp. 83–91.
Previts, Gary John, "Carman G. Blough: Architect of Financial Disclosure," *Journal of*
  Accountancy (January, 1982): pp. 92–96.
Previts, Gary John, "Accountancy in an Investor Fund Economy: Regulation and Reports
  to Portfolio Investors," *Research in Accounting Regulation* (1992).
Previts, Gary John, and Richard Brown, "A Content Analysis of the Journal of Account-
  ancy, relating to the Development of Government Accounting 1905–1979," Paper
  presented to the annual meeting of the Southeastern Region of the American
  Accounting Association, Charlotte, North Carolina (April 24, 1992).
Previts, Gary John, and Barbara Dubis Merino, *A History of Accounting in America* (New
  York: John Wiley & Sons, 1979).
Previts, Gary John, Lee D. Parker, and Edward N. Coffman, "Accounting History: Def-
  inition and Relevance," *Abacus* (March, 1990): pp. 1–16.
Previts, Gary John, and Terry K. Sheldahl, "From Rote to Reason: The Development of
  American Accounting Thought from 1830–1880," Section 113, *Collected Papers*
  of the Fifth World Congress of Accounting Historians, A. T. Craswell, editor
  (Sydney: Accounting and Finance Foundation within the University of Sydney,
  1988).
Ratner, Sidney, "Dewey's Contribution to Historical Theory," in *John Dewey, Philos-*
  opher of Science and Freedom, Sidney Hood, editor (New York: Dial Press,
  1950).
Sack, Robert J., "Commercialism in the Profession: A Threat to Be Managed," *Journal*
  of Accountancy (October, 1985): pp. 125–32.
Schlesinger, Arthur, Jr., "In Defense of 'Kiss and Tell,' " *Wall Street Journal* (May 11,
  1988): p. 18.
Scott, D.R., *The Cultural Significance of Accounts* (Lawrence, Kansas: Scholars Books,
  1976).
Skousen, Mark, "Roaches outlive elephants: An interview with Peter F. Drucker,"
  Forbes (August 19, 1991): pp. 72–74.
United States Senate, *The Accounting Establishment Subcommittee on Reports, Account-*
  ing and Management of the Committee on Government Operations (GPO: Wash-
  ington D.C., 1977).
Wessel, David, "White House Budget Proposal to Stretch Seams of 1990 Deficit-
  Reduction Law," *Wall Street Journal* (January 20, 1992): p. A2.
Wilkinson, George, "The Genesis of the C.P.A. Movement," *The Certified Public Ac-*
  countant (September, 1928): pp. 261–66; 279–85; (October 1928): pp. 297–300.

Willmott, Hugh, "Auditing Game: A Question of Ownership and Control," *Critical Perspectives on Accounting* (March, 1991): pp. 109–21.

Zeff, Stephen A., "Some Junctures in the Evolution of the Process of Establishing Accounting Principles in the U.S.A.: 1917–1972," *Accounting Review* (1984): pp. 447–68.

Zuckerman, M.B., "George Herbert (Hoover) Bush?" *U.S. News and World Report* (January 20, 1992): p. 68.

2

Eugen Schmalenbach as the Founder of Cost Accounting in the German-Speaking World

Marcell Schweitzer

THE NESTORS OF BUSINESS MANAGEMENT IN THE GERMAN-SPEAKING WORLD

The beginning of business management as a modern academic discipline in the German-speaking world (Austria, Germany, Switzerland) can be dated from the start of the 20th century. At this time highly reputable scholars were at work. They were pursuing research and teaching in business management that was methodologically sound for the most part, and viewed it as an epistemological task whose approach could be understood as being intersubjectively testable. The names of three scholars who are considered to be the *forerunners of our current discipline* of business management should be mentioned first (Albach [History], 249):

- *Eugen Schmalenbach* (1873–1955),
- *Wilhelm Rieger* (1878–1971), and
- *Heinrich Nicklisch* (1876–1946).

An important phenomenon for the review of past events is that these three forerunners were distinguished by different methodological perspectives as well as contextual design. Consequently a *Methodenstreit* resulted in which the question, Which of these three approaches should be used in the scientific design of business management? played a central role. Eugen Schmalenbach with his approach to business management clearly emerged from this scientific dispute as the dominating personality. Because his influence on current business management has been so lasting, I would like to provide an overview of his career and scientific work. In so doing, I will limit myself to his contributions in cost accounting, although his interests and research areas went far beyond this.

SCHMALENBACH'S CAREER

Youth, Profession, and Studies

Schmalenbach inherited a farmer's and craftman's blood from his father's side and an entrepreneurial spirit from his mother's side. His appearance was not sensitive and intellectual but angular and at home with nature (Cordes [*Schmalenbach*], 3 ff.). His father rose from a position as locksmith to the owner of a craftsman's business. He wanted to make an owner of a factory in the light-iron industry out of his son Eugen.

After having completed several years of high school, Schmalenbach spent a year at a company in the machine industry and then in the metal-processing industry as a business apprentice. There followed three hard years in his father's business. He withdrew from this "forced labour" (Cordes [*Schmalenbach*], 12) in 1896 and voluntarily joined the army. After that he returned to his father's company to share the business managership with his father. His chief duties were in operational accounting and cost estimating. Increasingly asking critical questions about business operations, he developed into the business research intellect of the firm. But his father could answer hardly any of his questions. Just at this time (1898) the Leipzig School of Commerce (*Handelshochschule*) was being founded. There he hoped to find answers to questions about cost estimating and business organization. Originally he had planned to improve his "quality as a factory owner" through his studies, enabling him to return to his father's business with a more solid preparation. This, however, never came about.

In the spring of 1898 Schmalenbach, 24 years old, went to Leipzig, where he was among the first students at the trade school. But even his professors were not able to answer his questions. Thus he began to write down and analyze his problems. This is how his first professional essay came about—a few months after he commenced his studies. It was followed in 1899 by a very long essay in ten parts on the problem of fixed costs (*Buchführung*). This work rates as an early masterpiece that reveals his high intelligence. After two years of study he had acquired a brilliant master's degree (*Diplom*) (Forrester [*Schmalenbach*], 7 ff.).

On the Way to a University Career

Schmalenbach's career in business administration began with a failure. In October 1900 he applied for an assistantship at the Cologne Trade School. His application was rejected. His only financial backing at that time was journalist work with the German newspaper devoted to the metal industry, the *Metall-Industrie-Zeitung*. In the period from 1899 to 1906 he published there a total of 130 articles and other contributions. Their level, however, varied, ranging from innovative scientific ideas to banalities. For a businessman his style was very lively and informative. Yet from time to time he wrote in a cynical and bitingly penetrating tone. As early as 1899 he had laid the cornerstone of his main ideas in an article (*Buchführung*) on the function of a business in optimizing macro-economic efficiency. After realizing that journalism would by no means become his livelihood, he followed the advice of the well-known economist Karl Bücher and took up studies in national economics in 1900.

In early 1901 Schmalenbach became Karl Bücher's assistant and librarian. He received in the fall of 1902 his first independent university teaching position involving bookkeeping courses. As an assistant in the fifth semester, he managed to perform the unimaginable: to write his dissertation and the German habilitation. On the ninth of March 1903 the Cologne Trade School was ready to recognize his habilitation, although Schmalenbach was not yet a Ph.D. The habilitation was entitled "Transfer Prices in a Business" (*Die Verrechnungspreise im Betriebe*). Schmalenbach dropped his study of national economy, relinquished his assistantship, and became an instructor (*Privatdozent*) in Cologne; a year later his position in the technical science of trade (*Handelstechnik*) with a special focus on business arithmetic (*kaufmännisches Rechnen*) became contractual (*planmäßiger Dozent*). On the first of October 1906, when he was thirty-three years old, he was given a professorial position—highly unusual in the German-speaking world. He was a professor without having a high-school diploma or having completed the Ph.D. exam. But he was a gifted researcher and a reputable teacher. Eight and one-half years after first setting foot in the university he had become a professor. His Ph.D. was finally conferred as an honor at the opening ceremony of the University of Cologne in 1919 (Cordes [*Schmalenbach*], 25 ff.).

In the next years several universities at home and abroad expressed a serious interest in Schmalenbach. Professorships in Stockholm (1908), Frankfurt (1912), Berlin (1922), and Jena (1923) were rejected. After 1933, when he was experiencing political persecution, the universities of Dorpat in Estonia (1933), Istanbul (1937), and Bern (1939) called on his services to no avail (Cordes [*Schmalenbach*], 44 ff.).

Persecution during the Third Reich

Hitler's rise to power on the thirteenth of January, 1933, brought an abrupt turning point to Schmalenbach's life. Because of his Jewish wife and his children he had to reckon with the worst. He searched for a way out by taking a research semester and then by becoming professor emeritus. He requested to be relieved of his research and teaching duties on the first of October, 1933. The responsible minister for education even expressed recognition of and a special thanks for his academic accomplishments (Cordes [*Schmalenbach*], 151).

In his free time as a retired professor he was active as a consultant, wrote new books, and reworked those already published. In 1941 he converted the Treuhand AG company, an auditing business founded by him, into a schooling enterprise that offered experience in the practical side of business management. In this way he returned to pragmatic knowledge. The increasing campaigns against Jews and anti-Jewish sentiment in the population had a devastating psychological effect on Schmalenbach: his zeal for work diminished sharply and finally became completely paralyzed.

The officials distanced themselves from Schmalenbach step by step, but his students and friends held to him just as they always had. From 1939 on, the political situation became more and more unbearable for Schmalenbach, finally forcing him to disappear in hiding with his wife. In spite of the existence of informers, he remained in hiding until the end of the war and thus survived (Forrester [*Schmalenbach*], 13 ff.; Cordes [*Schmalenbach*], 177 ff.).

Work in Old Age

Directly after the end of World War II Schmalenbach worked on his two books on decision-oriented transfer prices, what Schmalenbach terms *"Pretiale Lenkung"*—with the word "pretial" derived from the Latin word *"pretium,"* meaning price (*optimale Geltungszahl, Pretiale Lenkung*). In addition to this he dedicated himself once again to work in committees and to questions of compensation for war losses and individual problems of currency restoration. He wanted to couple the upcoming currency reform with his own tax reform.

Along with other Cologne professors he prepared the reopening of Cologne University. In the winter semester of 1945/1946 he held a course on "balances and finances" that was to be the last he held. In the next five years Schmalenbach only offered seminars for graduate students and was a sought-after speaker and counselor. At age seventy-seven he finally gave up all academic activities. It is worth mentioning that he was called on to be an auditor in 1946. At that time he was also offered the office of Minister for Economic Affairs (*Wirtschaftsminister*) in North Rhine Westphalia, which he turned down (Cordes [*Schmalenbach*], 185 ff.). A very important event for Schmalenbach was the reappearance of the *Journal for Research in Trade* (*Zeitschrift für handelswissenschaftliche Forschung*) in 1949, in which he was named as a founder. It was in this journal that Schmalenbach published his last article, in August, 1950. In 1963 the journal was renamed *Schmalenbach's Journal for Business Research* (*Schmalenbachs Zeitschrift für betriebswirtschaftliche Forschung—ZfbF*) in his honor.

Schmalenbach's last three monographs were dedicated to the market economy. More than seventy years old, but with professional maturity and in a clear language and lively style, he wrote the two-volume *Managing Business Through*

Transfer Prices (*Pretiale Wirtschaftslenkung*) as well as his final work, *In Memory of the Free Market* (*Der freien Wirtschaft zum Gedächtnis*). Two other monographs that he had planned did not appear: *Managing Business Through Decision-Oriented Transfer Prices in the Free Market* (*Pretiale Lenkung in der freien Volkswirtschaft*) and *Managing Business Through Decision-Oriented Transfer Prices in the Planned Economy* (*Pretiale Lenkung in der Planwirtschaft*) (Cordes [*Schmalenbach*], 195 ff.).

SCHMALENBACH'S CONTRIBUTIONS TO BUSINESS MANAGEMENT

Schmalenbach's View of Science

In accordance with his practical view, it follows logically that Schmalenbach had a pragmatic orientation to business management as a science. Business management, which at that time was still designated as the "economics of private firms" (*Privatwirtschaftslehre*), was thus an applied science that was to serve a practical purpose. In his view it was thus necessary for a business researcher to have practical experience before he could work as a researcher. The business researcher in this view could under no circumstances be a bookworm; instead he should be a practical field worker who contributes to solutions to practical economic problems.

In a *Methodenstreit* that had been waged between the national economists Weiermann and Schönitz on the one hand and Schmalenbach on the other, Schmalenbach distinguished between a "philosophical science" and a "technologically oriented science." The latter of these two views he designated as an "applied art" (*Kunstlehre*) (*Privatwirtschaftslehre*, 306). The chief task of such an applied science is to formulate rules that depict how a business can be run efficiently. The principle of efficiency represents the basic systematic idea of the discipline. This view of science largely overlaps with today's conception of business management as a decision-oriented discipline (Kilger [*Kostenlehre*], 533). If we hold to a division of scientific goals into three areas—descriptive, theoretical, and pragmatic—Schmalenbach's applied science clearly serves the pragmatic goal. All theoretical parts that he needs to obtain this goal clearly have to satisfy the empirical criterion of validity. Today's system-theoretical conception of the discipline adheres to a more abstract form of this basic approach. The development of a closed system or a body of theory that is both formally and completely structured is of secondary importance to Schmalenbach. His central postulate is aimed at a pragmatic scientific goal, and furthermore, embraces the use of a multitude of methods. For him it is less fruitful and efficient to talk about methods than to work with all appropriate methods (Cordes [*Schmalenbach*], 281).

With hindsight we can say today that Schmalenbach had no precise concept of theory. Strictly speaking, he was satisfied with quasi-theories to supply his

practical problems with solutions. Schmalenbach would have had great difficulties with the demands made on a theory today, for instance, like those formulated by advocates of critical rationalism.

Schmalenbach realized both rationally and intuitively that following an efficiency principle presupposes the formulation of precise goals. These goals can
either be of a microeconomic or macroeconomic character. In this sense he thus
distinguished between microeconomic and macroeconomic efficiency. He personally finally embraced macroeconomic efficiency whose basis can be understood today as a precisely defined welfare function. All businesses with their
individual goals hence are viewed as serving the entire economy, i.e., a higher
welfare purpose. This basic position of Schmalenbach's is without a doubt the
outflow of the harmony views of classical economic liberalism. He is nonetheless aware of the problem that many conflicts can exist between the correct
microeconomic and macroeconomic control of a system. Schmalenbach demands that education and economic policy be used towards a higher macroeconomic purpose and in this way macroeconomic efficiency. Schmalenbach
never clearly defined his concept of macroeconomic efficiency (*Gemeinwirt-
schaftlichkeit*). For this reason Wilhelm Rieger (*Privatwirtschaftslehre*) attacked
it harshly. Rieger represented the opposed position that the individual business
should follow the goal of maximizing profits. Moreover, he claimed that Schmalenbach's concept of macroeconomic efficiency could only work in a planned
economy. Finally, he pointed out that not a single instance was named in which
a measure taken by a business could be judged as macroeconomically efficient.
The problem can be interpreted from today's perspective as if individual business goals were derived from macroeconomic policy goals; we would have to
assume that the macroeconomic policy goals serve the public weal to the greatest
possible extent. Schmalenbach provided no answer to this question. Instead he
always assumed microeconomic goals in all his investigations in which goals
were involved.

The Scholar's Research Fields

Because I would like to dedicate myself in my later discussion chiefly to
Eugen Schmalenbach's contributions to cost accounting, I will mention briefly
the other research areas that the scholar was concerned with here.

The first research area I would like to name is *financial accounting*. In this
area Schmalenbach developed a dynamic conception of financial accounting
theory (*Grundlagen; Dynamische Bilanz*) in which efficient measurement became the central purpose of balance statements. He interpreted a balance statement consistently as a balance for calculating profits and derived accounting
principles from it. He also concerned himself with the problems of the fictitious
character of inflationary profits and with the question of maintaining the real
value of money capital. Furthermore, he developed numerous proposals in the
areas of accounting regulation and balance-sheet auditing.

A further research area is corporate finance (*Beteiligungsfinanzierung; Kapital*). Within this framework he focused on capital budgeting and problems of finance. In addition, he handled individual questions of the valuation of a going concern, of forms of holding interests, and of business constitution.

Another research area is management and business organization. On this issue he posed questions of the divisional structure of the business and of competence and responsibility, as well as analysing the problems of organization of top management (*Dienststellengliederung*). It should be stressed that he introduced his contribution to management through decision-oriented transfer prices as the principle of management in organization there.

The appropriate institutional economic framework should be mentioned as the final research area (*Wirtschaft*). It follows from Schmalenbach's view of science that he postulated a free economy that was geared to the public welfare. Within this framework he examined strengths and weaknesses of the free economy and tried to discover what chances for survival such an economic arrangement can have.

SCHMALENBACH'S CONTRIBUTIONS TO COST THEORY AND COST ACCOUNTING

The Essentials of Cost Theory

The earliest scientific question posed by Schmalenbach was cost theoretical in nature. As early as 1899, he was analyzing the structure of fixed costs, which consequently led to the decomposition of total costs into fixed and variable costs (*Buchführung*). The most important determinant of variable costs for him was volume. The purpose of his theoretical analysis was to refute the view that was current at that time, i.e., that total costs were proportional. After breaking down total costs into fixed and variable costs he came to the conclusion that fixed costs should be excluded from cost estimating and pricing policy. Later Schmalenbach made his view of fixed costs more precise and allowed semi-fixed costs to count. It is also important that he defined the fixed and variable character of costs with respect to the individual determinant. By focusing on another determinant of cost he found it was quite possible for the fixed and variable character of costs to change.

At a very early stage in his career Schmalenbach described the increasing size of the firm as one important reason for the growth of fixed costs. In this way he succeeded in analysing economies of scale and diseconomies of scale. This question in turn is a central element in the law of mass production, which was discovered by his teacher Karl Bücher in 1910 [Gesetz]. It is still an open question whether Schmalenbach influenced his teacher Bücher in the discovery of this law while he was his assistant. The contextual explanation of cost functions and the demarcation of the important categories of subproportional, supraproportional, and regressive costs was of great significance for further developments. With this he laid both the formal and the contextual foundations for later cost theoretical discussions in the subject.

The Scientific Foundation of Cost Accounting

The Objectives of Cost Accounting

Schmalenbach's approach begins with the theoretical insight that the design of cost accounting is dependent on the goal set by the firm. Schmalenbach named the following as purposes of cost accounting (*Selbstkostenrechnung*, 347 ff., *Preispolitik*, 119 ff.):

* supervision of efficiency,
* observation of changes in structure,
* cost estimating for pricing policy,
* management, and
* miscellaneous purposes.

While Schmalenbach relegated the determination of transfer prices to the secondary purposes of cost accounting, today we assume that this problem counts as one of the chief purposes of cost accounting. The concept "cost accounting" is understood in every connection as cost estimating on a unit basis.

The Subclassifications of Cost Accounting

In general Schmalenbach had two different subclassifications of cost accounting in mind. Because he was not graced either in linguistics or with a methodical mind, he tended to include components that had caught on in practice. Thus we find he chose to break cost accounting into cost category accounting, cost center accounting, and cost estimating, while placing a special emphasis on the two first categories. With further consideration, Schmalenbach succeeded in a second breakdown of cost accounting (*Preispolitik*, 171 ff.):

* simple accounting based on historical costs versus accounting based on decision-oriented costs,
* preliminary versus statistical costing,
* systematic cost estimating versus cost estimating based on incomplete accounting records, and
* process costing versus job order costing.

In the second breakdown he was aware of some overlapping, but accepted it for practical reasons. His real concern was in a demarcation between accounting based on historical costs and accounting based on decision-oriented costs.

The Fundamental Idea of Accounting Based on Decision-Oriented Costs

The focus on decisions in Schmalenbach's cost accounting is made especially clear in his conception of accounting based on decision-oriented costs. He required that goods in cost accounting be priced at the "correct" value, with the correct value defined as the amount that results from "the most efficient of all efficient possibilities chosen" (*Preispolitik,* 9). The correct value, which Schmalenbach designated as the decision-oriented transfer price (*optimale Geltungszahl, Kalkulationswert, Betriebswert*), was to express the advantage over the alternative use of goods (*optimale Geltungszahl,* 14). But his main concern was in the creation of a theory of value. The value of goods did not correspond to the historical cost of the goods. And even the goods' selling price deviates from their value. Strictly speaking, he conceived of value as a relation in which the accounting objective and the decision field play a significant role. This conception of value exactly corresponds to a decision-logical conception of value if we replace the accounting objective with an objective function. If value concerns the cost side, this conception of value is defined as "cost-value" cost concept.

Individual Contributions to Cost Accounting

The Division Between Basic and Objective-Oriented Cost Accounting

Because on the one hand every approach to value is dependent on the accounting objective, and on the other hand various accounting objectives must be followed, the question of how to satisfy this variety of objectives arises. One way to do this would be to develop as many accounting systems as there are objectives and corresponding approaches to value. A second way would be the most "efficient" and would consist of developing a basic accounting system (*Grundrechnung*) with no particular objective, whose data could be evaluated for various accounting objectives in different objective-oriented accounting methods (*Zweckrechnung*) (*Pretiale Lenkung,* 66 ff.). The basic accounting system would have to be constructed in a way independent of objective, yet in a way that allows its data to be evaluated for all possible purposes. Completely independent of Schmalenbach, the American B. E. Goetz made a comparable proposal for a basic accounting system in 1949 [Planning]. Later this idea reappeared in P. Riebel's approach to contribution costing based on relative direct costs (*Deckungsbeitragsrechnung*).

The concept of a basic accounting system requires really a data bank system that is built independently of the individual application. If the data bank system is complemented by a model bank system and a method bank system, objective-oriented accounting methods (decision models) that do each individual decision problem justice can be formulated. With this idea of a basic accounting system

Schmalenbach came up with exactly the development that plays a significant role in today's computer-based cost accounting. Without understanding the current possibilities provided by electronic data processing and information systems, Schmalenbach possessed extraordinary vision with his idea of structuring cost accounting systems on basic and objective-oriented accounting.

The Structure of Decision-Oriented Transfer Prices

The decision-oriented transfer price is a cost value whose determination follows the idea of marginal utility theory. After this the additional costs of each final production unit have a special meaning. The decision-oriented transfer price can be either a marginal-cost rate or a marginal-utility rate. It is a marginal-cost rate if no bottlenecks in production occur. If, however, bottlenecks slow production, it is a marginal-utility rate (Schmalenbach [*Preispolitik*], 24). At first Schmalenbach designated the marginal-cost rate as the "proportional rate." Later he replaced this concept with "marginal costs."

In Schmalenbach's view, the relationship of marginal costs to pricing policy is summed up in the fact that a supplier of goods both in a micro- and macro-economic perspective should demand at least the marginal cost as the price. In this way an influence on demand was guaranteed. Given supraproportional total costs, the marginal-cost price should curb demand and given cost subproportionality, it should increase demand. As long as no capacity bottlenecks occur, Schmalenbach expected the minimal cost volume in the business to obtain through the price mechanism. Hence, cost estimating in marginal-cost prices was meant to control the business experiencing underemployment into a cost-favourable employment situation.

As soon as production bottlenecks occur, a price at the marginal-cost rate no longer suffices. Instead, the marginal-utility rate must be used for cost estimating. The decision-oriented transfer price as a marginal-utility rate consists of the marginal cost plus the lost marginal profit given fully exploited capacity. Today the lost marginal profits are called "opportunity costs" or "shadow prices." Simultaneous optimization models that were developed in the United States during World War II and later systematically extended, completely established Schmalenbach's concept of a decision-oriented transfer price. Shadow prices, which can be calculated in these optimization models, are exactly those lost values that represent the marginal components in the decision-oriented transfer price, given the restrictions and a chosen objective function.

Strictly speaking, Schmalenbach calculated his decision-oriented transfer price only for one bottleneck. With several bottlenecks he could solve the valuation problem only with "estimated transfer prices." Without a knowledge of either linear or nonlinear programming, Schmalenbach thus discovered shadow prices that served in the calculation of his decision-oriented transfer price. Without intending to belittle the merits of George B. Dantzig's (Programming) work, we can say that Schmalenbach recognized and partially solved the duality problem parallel to Dantzig, although he did not possess a knowledge of exact optimization procedures (Schneider [*Betriebswirtschaftslehre*], 222).

The Use of Decision-Oriented Transfer Prices as a Management Principle

In every business the management must decide on the general direction to be taken. How this is to be done is the second task of the management. As an instrument of supervision and management, the accounting system supplies management with important information concerning decisions, e.g., for the way in which the march is executed. According to Schmalenbach, management through decision-oriented transfer prices is a very important management instrument (Pretiale Lenkung). He advocated an extensive delegation of decision competence on the division head level, as well as the participation of the division heads in the success of the division. For this purpose he proposed a divisional income statement in which costs and performance were valued with transfer prices. The decision-oriented transfer price should be used in such a way that scarce resources are optimally allocated. Only those costs that could be influenced by the division head were to be allocated by the departments.

''Management through decision-oriented transfer prices'' is not only a slogan that Schmalenbach brought into the discussion, it is the foundation of modern transfer price theory. Schmalenbach's theory of management through decision-oriented transfer prices, formulated in 1948 (Pretiale Lenkung), rates today as the heart of modern business policy. These ideas have their roots in the Schmalenbach works written at the beginning of the century. The increasing breakdown of the business into divisions and the growing use of optimization models allowed transfer price theory to be built up systematically. Coming in at the end of this development was the profit-center conception, which was analysed theoretically by Schmalenbach in research work over decades well before its practical test.

The Development of a Basis for Standard Costing

Fundamental to the development of flexible standard costing and marginal standard costing is the decomposition of total costs into fixed and variable components (*Buchführung*, 8 ff.). Schmalenbach became very interested in cost decomposition very early in his career. He proposed the following methods to decompose costs:

- mathematical cost decomposition, and
- cost decomposition based on bookkeeping accounts.

While mathematical cost decomposition in part led to confusion because it resulted in negative residual costs given cost progression, the second method proved to be a relatively easy instrument of cost decomposition (Kosiol [*Kostenauflösung*], 345). But Schmalenbach did not come further than this theoretical basis for standard costing. Standard costing was later developed by Michel (*Plankostenrechnung*) and others in the machine-building and textile industries. During World War II development stagnated in the German-speaking world, while in America standard costing was systematically developed. After the Second World War, these developments were successfully used and refined in the German-speaking countries. Schmalenbach's merit can thus be seen in his having established the theoretical basis for the developments of efficient standard costing.

Schmalenbach and Contribution Costing

Schmalenbach had also thought through the principles of contribution costing very early in his career (*Kalkulation*). The breakdown of total costs into fixed and variable costs that provided the key to the development of marginal costing is also fundamental there (Kilger [*Kostenlehre*], 538 ff.). Marginal costing based on variable costs, developed in the German-speaking world parallel to the development of direct costing in the United States, led to contribution costing on the basis of variable costs, given the inclusion of the revenues. It was quickly proved that contribution costing led to a higher level of efficiency than decisions on a full-cost basis, especially for short-run decisions. Although in economic practice contribution costing came up against strong resistance because it frequently leads to price declines and thus to price wars (*Preispolitik,* 174), Schmalenbach never gave up propagating this accounting concept. Schmalenbach was guided by the correct idea that the use of contribution costing clearly leads to an optimal product mix. He went one step further and solved the valuation problem with the decision-oriented transfer price, thus introducing opportunity costs into his concept of contribution costing.

Schmalenbach's approach to contribution costing did not make great headway. The real impetus came after World War II from the United States, where the same idea was being developed simultaneously as "direct costing." In the next few years especially the application of shadow prices from simultaneous optimization methods proved to be very productive, leading to the complete establishment of the basic approach of the decision-oriented transfer price.

His Approach to Activity Based Costing

Schmalenbach had required a differentiated analysis of fixed costs to ascertain their determinants as early as 1899 in connection with the inadequacy of book-keeping and the treatment of fixed costs (*Buchführung,* 4 ff.). In recent discussions of activity-based costing just these determinants (cost drivers) are emphasized. Researchers are trying to find cost determinants (i.e., cost drivers) for their corresponding activities; then the overhead should be allocated correctly through the causation principle to these cost determinants. In the developments in cost accounting that followed, this theme was not followed up. Only with the recent discussions on activity-based costing has Schmalenbach's early idea been remembered.

CONCLUSIONS

Schmalenbach possessed neither a pronounced methodical mind nor a meticulous bent for the theoretical. Nonetheless he not only assisted economic practice greatly with his pragmatic approach to problems, but also put business management as a science on the right path to the successful decision-oriented discipline that we know today. During the discipline's pioneer phase, he steered the attention of later generations of researchers to the central microeconomic problems through his unusually wide-ranging work. His most important concern—the one dominating all others—was value theory as an instrument of optimal management. His principle of management via decision-oriented transfer prices, *pretiale Lenkung,* was and remains the central component of the management of a multidivisional business organization. Due to this principle, and with the help of cost accounting and business organization, management is strictly market-oriented. His goal was a flexible, competitive, and innovative business. He strove to shape an economy that has the price mechanism as its central instrument of control and in which all businesses participate in the macroeconomic goal of obtaining public welfare.

Schmalenbach's contribution to business management as an applied science has been manifested in business management's consistent development as a decision-oriented discipline. It, too, serves a pragmatic scientific goal, but is in practice interdisciplinary and integrates the descriptive, theoretical, and pragmatic. Nonetheless, in the modern, decision-oriented discipline of business management, theory receives a fundamentally greater weight than in Schmalenbach's work.

In conclusion, let me emphasize that the influence of Schmalenbach's applied science was felt well beyond the German-speaking world. The proof of this lies in the numerous translations of his works into other languages. His book *Dynamische Bilanz,* a dynamic conception of financial accounting, has been translated into English, French, Japanese, and Spanish. *Kontenrahmen,* his work on the standard chart of accounts, has been translated into Japanese and Russian. Also translated into Japanese are his book *Selbstkostenrechnung und Preispolitik* [Cost Accounting and Pricing Policy], and his work in memory of the free market, *Der freien Wirtschaft zum Gedächtnis.*

Schmalenbach's scholarly work has been recognized internationally and nationally through five honorary Ph.D.s, an honorary citizenship, and two honorary university senatorial positions (Forrester [Schmalenbach], 15). In addition, two biographies about Schmalenbach have appeared: one by the Scotsman David A. R. Forrester (*Schmalenbach*) and an extensive biography edited by the German Walter Cordes in 1984 (*Schmalenbach*). Both biographies characterize Schmalenbach as a brilliant scholar with vision who provided business management with an important foundation and innumerable stimuli. This goes especially for modern cost accounting. I think it is safe to assume that there will never again be another amateur gardener, handicraft enthusiast, inventor, and entrepreneur

(Forrester [*Schmalenbach*], 7) who will make in research and teaching comparable achievements in the field of cost accounting respectively in the field of business management.

NOTE

I would like to thank Dr. B. Friedl and Dr. D. A. Redman for their help in translating this paper.

REFERENCES

Albach, H. 1990. "Business Administration: [History] in German-Speaking Countries." In *Handbook of German Business Management*, cols. 246–270. Edited by Erwin Grochla, et al. Stuttgart: C. E. Poeschel, Springer.

Bücher, K. 1910. "Das [Gesetz] der Massenproduktion." In *Zeitschrift für die gesamte Staatswissenschaft* 66: 429–444.

Cordes, W. (ed.) 1984. *Eugen [Schmalenbach]. Der Mann—Sein Werk—Die Wirkung.* Stuttgart: Schäffer.

Dantzig, G. 1951. "[Programming] of Interdependent Activities: Mathematical Model." In *Activity Analysis of Production and Allocation*, pp. 19–32. Edited by Tjalling C. Koopmans. New York, London: Wiley.

Forrester, D. A. R. 1977. *[Schmalenbach] and After.* Glasgow: Strathclyde Converg.

Goetz, B. E. 1949. *Management [Planning] and Control: A Managerial Approach to Industrial Accounting.* New York.

Kilger, W. 1973. "Schmalenbachs Beitrag zur [Kostenlehre]." In *Schmalenbachs Zeitschrift für betriebswirtschaftliche Forschung* 25: 522–540.

Kosiol, E. 1927. "[Kostenauflösung] und proportionaler Satz." In *Zeitschrift für betriebswirtschaftliche Forschung* 21: 345–358.

Michel, E. 1941 (1937). *Handbuch der [Plankostenrechnung]*, 2nd ed. Berlin: Otto Elsner Verlagsgesellschaft.

Riebel, P. 1990. *Einzelkosten- und [Deckungsbeitragsrechnung]. Grundfragen einer markt- und entscheidungsorientierten Unternehmensrechnung*, 6th ed. Wiesbaden: Gabler.

Rieger, W. 1959. *Einführung in die [Privatwirtschaftslehre]*, 2nd ed. Erlangen: Palm & Enke.

Schmalenbach, E. 1928. *[Buchführung] und Kalkulation.* Leipzig: G. A. Gloeckner Verlagsbuchhandlung. Originally published in *Deutsche Metall-Industrie-Zeitung*, vol. 15 (1899): 98 ff.

Schmalenbach, E. 1963. "Die gewerbliche [Kalkulation]." In *Zeitschrift für handelswissenschaftliche Forschung* 15: 375–384. Originally published in *Zeitschrift für das gesamte kaufmännische Unterrichtswesen*, vol. 15 (1902/03): 150 ff.

Schmalenbach, E. 1911/12. "Die [Privatwirtschaftslehre] als Kunstlehre." In *Zeitschrift für handelswissenschaftliche Forschung* 6: 304–315.

Schmalenbach, E. 1949. *Die [Beteiligungsfinanzierung]*, 7th ed. Köln, Opladen: Westdeutscher Verlag. The first ed. appeared as *Finanzierungen* in 1915.

Schmalenbach, E. 1919. "[Grundlagen] dynamischer Bilanzlehre." In *Zeitschrift für han-*

delswissenschaftliche Forschung 13: 1–60, 65–101. Later published as a book, *Dynamische Bilanz,* in 1920 (see below).

Schmalenbach, E. 1919. "[Selbstkostenrechnung]." In *Zeitschrift für handelswissenschaftliche Forschung* 13: 257–99 and 321–56. Later published as a book, *Grundlagen der Selbstkostenrechnung und Preispolitik,* in 1925 (see below).

Schmalenbach, E. 1953. *[Dynamische Bilanz],* 11th ed. Köln, Opladen: Westdeutscher Verlag. The 2nd ed. appeared as *Grundlagen dynamischer Bilanzlehre* in 1920.

Schmalenbach, E. 1934. *Selbstkostenrechnung und [Preispolitik],* 6th ed. Leipzig: G. A. Gloeckner Verlagsbuchhandlung: The 2nd ed. appeared as *Grundlagen der Selbstkostenrechnung und Preispolitik* in 1925.

Schmalenbach, E. 1939 (1929). *Der [Kontenrahmen],* 6th ed. Leipzig: G. A. Gloeckner Verlagsbuchhandlung.

Schmalenbach, E. 1951 (1933). *[Kapital], Kredit und Zins in betriebswirtschaftlicher Beleuchtung,* 3rd ed. Köln, Opladen: Westdeutscher Verlag.

Schmalenbach, E. 1947. *Pretiale Wirtschaftslenkung,* vol. 1: Die [optimale Geltungszahl]. Bremen-Horn: Industrie- und Handelsverlag Walter Dorn.

Schmalenbach, E. 1948. *Pretiale Wirtschaftslenkung,* vol. 2: [Pretiale Lenkung] des Betriebes. Bremen- Horn: Industrie- und Handelsverlag Walter Dorn.

Schmalenbach, E. 1960 (1949). *Der freien [Wirtschaft] zum Gedächtnis,* 3rd ed. Köln, Opladen: Westdeutscher Verlag.

Schmalenbach, E. 1959. *Über die [Dienststellengliederung] im Großbetriebe,* Köln, Opladen: Westdeutscher Verlag.

Schneider, D. 1987. *Allgemeine [Betriebswirtschaftslehre],* 3rd ed. München, Wien: R. Oldenbourg.

3

Costing Activities: Alternative
Views of History

Claudia Gormly and Murray Wells

INTRODUCTION

We live in a world of contradictions. Comments like "Let the facts speak for
themselves" or "History will decide" are as familiar as the problems of interpreting historical events. The French have a different view from the English of
what happened at the battle of Waterloo; Christians and Jews have different
views about the significance of events in Jerusalem during the rule of Herod;
and the contributions of Lenin and Marx have been drastically reevaluated in
the light of recent events in Eastern and Central Europe.

It is difficult to see how the facts will be able to speak for themselves or how
history will decide anything when there are countless examples of recorded
history being colored by the perceptions of the historian (for an excellent example of various interpretations of the reasons for the adoption of the factory
system in Britain in the nineteenth century, see Jones, 1987).

The history of accounting suffers from the same dilemma—Schneider (1991)
provides a useful sample of cases where the "New School in the History of
Accounting" provides a different perspective from traditional views of history.
Again, alternative perceptions of events have led to different histories being
written about the same events or, in some cases, "A priori theorizing, it seems,
takes precedence over historical investigation" (Jones, 1987, p. 74). The writings of Tinker, Merino, and Neimark (1982; 1987), compared to the more "accepted" views of Littleton (1933) and Garner (1954), provide ample evidence

of the effects of different mind-sets (conceptual frameworks) leading to alternative accounts of historical events (for a more detailed examination of this phenomenon, see Cooper and Puxty, 1991).

This paper is a further exploration of that phenomenon. It explores the alternative views of the history of cost accounting presented by Wells (1978a) and Johnson and Kaplan (1987). In doing so, it should be noted that it is not a dispassionate view, as one of the present authors is also a party to the disputed views of the history of cost accounting. Furthermore, it is not a dispute between classical or traditional historians and adherents of the ''New School,'' for the three authors would (we believe) willingly accept their categorization as belonging to the capitalist, market economy school of thought. In that sense, the dispute is used to demonstrate the phenomenon of alternative histories within a broad economic and social context accepted by all the authors.

DISPUTED VIEWS

In *Relevance Lost* (1987) and in later publications, Johnson and Kaplan (J&K) maintain the view that the allocation of overhead costs to products is necessary and that the early engineers (c. 1880–1910) developed costing systems capable of generating relevant information for line managers. As more activities were undertaken internally by hired workers, managers lost the market signals previously generated by external prices. They had no record of the cost of manufactured goods. The early costing systems were attempts to simulate the market prices.

Relevance was later lost, according to J&K, when accountants adopted a single allocation base such as direct labor hours to spread general overheads over units of production. J&K concluded that the ''managerially relevant product costs'' had been generated by the systems used in metal working companies between 1880 and 1910, but by 1914 these had been replaced by systems that generated product cost information which, while supposedly useful for financial reporting, was managerially irrelevant and misleading.

J&K also claim that a key player in the development and widespread adoption of the so-called ''managerially relevant product costs'' was Alexander Hamilton Church. He was a keen advocate of more efficient engineering management. Of more direct relevance here were his widely acknowledged efforts to convince engineers of the need to include overhead costs in their calculations of product costs (for examples of that acknowledgement, see Vangermeersch, 1986). Johnson and Kaplan (1987) quote Church with approval:

[Church] believed that information about a product's cost should reveal the real resources used to make the product. (p. 55)

Church intimated over 80 years ago [that] a good product cost system will accumulate costs, by product and product line across the entire value chain so that the company will know its total cost (including selling and administration) of producing each good and service. (p. 247)

The motivation for this paper is that, contrary to that euphoric view of Church's contribution, Wells (1978b) had analyzed Church's system ten years earlier and concluded: "Although Church's system was the product of careful thought and an analysis of the apparent needs of manufacturers, it was shown to be incapable of achieving the stated purposes" (p. 148).

Those differences in views about the value of Church's system will be explored below. They provide yet another example of alternative views of history.

THE JOHNSON AND KAPLAN VIEW

J&K published *Relevance Lost: The Rise and Fall of Management Accounting* in 1987. In that book they examined the historical development and current practices of management accounting. Our interest here is limited to their arguments about cost accounting.

The impact of J&K on the thinking and practise of cost accounting in particular and management accounting in general has been acknowledged by many authors and it is not our intention here to go over that ground (see, for example, Wells, 1991).

J&K blame the narrow attitudes of accountants for taking cost accounting off the course originally and soundly navigated by engineers—the ultimate destination of which was to establish and record the real relationship between overhead costs and output on a per unit basis.

We agree that cost accounting, as currently practised, has little, if any, relevance to the decisions managers make. At best it is irrelevant, at worst it is misleading to the point that the output of the cost accounting system may lead to wrong decisions. The dispute described here is, therefore, not about the outcome—we agree that cost accounting has lost any relevance it might have had. Rather the dispute is with the historical interpretation of the events that lead to this unsatisfactory situation.

J&K (1987) lay the blame for the current irrelevance of cost accounting at the feet of accountants and they dispute the view that what engineers such as Church, Towne, Metcalfe and Taylor (see Wells, 1978a, p. 65) advocated was fundamentally flawed:"Many historians mistakenly associate the overhead allocation methods of these early mechanical engineers with the procedures used by 20th century financial accountants" (p. 53). The essential difference between the practices of the accountants and engineers, they say, was in relation to the allocation of overheads. The engineers "tried to trace all costs of the firm as direct costs of products" (p. 132). On the other hand, "auditors, and by implication accountants, commonly apportioned all indirect costs as a whole, allocating them to products according to a common divisor such as labor hours or labor cost" (p. 133).

There are two claims here that need to be addressed. The first and most significant is that the engineers developed "managerially relevant product costs." The chief support for that argument is drawn from the writings of Alexander Hamilton Church, who we noted above was one of the major contributors to the widespread adoption of cost accounting. He was also closely linked with the scientific management movement usually associated with Frederick Taylor (1911).

How then, did Church's "ideal" system perform under real conditions? In practical applications, Church's system appeared less convincing. J&K quote one firm which attempted an application in 1900 and found that the system "became quite unmanageable . . . [and] gave no convenient guide to action" (J&K, 1987, p. 128). J&K attribute this failure to the high cost of processing information.

THE WELLS VIEW

Contrary to the views expressed above, Wells had commented that, despite his prolific writing, Church "had only a limited practical influence" and quoted similar comments made by Garner and Solomons (Wells, 1978a, p. 80). There is, therefore, some doubt about Church's influence, and J&K do not cite any evidence of the extensive adoption of his methods. There is, however, ample evidence that by the end of the first decade of this century, the necessity to allocate overheads to products (mainly for pricing purposes) was widely accepted both in the United Kingdom and the United States (see Wells, *Bibliography,* 1978b, under "Allocation").

Establishing the importance of Church's contribution is relevant to the question of whether he should be used as representative of the time. However, the major point of this discussion is, why did Wells and J&K come to such different conclusions about the place of his proposals in the historical development of cost accounting systems? If his proposals were not capable of practical application at the time, then it will be necessary to see whether conditions are now sufficiently different for J&K to claim its superiority. One thing is immediately obvious—while Church was endeavoring to determine the "real resources used to make a product," he was willing to compromise his ideal for the sake of practicality:

It may be objected here that we are here breaking away from actual figures and entering the nebulous region of estimated charges . . . It is true that the element of judgement is very strongly involved in this general establishment charge analysis, but there is a difference between judgement and mere guess-work. (Church, 1913, pp. 134–135)

And later, he recommends that office and selling expenses be allocated to products on "a more or less arbitrary basis" (Church, 1913, p. 126).

J&K claim that the reason that Church, and others like him, had to compromise the "ideal" system was because the information technology of the time could not cope with the demands of the system. Wells, on the other hand, maintained that in practical terms the system could not work because it sought to do the impossible—that is to measure the "true" relationship between common costs and output. Wells claims that what Church, J&K and others overlook is that there is no relationship between common costs and output—by definition. The early engineers did not, therefore, simulate the market prices of intermediate goods because the circumstances in which they were manufactured were quite different (Wells, 1978a, p. 111). For a small, specialized or single-product manufacturer there may be a close relationship between total costs and output. For a large multi-product firm, however, it is unlikely that there will be any relationship between total costs and the output of individual products. Nor is there any need to identify such a relationship, if one did exist, other than to determine the total costs at different levels of total output—and that does not require any form of overhead or indirect cost allocation. Indeed, in commenting on the extensive literature survey that underpinned his study, Wells (1978a) commented: "Yet I did not find a single example in the literature of the time of an author who demonstrated that that [overhead] allocation was essential" (p. 101).

One further comment may be made in relation to this first claim. If, as J&K maintain, the engineer-managers had perfected the system between 1880 and 1910 (that is, they had effectively simulated the prices of intermediate goods), and the influence of accountants did not emerge until some time after 1914, who was Church criticizing in his writings of 1910–1913? The answer must be, other engineers. In particular, Church was critical of engineers who used the same single-base allocation methods of which J&K complain. Church (1909) stated that: "From the earliest days of manufacturing there has grown up a custom of considering labor as the main and only direct item in production, and of expressing all other expenditure in more or less vague percentages of wage cost" (p. 134).

According to Church, it was the engineers themselves, not accountants, who were originally at fault for basing overhead allocations on direct labour hours. Furthermore, again contrary to J&K's views, Wells maintained that Church did nothing to improve the system—he simply sought to replace one system of arbitrary allocations with another.

To summarize, the differences between J&K's claims that the engineers were "computing managerially relevant product costs" during the period 1880–1910 and the conclusions reached by Wells may be categorized as follows. Wells denied the usefulness of Church's system because:

1. The system contained examples of the very compromises and arbitrary allocations that J&K complained of in later systems.
2. The "ideal" system seems to have failed in actual applications.
3. The criticisms made by Church in 1910 related to systems developed and maintained by engineers, not by accountants.

The further claim that accountants abandoned the system and replaced it with their own, has already been addressed above. Wells had already concluded that accountants did not make any substantial contribution to the development of cost accounting, but rather that they entrenched the engineer's cost accounting system by using the output to value inventories for financial statements. This point is partially recognised in J&K: "But, the engineers and the accountants applied overhead to products for very different reasons" (J&K, 1987, p. 53). However the accountants did so by using the cost accounting systems already in existence. We found no evidence of accountants adapting the system—they continued to use a single, factory-wide allocation base such as direct labor hours, just as the engineers had. The purpose may have been different, but the system was the same.

Here we have an example of the alternative views referred to in the introduction. Drawing from many of the same sources and within the same broad social and economic context, Wells (1978a) concluded that the accountants simply adopted the systems already developed by the engineers. J&K, on the other hand, claimed that it was a mistake to associate the allocation methods used by the engineers with those used by accountants. Furthermore, while Wells concluded that those systems were not providing "managerially useful information" then and they do not do so now, J&K argued that those systems only lost their "relevance" once they were adopted and adapted by accountants.

WHY THE INTERPRETATIONS WERE DIFFERENT

We agree with Johnson and Kaplan (1987) that: "The ultimate question, is not who developed or required non-managerial sources of cost information but what prompted rational managers to voluntarily use such information in settings where it was clearly irrelevant" (p. 134). However, the time frame of that question is different. For whereas J&K suggest that the question of the relevance of allocated overhead costs arose only after accountants adopted a single allocation base sometime after 1910, Wells claims that the system was flawed from the moment it was adopted by engineers, manufacturers and accountants. In seeking to identify differences, we should be clear about common ground. For example, J&K (1987) state that allocating costs not directly affected by activity levels within a cost center has no value for cost control purposes. Costs not controllable by a cost center should not be included in that cost center's cost control report (J&K, 1987, pp. 231–32). In a later paper, Kaplan (1991) confirms this view: "no useful control or performance measurement purpose is served by contaminating a short run performance report with allocated indirect or common costs" (p. 206).

Those views coincide precisely with the conclusion reached in Wells (1976 and 1978). However, Wells went further and claimed that there was no purpose for which overhead costs need be allocated:

[I]f some other basis is used for valuing goods on hand at any time—their current market selling price has been advocated here—then that need [to allocate overhead costs] is removed, and all costs can then be regarded and accounted for simply as costs of the period in which they were incurred. (Wells, 1978a, p. 145; see also Wells, 1972)

J&K, on the other hand, still maintain the need to calculate unit costs of production based on allocated overhead costs for long run, strategic and product related decisions.

As indicated in the Introduction, the different conclusions arise because of the different mind-sets the authors brought to their studies. Kaplan's views are clear: "In order to make sensible decisions concerning the products they market managers need to know what their products cost" (Cooper and Kaplan 1988, p. 20). And:

ABC systems are designed by first identifying the activities performed by each support and operating department and then computing the unit cost of performing these activities. . . . Once the unit costs of all activities have been determined, we can accurately assign support and indirect product costs based on the number of activities performed for each individual product. (Kaplan, 1991, pp. 209, 210)

The "need" for product costs is not argued by J&K—it is asserted as if it is intuitively necessary. For example, the following extract indicates why it is important to reduce various overhead costs, but is used as an argument for the calculation of product costs. The former is not disputed but the reasons for the latter are not obvious:

When the expenses of support activities are traced directly to products, improvement in production processes to reduce set up times to improve material layouts, to focus the factory, or to reduce order processing costs produces an immediate and direct reduction in costs assigned to products. Any savings produced by continued improvement efforts to reduce defects or achieve just in time production capabilities can be directly attributed to the products where the improvements have been made. (Kaplan, 1991, p. 210)

In contrast, Wells examined the neoclassical and marginalist schools of economic theory underlying product related decisions—especially those of Marshall (1890), Jevons (1888), and J. M. Clarke (1923). He concluded that the relevant costs are those that will be changed by the decision and that no method of cost allocation can assist in identifying the marginal or differential costs (Wells, 1978b, p. 151). Rather, cost allocations are a form of averaging and, again by definition, average costs cannot be marginal or differential costs.

In explaining how some cost systems came to be adopted, it is necessary to understand the circumstances of the time. In that respect, again, there is agreement. The systems of cost allocation that came to be widely adopted in the United States and the United Kingdom were first given general exposure in contract engineering firms where unique "one-off" products were constructed to order (see Wells, 1978a, p. 74; J&K, 1987, p. 55). In those circumstances, the engineer had to have some readily available method for pricing the work, just as contractors do today. For those purposes, some rule of thumb such as "provide for overhead by multiplying direct labor by 150%" was as useful then as it is in the 1990s. A motor mechanic, plumber, electrician, or engineer has to be able to prepare the customers' accounts quickly and authoritatively without trying to recalculate an appropriate share of the overhead which each job should bear. It even makes sense to trace the overhead component of each job subsequently to see how much was recovered and what relationship that recovery bore to the overheads incurred. The mistake occurred when enthusiasts such as Church tried to use those data for other purposes such as "strategic product decisions." The average cost of production never could, and never will, be relevant for those classes of decisions where only the change in total costs and revenues are relevant. That is, the rough, average cost calculations provided a guide for pricing unique one-off products or services, but were of no use for the other purposes enumerated by Church and more recently by Johnson and Kaplan.

J&K also argued that Church's system would not have survived "because of high information collecting and processing costs," costs (J&K, 1987, p. 134), quite apart from any influence that financial reporting considerations may have exerted.

The claim that it was the high cost of information processing that was responsible for the undoing of managerially relevant cost accounting is critical to J&K's argument. It is in fact the pivot on which their whole thesis depends. In part, however, the view that the information processing technology could not cope with the demands of a full overhead costing system rests on the extent of the allocations proposed. Church had proposed that the allocation system extend to all overheads, including research and development and selling costs. J&K (1987) comment approvingly: "a thoroughly comprehensive method of recording shop work, including the connection of expenditure of all classes with the items of output on which they are incident" (p. 55).

Interestingly, the proposal by Wells (1978a) that the marginal costs should be assessed in relation to all "strategic product decisions" might also have been dismissed as requiring computational power that was not available at the time. Now, however, J&K's claim in relation to allocation-based systems would have even greater validity with respect to the simulations implied in Wells's suggestion:

the enormous expansion in computing capabilities has [meant that] extensive systems are now feasible to measure and attribute accurately the resource demands made by each product in a diverse line. (J&K, 1987, p. 5)

Curiously, despite J&K's claims, it is not obvious how any system, no matter how technologically sophisticated, can relate things that are not related. That is, while it is no doubt true that digital production controls can with great accuracy measure the weight of raw materials used in a unit of product, they cannot in any sense measure the consumption of overhead costs such as factory rent, or the factory supervisors time consumed by a unit of product.

J&K admit to the impossibility of relating all overhead costs to units of production and the inevitability of the use of subjective judgments and allocations. Product costs will be subjective and the result of an allocation procedure (J&K, 1987, pp. 249–250; see also p. 239).

And, in a later interview:

There are some problems here. We are never going to get the correct product cost to five decimal places because there are some jointness effects . . . that we just cannot split accurately. Our feeling is that these inaccuracies are relatively small in comparison with the distortions that currently exist in the costing systems. I want to get within 10% of the totally accurate product cost, right now we can easily be off by 100% or more. So I don't want to get into a hair splitting routine—we recognise that some of these costs are common to more than one product. (Maskell, 1988, p. 41)

How the manager knows whether the error factor in the calculated product costs are 10% or 15% or 50% is not explained.

More recently, Kaplan (1990) appears to have had second thoughts about the ability of information systems to cope with the demands being made of them:

Attempting to meet these diverse—even contradictory demands (of operational control and product costing) with a single system design seems well beyond the capabilities of any existing system. (p. 25)

[A]t this time and with our present state of knowledge of what is possible and beneficial from newly designed operational control and ABC systems I am sceptical that we can develop the detailed specifications for (a single fully integrated) system. (p. 26)

Those reservations have not, however, caused him to resile from the claimed benefits of Activity Based Costing (ABC). Under ABC, Cooper and Kaplan (1990) maintain that "virtually all" of a company's activities exist to support the production and delivery of today's goods and services. They should therefore all be considered product costs:

nearly all factory and corporate support costs can be split apart and traced to individual products or product families. These costs include logistics, production, marketing and sales, distribution, service, technology, financial administration, information resources, general administration. (p. 38)

There are, however, two exceptions:

1. Research and development on future products should be collected as project costs.
2. Costs of excess capacity should be treated as a period cost rather than be charged to individual products. (Cooper and Kaplan, 1990, pp. 43–44)

Cooper and Kaplan's reasoning for this treatment is to avoid situations where the allocation procedures lead to an apparent increase in product costs, due to a general downturn in activities. As many earlier authors pointed out, it would be foolish to produce cost reports that led to prices being increased during an economic downturn.

To have to admit "exceptions" to the previous view that "virtually all" costs are, ultimately, product costs is to admit the system's deficiencies. On what grounds were those items singled out? Are there other exceptions that should be considered? On what grounds?

The problem with admitting exceptions is that, without clear grounds for allowing exceptions, the system becomes, once more, dependent on subjective judgements. In the case of the two exceptions noted by Cooper and Kaplan, the rationale is purely pragmatic without any apparent theoretical support. They provide further strength to the conclusion reached above that the need for product costs was asserted by J&K without any clear indication of why and in what form information about product costs is required by line managers or other interested parties.

CONCLUSION

Wells (1978a) concluded that, except as a (rough) guide to pricing for unique products or specific services, product costs involving allocated overheads served no useful purpose. Because of his staunch advocacy of allocation procedures, Alexander Hamilton Church was seen to be typical of those engineers who, in the period circa 1880–1910 developed and proselytised a costing system designed to report "full (allocated) product costs" and, Wells argued, he was wrong.

Johnson and Kaplan examined the same period of history, looked at the same "facts," and concluded that the engineers of the time developed "managerially relevant product costs." They argued that the costing systems in place later became irrelevant because accountants adopted broad allocation bases, such as direct labour hours, for the purposes of inventory valuation in financial reports. J&K advocated a return to the kind of system developed by Church (although more recent statements by Johnson suggest the he, too, may be moving away from that position—see Johnson, 1991, p. 65).

The point of this paper is to ask why such different conclusions emerge from studies of the same "facts." The conclusion reached is that Wells approached his study with the view that accounting systems in general, and costing systems in particular, should accord with economic theory. As the systems developed by people like Church were at odds with economic theory, and as they were shown to be incapable of satisfying the purposes for which they were developed, Wells advocated a form of activity costing that did not involve any kind of averaging of costs over products.

J&K, on the other hand, appear to have approached their study with the preconception that full product costs are necessary for long-run product-related strategic decisions. Their dispute with allocation procedures lay in the use of a single, factory-wide allocation base such as direct labor hours. They did not dispute the need for allocating costs except in the case of the short-run evaluation of the performance of line managers, where controllability is the obvious criterion for the inclusion of cost items in a performance report.

The starkly different conclusions emerged from the two studies under review because of the different, unstated, assumptions or ''mind sets'' of the people undertaking the research. They should serve to remind us of the dangers inherent in interpreting history because the facts will not speak for themselves and history will not decide. Rather, the facts are more likely to tell us what the researcher wants us to be told, and history will only decide what the researcher has already decided.

REFERENCES

Church, A. H., "Organisation by Production Factors," *The Engineering Magazine* (October, 1909).

Church, A. Hamilton, "The Proper Distribution of Expense Burden," *The Engineering Magazine* (1913).

Clarke, J. M., *Studies in the Economics of Overhead Costs* (Chicago: University of Chicago Press, 1923).

Cooper, C., and A. G. Puxty, "Ready Accounting Writing," EIASM Workshop, Madrid (June, 1991).

Cooper, Robin, and R. S. Kaplan, "How Cost Accounting Distorts Product Costs," *Management Accounting* (April, 1988).

Cooper, Robin, and Robert S. Kaplan, "Measure Costs Right: Make the Right Decision," *CPA Journal* (February, 1990).

Garner, S. Paul, *Evolution of Cost Accounting* (University of Alabama Press, 1954.)

Jevons, W. Stanley, *The Theory of Political Economy* (London: Macmillan and Co., 1888).

Johnson, H. Thomas, "Managing by Remote Control," in Peter Temin (Ed.), *Inside the Business Enterprise* (Chicago: University of Chicago Press, 1991).

Johnson, H. Thomas, and Robert S. Kaplan, *Relevance Lost: The Rise and Fall of Management Accounting* (Boston: Harvard Business School Press, 1987).

Jones, S. R. H., "Technology, Transaction Costs, and the Transition to Factory Production in the British Silk Industry, 1700–1870," *Journal of Economic History* (March, 1987).

Kaplan, Robert S., "The Four Stage Model of Systems Design," *Management Accounting* (February, 1990).

Kaplan, Robert S., "New Systems for Measurement and Control," *The Engineering Economist* (Spring, 1991).

Littleton, A. C., *Accounting Evolution to 1900* (New York: Russell and Russell, 1933).

Marshall, Alfred, *Principles of Economics* (London: Macmillan and Co., 1890).

Maskell, Brian, "Management Accounting: Relevance Regained—An Interview with Professor Robert S. Kaplan," *Accounting* (UK) (September, 1988).

Schneider, Dieter, "A Critique of the 'New School in the History of Accountancy' by

Accounting History: The Paradigms of Depreciation and Price Calculation,'' Paper presented at the Accounting History Research Methodology Conference, University of Mississippi, December, 1991.

Taylor, F. W., *The Principles of Scientific Management* (New York: Harper Bros., 1911).

Tinker, Anthony M., and Marilyn Neimark, ''Role of Annual Reports in Gender and Class Contradictions at General Motors,'' *Accounting Organisations and Society* vol. 12 (1987).

Tinker, Anthony M., Barbara D. Merino, and Marilyn Neimark, ''The Normative Origins of Positive Theories: Ideologies and Accounting Thought,'' *Accounting Organisations and Society* vol. 7 (1982).

Vangermeersch, Richard (Ed.), *The Contributions of Alexander Hamilton Church to Accounting and Management* (New York: Garland, 1986).

Wells, Murray C., ''The Nature of Activity Costing'' in O. Finley Graves, *The Costing Heritage,* The Academy of Accounting Historians, Mono. 6 (1991).

Wells, M. C., *Accounting for Common Costs,* CIERA (Urbana, Ill.: University of Illinois Press, 1978a).

Wells, M. C. (Ed.), *A Bibliography of Cost Accounting: Its Origins and Development to 1914,* CIERA (Urbana, Ill.: University of Illinois Press, 1978b).

Wells, M. C., ''Accounting for Activities,'' *Management Accounting* (May, 1976).

Wells, M. C., ''The Allocation of Overhead—Why?'' *The Australian Accountant* (April, 1972).

4

The Development of the Certified Public Accountant System in the People's Republic of China

Xu Zheng-dan

The certified public accountant system in the People's Republic of China, also called "public auditing" or "independent auditing," was developed in the 1980s, suited for the objective requirement of the socialist commodity economy. In the past ten years, it carried out the policies of opening to the outside world and vitalizing the domestic economy, and played a positive role in developing the socialist economy. This article will generally discuss the certified public accountant system and its development before the founding of the PRC, the establishment, development and roles of the certified public accountants system after the founding of the PRC, and the main characteristics and prospects of current certified public accountants system in the People's Republic of China.

THE CERTIFIED PUBLIC ACCOUNTANT SYSTEM AND ITS DEVELOPMENT BEFORE THE FOUNDING OF THE PEOPLE'S REPUBLIC OF CHINA

The certified public accountant system is the result of a commodity economy having developed to a certain extent. In the early 20th century in China, the feudal economy system gradually disintegrated, and there were some development in the commodity economy as it came in contact with foreign countries. After World War I especially, foreign capitalists came in succession to China to invest. Domestic industry and commerce developed quickly, and there appeared some limited companies which separated investors from managers. In such an economy, some foreign certified public accountants came to China to develop the operations of certified public accountants. For example, Deloitte Haskins & Sells and Price Waterhouse set up branches to develop their business in Shanghai. In 1918, the Beijing government issued the "Provisional Rules for Accountants," and Xie Lin, the general accountant of the Bank of China, became the first man who was qualified as a certified public accountant in China. The Kuomintang government issued the "Rules of Certification for Accountants" in 1928, the "Regulations for Accountants" in 1930, and the "Law of Accountants" in 1945. These rules, regulations and laws stipulated acquirement of qualification, scope of services, responsibilities and ethics of a certified public accountant.

After the issuing of the "Provisional Rules for Accountants," the number of certified public accountants (CPAs) increased year by year. According to statistical data, the number of persons who were qualified as CPAs is as follows:

Year	Number of CPAs
1918–1921	13
1922–1924	101
1925–1927	171
1927–1929	268
1929–1930	184
1931–1937	1,036
1938–1947	1,583

The total number was more than 3,000, excluding re-qualified persons.

At that time, there were some famous public accounting firms established by Chinese CPAs. For instance, Zhengze Public Accounting Firm, created by Xie Lin in 1918; Xu Yong-zuo Public Accounting Firm, created by Xu Yong-zuo in 1921; Xu-lun Pan's (Li Xing) Public Accounting Firm, created by Pan Xu-lun in 1927; and Gong Xing Public Accounting Firm, set up in 1932. The above four public accounting firms were the so-called "Big Four Public Accounting Firms." The Xu-lun Pan Public Accounting Firm was well-known in Hong Kong, Macao, Singapore, and the Philippines. It headquartered in Shanghai and had branches in Nanjing, Chongqing, Guilin, Wuhan, and Tianjing. Its services covered all of the provinces in China and its staff was more than one thousand.

Following are brief explanations of the scope of services before the founding of the People's Republic of China.

The accountant who acquired CPA qualification could run a public accounting firm himself independently or form a joint accounting firm with other CPAs to develop the services of certified public accountants. According to the "Law of Accountants," the following defines the scope of services for CPAs:

1. Handling affairs of organization, management, checking, investigation, arrangement, settlement, testification and appraisal on accounting ordered by government agencies or entrusted by clients;
2. Filling the post of examiner, settlement officer, bankruptcy manager, testament executer and other trustees;
3. Paying taxes, registering matters and making documents of accounting and business for clients.

The scope of services for CPAs specifically includes company register, trademark register, engagement and appraisal entrusted by clients; holding the post of standing accounting consultant for enterprises and institutions; examining accounts entrusted by clients and presenting certificates to concerned parties; handling affairs of property settlement for bankrupt enterprises and presenting reports; designing accounting systems, and training accountants and auditors; etc.

For the purpose of promoting the certified public accountant system, Shanghai founded an association of accountants in 1925. After that, many provinces founded similar associations succesively, and there appeared the Federation of Accountants Association of China.

THE ESTABLISHMENT, DEVELOPMENT AND ROLES OF THE CERTIFIED PUBLIC ACCOUNTANT SYSTEM IN SOCIOECONOMIC ACTIVITIES AFTER THE FOUNDING OF THE PEOPLE'S REPUBLIC OF CHINA

At the beginning of the founding of the People's Republic of China in 1949, the government adopted a policy to support and guide private enterprises to develop production. CPAs, therefore, continued to render their services, checking accounts for private enterprises and presenting auditing reports to the board of directors and concerned parties, and handling other business affairs of the CPA.

From 1953, the State began to carry out the socialist transformation of capitalist industry and commerce, i.e., to reform private ownership of the means of production into socialist public ownership step by step. In 1956, the socialist transformation was basically completed, and the socialist public ownership economy held absolute predominance in the national economy. In the long period after that, China has carried out a unique model of a planned production economy and a restricted commodity economy. In such a situation, the position of CPA firms closely related to a commodity economy lost their existing social context, and gradually disappeared.

The Third Plenary Session of the Eleventh Central Committee of the Chinese Communist Party, convened in December 1978, determined the strategies for opening to the outside world and vitalizing domestic economy policies, and defined theoretically the socialist economy as a planned commodity economy. Opening to the outside world implies that, proceeding from China's actual conditions, development of foreign trade, adopting various forms to make full use of foreign capitals, introducing foreign advanced technologies, studying and applying foreign scientific methods of operational management, and so on. Vitalizing the domestic economy mainly implies expanding the operational right for enterprises, enhancing their vitalization, and furthering the society's productivity. The implementation of the policies of opening to the outside world and vitalizing the domestic economy has promoted the development of a planned commodity economy. It has particularly promoted and given great impetus to the initiations of joint ventures, cooperative enterprises and sole foreign-capital enterprises in China.

In July 1979, the government issued the "Law of Joint Ventures in the People's Republic of China" accompanied by "Executive Regulations." These stipulated that the certificates of paid-in capital of all parties to joint ventures, and the annual financial statements and liquidation accounting statements of joint ventures, "will be valid only after being attested and verified by Chinese certified public accountants and after presenting certificates" (Article No. 90, Executive Regulations). The Detailed Rules and Regulations of the Law of Joint Ventures in the People's Republic of China, issued in December 1980, also stipulated that joint ventures should present the auditing reports made by CPAs registered in China when they submit the tax return of income taxes and financial statements to the local taxation agencies (Article No. 20, Detailed Rules and Regulations). The initiation of foreign-funded enterprises, the development of a planned commodity economy, and requirements of the government's laws and regulations impelled the reestablishment of the certified public accountant system in China. On January 1, 1981, the first certified public accountant firm was established in Shanghai. All provinces in China have since recruited the CPA system and set up certified public accountant firms in succession.

In July 1986, the State Council issued the "Regulations of the People's Republic of China on Certified Public Accountants" (abbreviated to RCPA), which includes six chapters and thirty articles stipulating the examination, registration, scope of services, rules of work and establishment of a public accounting firm, etc. The issuance of RCPA has promoted the certified public accountant system of the People's Republic of China, and opened up a new area of accounting theory and practice.

Following is an explanation of scope of services stipulated in Articles No. 11 and 12 of RCPA:

A. Certified public accountants can render the following accounting and auditing services:

    1. Examination of accounting records, financial statements, and other financial information, and issuance of auditing reports;

    2. Verification of paid-in capital of an enterprise and issuance of capital verification reports;

3. Participation in administrating the liquidation affairs for the dissolution and bankruptcy of enterprises;

4. Participation in mediation of economic disputes, asistance in identifying evidences in economic lawsuits;

5. Other matters concerning accounting and auditing.

B. Certified public accountants can render the following accounting consultancy services:

1. Design of financial accounting systems, serving as accounting consultants, and provision of consultancy services in accounting, finance, tax, and business management;

2. Agency service in tax declaration;

3. Agency service in application for registration, assistance in drafting contracts, articles of association, and other commercial documents;

4. Training of financial accounting personnel;

5. Other accounting consultancy services.

The regulations stipulate that government agencies, enterprises, non-profit business units, or individuals may engage CPAs for the services specified in the above articles.

The number of public accounting firms and CPAs in China has been growing steadily due to the development of a planned commodity economy, the rapid increase of foreign-funded enterprises, and the issuance of RCPA. Following are the numbers of public accounting firms with CPAs and staff in recent years:

Year	Firms	CPAs	Staff
1986	80	1,000	2,500
1989	200	2,000	7,000
1991	1,456*	6,700	10,000
1992	1,500	10,000	15,000

*The number of firms includes 955 branches.

The establishment of the certifed public accountant system in China has promoted interchanges and business cooperation with international certified public accountant firms and foreign accounting associations. During the last decade, big foreign accounting firms set up permanent representative agencies separately in Beijing, Shanghai, Guangzhou, and Fuzhou. Coopers & Lybrand, for example, conducted an auditor training course at Shanghai University of Finance and Economy in 1980, and then set up two permanent representative agencies in Shanghai and Guangzhou in January and April 1981. Deloitte Haskins & Sells set up a permanent representative agency in Shanghai in October 1981. Price Waterhouse & Co. set up a permanent representative agency in Beijing in November 1981; Arthur Andersen & Co. set up a permanent representative agency in Beijing in 1982; and Peat Marwick Michell & Co. set up a permanent representative agency in Beijing in 1983. At present, the six big accounting firms have set up sixteen permanent representative agencies in China. These agencies act as consultants to foreign investors in accounting, auditing and taxation, etc. They also accept clients' trusts and cooperate with Chinese certified public accountants to audit jointly foreign invested enterprises, then present auditing reports separately. The auditing reports presented by foreign accountants are invalid to Chinese agencies in China. The firms, furthermore, accept staff from Chinese accounting firms to practice and accept training abroad. All these have made valuable contributions to improve the foreign investment environment and promote the development of certified public accountants in China.

For the sake of protecting the legal equity of CPAs, exchanging their experiences and furthering contacts with other accountants at home and abroad, the Association of Certified Public Accountants of China was established on November 15, 1988, in Beijing. After that, there appeared many local associations of certified public accountants in China. The associations are professional bodies composed of CPAs. The associations are also the trade associations in which CPA and public accounting firms can be self-educated and self-managed. The establishment of the associations has impelled an exchange of working experience between certified public accountants in China, improved the quality of services and professional ethics of CPAs, and also promoted connections and contacts with international associations, such as the Federation of International Accountants, the International Accounting Standards Committee, and the Federation of Accountants in Asia and the Pacific area, thus enhancing interchanges with international accounting circles.

The reestablishment of the certified public accountant system has played a positive role in carrying out the policies of opening to the outside world and vitalizing the domestic economy, improving the management quality in enterprises, training accountants and auditors in international business, and promoting the research of accounting theories.

Firstly, in international business, the establishment and development of the certified public accountant system has improved the investing environment for foreigners and helped implement the open-door policy. According to international conventions, the financial statements and the other financial materials of enterprises will become valid only after being examined and verified by certified public accountants. The certified public accountant system is an indispensable measure for organization, operation, and liquidation of enterprises. As of June 1991, there were 34,000 foreign-invested enterprises in China, with capital of $20 billion U.S. dollars. The number of enterprises as well as their capital is constantly increasing. Over the past decade, CPAs have conducted a great deal of business for foreign-invested enterprises, including verification, auditing and feasibility studies for joint ventures, cooperative enterprises, sole foreign capital enterprises, material processing, parts assembling, sample-making, and compensation trades and foreign debt items. CPAs have held the post of permanent accounting consultants, participated in negotiations with foreign investors, designed internal control systems and accounting systems (including accounting computer software), and trained accounting and auditing personnel, etc. The certified public accountant system has thereby played an important role in the open door policy and in developing economic contacts with foreign countries.

Secondly, in internal affairs, CPAs have performed the following: (1) to suit the needs of the reforms of the economic system, verifying capital and auditing for joint operations, contract operations, and verifying capital, checking accounts, property appraisal for leases, sales transactions, issuance of bonds and stocks; (2) to suit the development of various components of the economy, verifying capital, declaring taxes, property appraisal account checking, annual examination and re-registration for collective, private, and individual firms and united enterprises of various economic components; (3) consulting, designing accounting systems and accounting computer programs, training accounting and auditing personnel for enterprises, and holding the post of standing accounting consultants in enterprises. All these works have promoted the development of the economy, protected the legal equities of the state and enterprises, and improved the management quality of enterprises.

Thirdly, as the CPAs need advanced professional technology and ethics, they should continue to develop professionally and accept further education in accounting and auditing concerning foreign business, laws of economy, international accounting, investing management, enterprise management, computerized accounting, psychology, etc., thus improving the quality of CPAs in accounting and auditing theories and practices. The establishment of the certified public accountant system, therefore, can not only achieve improvement in practice but also enhance knowledge and training of talents in accounting and auditing.

The execution of the certified public accountant system, in brief, is necessary for the development of a planned commodity economy and opening to the outside world and vitalizing the domestic economy policies. The reestablishment and recovery of the certified public accountant system is an inevitable outcome of transforming the economic system in China from one of a product economy to one of a planned commodity economy.

THE FEATURES OF THE CERTIFIED PUBLIC ACCOUNTANT SYSTEM IN THE PEOPLE'S REPUBLIC OF CHINA

There are some common characteristics in the certified public accountant system of the People's Republic of China and those of other countries. In China, however, it is a result of the planned commodity economy and should be suitable to the Chinese situation. It has, therefore, some particular features in contrast to other countries. I will outline these features in brief.

Qualifications of Certified Public Accountants

Professional level and ethical quality are important factors in determining auditing quality. At the beginning of restoring the certified public accountant system, China put great attention on reviewing the qualifications of CPAs and strictly controlling them. In the ''Regulations of the People's Republic of China on Certified Public Accountants,'' it is stipulated that a candidate for CPA must pass the examination or evaluation of CPA, and ask the public accounting firm he or she has served to report to the Ministry of Finance or the provincial public finance department or bureau for approval and registration. Once a CPA is approved for registration by a provincial department or bureau, the said department or bureau shall report to the Ministry of Finance for recording purposes. The Ministry of Finance will prepare and issue, on a uniform basis, a CPA certificate to those approved for registration.

In China, examination and evaluation of CPAs shall be directed, organized and supervised on a uniform basis by a the national examination board approved by the Ministry of Finance.

The professional examination of CPAs is a uniform national examination and a kind of national examination for professional qualification. The candidate sitting for the CPA examination must be a Chinese citizen who loves the People's Republic of China and supports the socialist system. The candidate must be a college graduate, or a person with an equivalent academic education, who has worked in the accounting or auditing field for more than three years, or must be a postgraduate who has worked in the field for more than one year. The contents of the examination include accounting, financial management, auditing, economic law, etc., and the candidate shall have knowledge about current laws, regulations, and systems which have close relationship to the field of CPAs. A candidate who passes all the examinations has the essential qualification of a CPA and can obtain a certificate of quality in all the courses. A candidate who has the certificate of quality takes part in a public accounting firm, then the firm can apply to the Ministry of Finance or the provincial public finance department or bureau for approval and registration. After approval and registration, he or she becomes a CPA. If a candidate who has the certificate of quality is not approved as a CPA in five years, his certificate of quality will cease to be effective at the sixth year.

The first CPA examination in China was held in December 1991.

An applicant for registration as a CPA can be waived from the examination requirements and qualified through an evaluation process. The applicant must be either a senior accountant, an accounting professor or associate professor, a research fellow, or associate research fellow who has practical accounting experience; or someone with a college or equivalent education who has worked in the financial or accounting field for more than twenty years and possesses professional expertise.

The method of evaluation is to review and check the following documents:

diploma of education, certificate of professional title, published professional works, translations, or articles published in provincial or national professional journals, certificate of performance on practical accounting work, etc. The implementation of the evaluation process is undertaken by a provincial examination board. The result of evaluation shall be reported to the national examination board for review.

According to the "Regulations of the People's Republic of China on Certified Public Accountants," if a CPA leaves a public accounting firm, the firm shall request approval from the controlling public finance bureau and shall return the accountant's Certified Public Accountant Certificate to the public finance department or bureau. If such an accountant wishes to perform professional services again, he or she shall apply again according to stipulations.

No staff currently working in governmental agencies may be registered to practise as a CPA, according to the regulation.

The Relationship between CPAs and Public Accounting Firms

In China, a public accounting firm is a legal body approved by the state to engage independently the services of CPAs according to the law. The firm shall balance its revenue and expenses itself, keep an independent accounting record and pay taxes according to the law. Collective and individual persons cannot open a public accounting firm. The opening of a public accounting firm shall be reported to the Ministry of Finance or to the provincial public finance department or bureau for review and approval. A public accounting firm may accept engagements in other administrative areas within the country. The Ministry of Finance and the provincial public finance department or bureau are reponsible for supervising the business of public accounting firms. A CPA must be with a public accounting firm. The services rendered by a CPA must be accepted by a public accounting firm and not by the CPA individually. A report issued by a CPA shall be signed by the accountant and shall bear the seal of the public accounting firm, thus guaranteeing the independence, objectivity, and impartiality of the opinions in the report and its responsibility for the performance of the CPA.

The public accounting firm shall collect fees on a uniform basis for services rendered by CPAs. The standard of fees shall be worked out by the provincial public finance department or bureau. In China, the aims of services rendered by public accounting firms is not only to collect service fees, but also to meet the needs of the economic management. Public accounting firms are required to learn from each other, help each other, and yield to each other. Any conflict amongst them shall be resolved by consultation. A public accounting firm should not engage services by discounting the standards of service fees or offering some promises or by other inappropriate means.

The Working Rules of Certified Public Accountants

A CPA shall observe the following rules when he or she renders services:

a. Observe the relevant rules, laws and regulations of the State, according to the relevant agreements, contracts and articles of association;

b. Scrupulously abide by the principles of impartiality and objectivity in seeking the truth from facts and being responsible for the correctness and legitimacy of the contents of the report issued;

c. Decline to render services to any client if there is any conflict of interest between them, and report the situation to the public accounting firm. The client or other relevant person has the right to ask for such a declination;

d. Strictly keep the confidentiality of the data and information obtained or accessed in performing services;

e. Indicate the situation clearly in the report issued when he or she finds fabrication of information, fraud for personal gain, or other violation of the State laws or regulations. Clients' requests for false or inappropriate attestation shall be rejected;

f. If a CPA is negligent in his professional conduct, the public finance agency that approved the registration shall cancel it and revoke the CPA certificate and report to the Ministry of Finance for recording;

g. If a CPA violates the rules of work with harmful results, the public accounting firm shall make an accurate report, and the public finance agency in charge shall impose on the accountant the following sanctions according to the seriousness of the case: warning, fine, provisional prohibition from practice, or revocation of the CPA certificate. A CPA who violates the criminal law shall be committed to the judicial authority for punishment according to the law.

Auditing Standards and Accounting Standards for Certified Public Accountants

Because the time since restoring the Chinese certified public accountant system is short, a series of auditing standards has not been established. While developing CPA services, the Institute of Certified Public Accountants of China and the Accounting Business Administration Department of the Ministry of Finance are working out some rules on auditing and verification, and have posed trial programs or codes giving primary guides for CPAs when auditing and verifying. When executed, these work rules, in my opinion, will be more perfect, and gradually will become a standard for auditing and verification. Rules currently under examination and being worked out in the field include the following: Rules of Examination and Verification of Accounting Statements on CPAs, Rules of Auditing and Verification Plan on CPAs, Rules of Auditing Report on CPAs, etc.

The standards of auditing and verification on CPAs shall accord with the Chinese situation and meet the needs of a developing socialist commodity economy system, while absorbing auditing standards of Western countries by anal-ysis, including auditing standards of America, Britain, Canada, Australia, and Japan, and international auditing standards.

Accounting standards are an important basis for evaluating financial positions and profit and loss positions when a CPA performs an audit and verification. Now the accounting standards of China are being worked out by the Accounting Business Administration Department of the Ministry of Finance. In auditing joint ventures using Chinese and foreign investment, the accounting principles and methods CPAs now employ are mainly according to the "Accounting Regula-tions of the People's Republic of China for Joint Ventures Using Chinese and Foreign Investment" (abbreviated to "ARJV") promulgated on March 4, 1985, by the Ministry of Finance of the People's Republic of China; "Classification of Accounts and Accounting Statements of Industrial Joint Ventures Using Chi-nese and Foreign Investment" (abbreviated to "CAAS") promulgated on April 24, 1985, by the Ministry of Finance of the People's Republic of China; and "Supplementary Regulations on Accounting Dealing with Foreign Currencies for Joint Ventures Using Chinese and Foreign Investment," promulgated in December 1987 by the Ministry of Finance of the People's Republic of China.

"ARJV" proposes basic requirements for general provisions, accounting of-fices and accounting staff, general principles for accounting, accounting for paid-in capital, accounting for cash and current accounts, accounting for inventories, accounting for long-term investment and long-term liabilities, accounting for fixed assets, accounting for intangible assets and other assets, accounting for cost and expenses, accounting for sales and profit, classification of accounts and statements (there are other regulations in detail), accounting documents and ac-counting books, audit and accounting files, dissolution and liquidation, etc. This accounting system is applicable to joint ventures in all lines of business and industry, including transportation, agriculture and stock raising, commerce and trade, the catering trades and services, the tourist and hotel trade, construction and engineering services, leasing, etc. These accounting principles (including accounting policies and accounting assumptions) and methods regulated in the above accounting systems have taken into account the characteristics of the joint ventures, and their contents are fundamentally close to international accounting standards and conventions. For example, it is required to employ the principles of double entry bookkeeping, historical cost for valuation, accrual basis, match-ing of revenue with cost or expenses, strict distinguishing of capital expenditure and revenue expenditure, keeping the consistency of accounting methods from one period to the other, and accounting information provided being correct, faithful, complete and timely.

In "CAAS," accounts are classified into five groups: assets, liabilities, capital, cost, and profit and loss. This classification resembles Western enterprises. The kinds of accounting statements of joint ventures are much the same as Western enterprises' basic statements, including: a balance sheet reflecting financial po-sition of an enterprise at the end of every accounting period, an income statement reflecting operating results of an enterprise in every accounting period, and a statement of changes in financial position reflecting the position of sources and applications of working capital of an enterprise in every accounting year. The structures of these statements resemble the structures of Western accounting statements. There are some supplementary statements to these basic statements, including: (1) The supplementary statements of balance sheets are a statement of inventories, a statement of fixed assets and accumulated depreciation, a statement of construction in progress, a statement of intangible assets and other assets, and a statement of accounts in foreign currencies; and (2) Supplementary statements of income and statements of profit distribution; statements of cost of goods manufactured and cost of goods sold; statements of production cost, sales, and cost of sales for main goods; statements of manufacturing expenses; statements of selling expenses; statements of general and administrative expenses; statements of non-operating income and expenses, etc. These supplementary statements reflect the specific position of relevant items in basic accounting statements, according to the accounting principle of full disclosure.

In April 1991 the State promulgated "The Income Tax Law of the People's Republic of China for Foreign-funded Enterprises and Exclusively Foreign-owned Enterprises." In June of the same year, the State promulgated "The Specific Executing Regulations of the Income Tax Law." The State is working out "The Accounting Regulations of the People's Republic of China for Foreign-funded Enterprises." We can foresee that the standards and basis by which CPAs abide when performing audits will become more and more perfect and complete.

FORECASTING THE FUTURE OF THE CERTIFIED PUBLIC ACCOUNTANT SYSTEM OF THE PEOPLE'S REPUBLIC OF CHINA

In China, the business of certified public accounting is a newly developing line. Since the short period of restoration, it has played a full role in promoting opening to the outside world, strengthening indirect economic supervision of profit and non-profit-oriented organizations, maintaining the financial and economic discipline of the state, enhancing enterprise management levels, training and fostering talented accountants, etc. While the state thoroughly carries out the policies of opening to the outside world and vitalizing the domestic economy, the certified public accountant system will further develop and have a great future.

I will now give a forecast analysis of the future of the certified public accountant system in China, according to the present situation and the developing trends of the Chinese national economy.

Continuing the development of opening to the outside world and intensifying activation on the inside, CPAs will surely develop greatly in quantity and quality. Up to June 1991, the State had approved 19,519 units of Chinese foreign joint ventures; 9,977 units of Chinese-foreign cooperative enterprises; 4,515 units of exclusively foreign-owned enterprises; in total, 34,011 units of foreign-funded enterprises. It is estimated that the foreign-funded enterprises will increase by some 60,000 units in the next five years. Therefore, according to the requirements of opening to the outside world, the existing number of CPAs is far from the future need for verifying capital and audits. In the field of internal services, in the development of domestic capital markets, joint operating enterprises, corporations, and securities markets, there are many verification services that CPAs are needed to perform. So, according to either external or internal services, the number of CPAs will surely continue to multiply, and the quality of services will also be rapidly enhanced. Thus, the CPA will meet the growing needs of the society's economic activities. The contents and auditing methods in CPA service activities will have the following developments.

Audit and verification services as well as consultation services to operation and management will develop concurrently. Today, the contents of audits and verifications performed by CPAs are mainly checking and examining accounts, documents, properties, liabilities and accounting statements in order to judge the truthfulness and legality of the accounting information and statements. As the enterprise managements and relevant agencies (i.e., banks, taxation offices) focus attention on operation efficiency, effectiveness, and economy of enterprises, the future service area of CPAs in China will expand to the field of consultation services to operation and management, including consultation to investment decisions, operation decisions, supply, production and sale organizing and management, personnel administration, enterprises mergers, etc. It should be pointed out that developing consultation services for operation and management is a worldwide developing trend in CPA service activities. In some international accounting firms, the revenue collected from consultation services has reached about 50% of the total revenue. Therefore, developing these kind of services is important for Chinese CPAs.

Intensifying internal control and system-based audit will be developed concurrently. Internal control is an effective means for strengthening management, enhancing operation efficiency, protecting property safety, and realizing operation policies and targets. Internal control is a management system of organizing, restricting, assessing and adjusting economic activities by employing accounting, statistics, and other methods. Modern internal control has promoted the development of auditing methods, that is, employing "system-based audit" in auditing methods. It begins with evaluating internal control, including familiarizing, testing and assessing the internal control system, then deciding the focus, area, and extent of the sample audit according to the results of the evaluation. This system not only shortens the time of audit under the premise of guaranteeing auditing quality, this shortening of time allows limited auditors to undertake and perform more auditing tasks, but also can save depletion of auditing resources and decrease the burden of audit fees. This modern system of auditing is now being employed in audits performed by Chinese CPAs, and will surely be widely employed in auditing services further.

Computer-aided auditing techniques and conventional auditing techniques will be combined. The development of modern auditing requires CPAs to be familiar not only with conventional auditing techniques and methods, but also with computer-aided auditing techniques. Since the late 1970s a large amount of computerized accounting software has been introduced and developed. Today, many large and medium enterprises have completed computerized management on accounting. CPAs are requested to employ computer-aided auditing techniques in audit and verification work. Therefore, Chinese CPAs and their management departments should put much more attention on research of auditing techniques for computerized accounting, according to the characteristics of computerized accounting using minicomputers in China. They should develop general auditing software and special programs, employ ''audit through computers'' and ''audit with computers,'' to meet the needs of computerized auditing from now on.

In the past, some Chinese public accounting firms cooperated with foreign accounting firms to perform audits on some joint ventures. They also have cooperated with Hong Kong Ernst & Whinnry to open the Zhong An Finance and Accounting Consultation Firm, and have reached agreements with Arthur Andersen & Co. and Price Waterhouse & Co. to cooperatively open public accounting firms in China. In the future, with the rapid increase of foreign-funded enterprises in China, Chinese public accounting firms will further cooperate with foreign accounting firms in China to perform services, and to open public accounting firms. At the same time China has gradually set up overseas international enterprises. For example, by November 1991, Shanghai had opened 113 overseas enterprises of proprietorships and joint ventures. So, after several years, it is possible that branches of Chinese public accounting firms or independent public accounting firms will open abroad in the areas where there are significant economic contacts with China.

In brief, the business of Chinese certified public accounting is progressively active and growing, and has a glowing future. We believe that it will quickly prosper and play a much more important role in the economic activities of China.

5

Development of a "Philosophy of Disclosure" in Accounting Institutions of Japan

Tsunehiro Tsumori

INTRODUCTION

As proved by the valuable results of researches on the existing records of accounts, business accounting has taken a long and winding path to the present double entry bookkeeping system through much trial-and-error for hundreds of years since the beginning of the thirteenth century (Izutani, 1980). At first it was formulated as an income determination system for individual companies. With the establishment of the modern corporation system, especially in the first half of the 19th century, business accounting, which had been working as the income determination system for individual companies, assumed a new role as a social control system, i.e., the distributable income determination system to "protect creditors" (Littleton, 1933, pp. 242 ff.; Yamey, 1950; Tsumori, 1962). In the first half of the 20th century, a financial disclosure system to "protect investors" was established (Previts & Merino, 1979). With this as a start, business accounting took a role as the newer social control system. Needless to say, this transition to the modern business accounting system is essentially indicated by the establishment of the "disclosure system."

Japan was modernized after the Meiji Restoration in 1868, which opened Japan to foreign dealings after isolation for over 200 years. After the Restoration, Japan had an eager appetite for new accounting thought as thirsty people looking for a spring to sustain them. At first Japan built the foundation of modern accounting practice by learning from the Anglo-American experience (Kimura,

1950, pp. 9 ff.; Hisano, 1987 [1], [2]; Chiba, 1987). Later it established the modern accounting system in the Commercial Law and in the Corporate Income Tax Law by learning from the experience of Germany (Kimura, 1950, pp. 41 ff.; Takatera, 1974). After World War II, Japan acquired a lot from the U.S. experience in each area of accounting in the so-called "triangular system" (Arai & Shiratori, 1991, p. 3) composed of the Commercial Law, the Securities & Exchange Act, and the Corporate Income Tax Law. A new convention was built on the old domestic convention as a foundation by introducing the experiences of foreign countries, and then this new convention became tradition as a foundation for the creation of a yet newer convention. This process has been consistently repeated. In other words, this was the process of integration or "harmonization," on the basis of the Japanese tradition, between the Anglo-American system and the Franco-German one; it was the process of a kind of model of Horatian "concordance of discord (*concordia discors*)." The same process took place with regard to the introduction of the "thought of disclosure" and "disclosure system."

Recently, as the international harmonization of accounting standards has become an important issue, the role that the disclosure system plays has strikingly become significant, and the focus of accounting standards has been moving from the issue of measurement to that of disclosure (Tsumori, 1988 [2], pp. 93–94; Johnson, 1992, p. 101). The purpose of this paper is to examine the experience of the integration or harmonization between the Anglo-American system and the Franco-German one in Japan, with special focus on the development of the "thought of disclosure" in the historical stage.

From the perspective of world history, we have valuable experiences from hundreds of years, but tasks still remain for the next century. Such experiences and tasks suggest that it is necessary for us to attempt to analyze the historical experiences and reality of each country and to distinguish, carefully and elaborately, the general experiences which are common and which can be harmonized among countries from the peculiar experiences inherent to each country. The 21st century will come soon. It is high time that accounting researchers be required to review the experiences of each country from the perspective of world history. I hope this paper can offer helpful suggestions on such issues.

THE CHARACTERISTICS OF THE FINANCIAL STATEMENTS SYSTEM BEFORE WORLD WAR II

The establishment of the modern institution for financial statements in Japan was started in the midst of the Crash of 1929. In this sense, this attempt to establish the institution had a common foundation with the movements launched in the advanced capitalistic countries to reform the accounting institutions all together at that time, e.g., the movement to set accounting standards in the United States, the reform of the Companies Acts in the United Kingdom, and the establishment of the Stock Corporation Law in Germany (Kurosawa, 1987, p. 8).

The moment of this reform in Japan was the "Working Rules for Preparation of Financial Statements" established in order to "improve and unify financial statements" for the "purpose of the rationalization of industry" by the Financial Management Committee of the ad hoc Industrial Rationalization Board of the Ministry of Commerce and Industry (MCI). After the "Working Rules for Preparation of Financial Statements" was set as a starting point, the "Working Rules for Preparation of Financial Statements of Military Munitions Factory and Plant" and "Guidance for Preparation for Financial Statements of Naval Munitions Factory and Plant" were published one after another in 1940. Furthermore, for the purpose of unifying them, "Draft of Working Rules for Preparation of Balance Sheets of Manufacturing Industry," "Drafting of Working Rules for Preparation of Inventories of Properties of Manufacturing Industry" and "Draft of Working Rules for Preparation of Income Statements of Manufacturing Industry" were published by the Conference for Unification of Financial Statements of the Cabinet Planning Council in 1942. While these series of working rules were set for different purposes, they all had common historical characteristics in terms of sharing aspects of both the structure of computation and the institutional framework.

At first, with regard to the aspect of accounting measurement, the "Working Rules for Preparation of Financial Statements" (1934) published by the MCI was different from AAA accounting principles and AIA accounting principles which were developed almost at the same time in the United States, and yet based on the assets and liabilities view of earnings. This is obvious from the fact that the "Working Rules for Preparation of Financial Statements" was composed of "Balance Sheet Rules," "Inventories of Property Rules, and "Income Statement Rules" in that order. This was because both the "Balance Sheet Rules" and the "Inventories of Property Rules" were respectively set as the detailed rules for the year-end preparation of balance sheets and inventories of property provided in Article 26 of the Commercial Law (1899), which was based on the assets and liabilities view of earnings with inventories of property in the center.

The view of earnings that was expressed in "Draft of Working Rules for Preparation of Financial Statements of Manufacturing Industry" compiled by the Cabinet Planning Council was also essentially the same as the "Working Rules for Preparation of Financial Statements" by the MCI. That is, this draft had the same contents as the "Working Rules for Preparation of Financial Statements" by MCI mentioned above, and consisted of three parts in the following order: "Draft of Working Rules for Preparation of Balance Sheets of Manufacturing Industry," "Draft of Working Rules for Preparation of Inventories of Property of Manufacturing Industry," and "Draft of Working Rules for Preparation of Income Statements of Manufacturing Industry." Each draft provided the "standard procedures for the preparation [of] the corresponding statement" (Cabinet Planning Council, 1941 quoted in Kurosawa, 1987, pp. 186, 170).

In providing rules, however, both the working rules by the MCI and the draft by the Cabinet Planning Council adopted a different order from that of the commercial law: balance sheets at first, and then inventories of property in the working rules and the draft; inventories of property at first, and then balance sheets in the commercial law. In the working rules by the MCI, furthermore, income statements should be divided into four parts, and alienation began from the traditional principle of property determination.

Among the characteristics of these working rules, the aspect of the institutional framework is more remarkable than that of accounting measurement structure.

The "Working Rules for Preparation of Financial Statements" by the MCI mentioned above was intended to "improve and unify financial statements," to "objectify the principles in accounting itself," and to "generalize the common working rules of action for all business" (Kurosawa, 1990, p. 223). It was also "a forerunner of 'Financial Accounting Standards for Business Enterprises' to be developed after the Second War" together with the "Working Rules for Preparation of Inventories of Property" published in February 1936 (ibid., p. 208).

However, they were intended, at best, to "standardize and unify financial statements" for "the purpose of rationalization of industry" to cope with the economic recession at that time. Therefore they provided only "an improvement and unification judged from the viewpoint of management" (Iwata's speech at round-table discussion, May 15, 1948, pp. 68–69).

In addition, "Working Rules for Preparation of Financial Statements of Army Munitions Plant and Factory" by the Ministry of the Army, "Guideline for Preparation of Financial Statements of Navy Munitions Plant and Factory" by the Ministry of the Navy (these two were published one after another in April 1940), "Draft of Working Rules for Preparation of Balance Sheets," "Draft of Working Rules for Preparation of Inventories of Property" and "Draft of Working Rules for Preparation of Income Statements" (these three were published in November 1941) were all published "for economic control from the national standpoint" (ibid., p. 69).

Thus the working rules formulated in this period, e.g., "Working Rules for Preparation of Financial Statements," could not avoid being considered as defective rules lacking the fundamentals (especially such as the thought of disclosure) to a modern accounting system.

In history, the philosophy of business that "had ruled all the [Japanese] companies" since the Meiji Restoration in 1868 had been the "principle of the traditional paternalistic domination of business." The "accounting thought based on" this principle considered accounting as the "private instrument for the dominators of business" or the "system to protect business secrets" (Kurosawa, 1990, pp. 222–223).

In the 1930s when the working rules such as the "Working Rules for Preparation of Financial Statements" were published one after another, there rose the strong tendency toward financial disclosure in the advanced capitalistic countries such as the USA and the UK. The publication of these Working Rules in this world-wide tendency should have been the best chance to abolish the closed and secretive accounting system and thought prevailing in Japan since the Meiji Restoration, and to establish the modern disclosure system of financial statements and the thought of disclosure. But this reform was, at last, impossible because of the exclusive domination of stocks by family partners in so-called *zaibatsu* companies, the undeveloped securities market, the absence of democracy, and the irresistible stream toward the controlled wartime economy.

Therefore, when Japan lost World War II, the accounting system was still "involved mainly in setting and classifying financial statement items or in setting and unifying the standards of valuation" (Iwata's speech, May 15, 1948, p. 69), and "based on the orientation to the technical improvement of accounting" (Kurosawa, 1955, p. 131).

ESTABLISHMENT OF "FINANCIAL ACCOUNTING STANDARDS FOR BUSINESS ENTERPRISES" AFTER WORLD WAR II

The establishment of "Financial Accounting Standards for Business Enterprises (FASBE)" published in July 1949 is symbolic of changes in the Japanese accounting system after World War II. On the one hand, the FASBE was set to keep up the legacy-tradition of the prewar accounting system, particularly the "Working Rules for Preparation of Financial Statements" (published in August 1934) and "Rules of Assets Valuation" (published in February 1936) compiled by the ad hoc Industry Rationalization Board of the MCI. On the other hand, in the special situation under occupation, the FASBE was also influenced by "accepted accounting practices in occidental countries" (GHQ, Instruction, 1947, in Arai, 1989 [1], p. 74), especially by generally accepted accounting principles in the United States. As a result, while the FASBE still maintains common characteristics with the "Working Rules for Preparation of Financial Statements" and the "Working Rules for Property Valuation," it has new characteristics fundamentally different from those of the prewar accounting system with regard to the accounting measurement structure and the institutional framework.

As to the aspect of the accounting measurement structure, the FASBE takes a totally different approach from that of the "Working Rules for Preparation of Financial Statements" systematized with balance sheets and inventories of property in the center, and adopts the financial statements system with income statements in the center.

That is, as stated above, the system of the prewar "Working Rules for Preparation of Financial Statements" was composed of the following rules: (1) balance sheets, (2) inventories of property, and (3) income statements, in that order. The system of the FASBE, on the contrary, is composed of (1) general principles, (2) income statements rules, and (3) balance sheets rules, in that order. In addition, the system of FASBE includes the provision of "Surplus Statement," which didn't appear in the "Working Rules for Preparation of Financial Statements."

Furthermore the FASBE defines "Nature of Income Statements" at the beginning in Part II of its "Income Statements Rules," and then provides the principles of accrual basis, the principles of gross amounts representation, and matching principles. The FASBE also provides the "principles of distinction between capital surplus and earned surplus" in its "General Principles (3)." This is the first provision of the distinction in Japanese accounting history. In addition, rules of determining and reporting surplus are institutionalized in the "Income Statements Rule (6)–(8)." "The introduction of [the concept of surplus and] the surplus statements" is called "the core of the modernization of accounting" (Kurosawa, 1955, p. 133).

These changes mean two things. Firstly, the prewar "Working Rules for Preparation of Financial Statements" was "mainly involved in setting and classifying items in financial statements or setting and unifying valuation standards." On the contrary, the FASBE "alienates from the thought of [merely] technical improvement of accounting" (ibid. p. 131), and is obviously the norm of accounting systems based on a certain view of earnings. Secondly, the FASBE alienates from accounting thought based on the assets and liabilities view of earnings, and moves toward the revenue and expenses view of earnings which prevailed in the USA after the 1930s.

Thus, it is true that the FASBE had epoch-making contents and significance at that time in terms of the accounting measurement structure.

However, the changes in the aspect of the institutional framework have more important meanings than those in the aspect of the accounting measurement structure. The main point of these changes is that they were the first attempts to introduce the "philosophy of disclosure" of the American model which had never been institutionalized before the war in Japan, although incompleteness still remains in the FASBE. These are embodied in the "General Principles" of the FASBE.

The FASBE consists of seven "General Principles" as follows:

1. Principle of truthfulness

2. Principle of regular bookkeeping procedures

3. Principle of distinction between capital surplus and earned surplus

4. Principle of clearness

5. Principle of consistency

6. Principle of conservatism

7. Principle of single book of accounts.

The interrelation between 1, 4, and 5 is especially remarkable, because the "philosophy of disclosure" is intensively embodied in each of these three prin-

Figure 5.1
Institutional Framework of Modern Accounting Standards

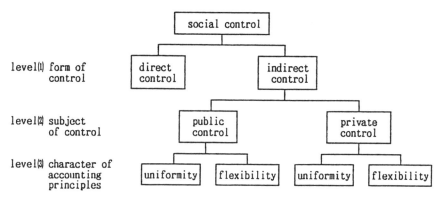

ciples and in the interrelation among them, and because, in addition, this philosophy of disclosure and the system based on the philosophy formulate the core
of the FASBE after the war in Japan. Before we discuss how these three principles are interrelated in the FASBE, it is necessary to summarize the relationship between the accounting standards of the American model and the
philosophy of disclosure.

In order to establish the modern accounting standards, it is necessary to pose
and solve at least the following questions related to the institutional framework
(see also Figure 5.1):

1. Choice of the form of social control: should direct or indirect control (disclosure
   system) be chosen?

2. Choice of the subject of social control (subject of accounting standards-setting); if
   indirect control is chosen: should public or private control be chosen?

3. Choice of the characteristics of the accounting standards: should uniform standards
   (so-called "strait jacket" or "Procrustean bed") or broad standards which allow the
   broad rights to select accounting policies be chosen? (Tsumori, 1981, pp. 65–73)

Each country has answers to these questions. For example, in the United
States, the disclosure system as the form of indirect control was chosen with
regard to the first question, private control with regard to the second one, and
the "GAAP" as the broad accounting standards to the third question. Also, in
Japan after the war, (1) disclosure system, (2) public control, and (3) broad
flexible standards were chosen. As a result, the Japanese system of FASBE is
essentially similar to the accounting standards of the American model.

As to the institutional framework of the accounting standards of the American
model, which is the prototype of the FASBE in Japan, the structure of the
framework can be summarized as follows.

First of all, flexibility is the fundamental characteristic of the accounting standards of the American model. As known, alternative accounting policies (principles or procedures) are accepted to the same accounting event. "Within the limits of such accepted alternative principles (broad principles), the right of corporations to select detailed methods of accounting deemed by listed corporations to be best adopted to the requirements of their business can never be restricted" (May, 1943, p. 80).

However, in order to accept alternative accounting policies to the same accounting event and allow options within the rather broad limits, it is necessary to (1) disclose the accounting policy selected to the users of financial statements, and (2) apply consistently the same accounting policy. Without (1), it would be impossible for users to make their own decisions. As to (2), if consistency was interrupted and the accounting policy was unreasonably changed, the basic framework of income determination (so-called *die Zweischneidigkeit der Bewertung*) would be destroyed.

As discussed above, the second characteristic of the accounting standards of the American model appears in (1) the disclosure of accounting policy selected, and (2) in the consistent application of accounting policy.

But the interruption of consistency is, rightly or wrongly, the convention in practices. Consequently the the disclosure of changes in the accounting policy, which is the third characteristic of the accounting standards of the American model, becomes a rule.

The fundamentals of such accounting standards of the American model are, needless to say, the philosophy of disclosure or thought of disclosure. Reconsideration from the standpoint of the philosophy of disclosure will prove that the accounting standards consist of the dual institution of disclosure: (1) disclosure of quantitative data, and (2) disclosure of accounting policy. In other words, they consist of the disclosure of accounting data on the one hand, and of the consistent application of accounting policy and disclosure of applied accounting policy on the other (ibid., p. 76).

In this case, the disclosure of quantitative data and the disclosure of accounting policy might look like disclosure on the same level at first sight. But the two are never on the same level. The disclosure of quantitative data is not necessarily connected with the disclosure of accounting policy. The disclosure of quantitative data is essential for financial disclosure, and financial disclosure without quantitative data is of course meaningless. On the contrary, the disclosure of accounting policy is not always accompanied by financial disclosure and is not the indispensable element of financial disclosure. It is the secondary disclosure additionally introduced for the reinforcement of the disclosure of quantitative data as the result of permitting certain flexibility in quantitative data. That is, it is only an additional disclosure or supplemental disclosure. The accounting standards of the American model are the combination of such application of thought of disclosure and a particular income determination structure, in other words, the composition of disclosure and accounting measurement (Tsumori, 1982, p. 10).

When the FASBE was first published, this structure of the accounting standards of the American model had already been embodied in the three principles mentioned above (principle of truthfulness, principle of consistency, and principle of disclosure) in its General Principles. The form of embodiment is as follows.

Firstly, it can be thought that "truthfulness" in the principle of truthfulness does not mean absolute truthfulness at all, but "relative truthfulness." That is, while it essentially starts from traditional "truthfulness" (*der Grundsatz der Bilanzwahrheit*) in the accounting system of the German model, at the same time, it also introduces the "true and fair view" or broad principles of the Anglo-American model. Consequently the principle of truthfulness can be understood as a flexible principle (e.g., "Value of Assets of Balance Sheets (A)" in the Balance Sheets Rules).

Secondly, the fifth principle, the principle of consistency, requires the consistent application of accounting policies every term and the disclosure in footnotes when the accounting policies are changed for valid reasons. This principle basically follows the preceding principle of consistency in the United States, and it also reflects the "principle of consistency in balance sheets" (*der Grundsatz der Bilanzkontinuität oder Bilanzstetigkeit*) in the Balance Sheet Law of the German model to some extent.

Suppose that the principle of consistency in the FASBE totally follows that in the USA. This principle would normally have to be complemented by the philosophy of disclosure as discussed above. The FASBE prescribes the "principle of clearness" as such. At least when the FASBE was published, however, it could be observed in the contents of the FASBE that the principle of clearness in the FASBE had the same characteristic as the principle of clearness in balance sheets (*der Grundsatz der Bilanzklaheit*) in the Balance Sheets Law of the German model or a formalistic principle on presentation, but that the characteristic of the philosophy of disclosure was rather less apparent.

Therefore it is obvious that the FASBE, indeed, prescribes the three principles (truthfulness, consistency, and disclosure) in compliance with the accounting standards of the American model. Nevertheless, the relation among the three principles is not necessarily a copy of the American model, but has similar characteristics to the Balance Sheets Principles of the German model. It can be concluded, in other words, that the accounting thought of the American model which was newly introduced after the war is mixed with the prewar "traditional" accounting thought which had been formulated following the accounting norm of the German model. This holds true not only for the three principles but also for other principles such as the principle of regular bookkeeping procedures and the principle of conservatism.

Consequently this mixture or compromise between the German and American model makes the relation among principles in the General Principles relatively difficult to understand, and underlies the later changes in the FASBE.

CONTRADICTORY STRUCTURE OF THE "FINANCIAL ACCOUNTING STANDARDS FOR BUSINESS ENTERPRISES"

As discussed above, the General Principles in the FASBE have a characteristic of compromise, basically based on the accounting standards of the American model on the one hand, but following the accounting norm of the German model on the other. As a result, the General Principles are rather difficult to understand. This is because there were two views on accounting thought in the Investigation Committee on Business Accounting Systems, which was the standards-setter when the FASBE was set.

From one view, it was attempted to formulate the General Principles with two crucial principles in the center (Kurosawa, 1979 [5], p. 98). These two crucial principles are the principle of truthfulness and the principle of regular bookkeeping procedures.

This view basically maintained the prewar tradition of Japanese accounting thought, and was strongly influenced by accounting theory in Germany. A representative of this theory was Professor Michisuke Ueno, the then chairman of the Investigating Committee on the Business Accounting System, and his accounting thought was named philosophy of truthfulness by Professor Kurosawa later. This thought was clearly shown in his lecture titled "The Meanings of Accounting in Economic Reconstruction in Japan" (1948), which made history.

According to him, the basis of the reconstruction of national economy after the war is "the rationalization of business management," which has to be underlain by accurate and clear accounting. In this case, the principle which is crucial to accounting is the principle of truthfulness, namely "there is no manipulation, there has to be no manipulation, and there has to be honesty everywhere" (Ueno, 1948, p. 5). Thus, "the spirit of doing no manipulation is the principle or theory of accounting, and no manipulation is the true spirit of accounting" (ibid., p. 5). "Only the principle of accounting can prove that measurements are accurate and reliable, and that there is completely no mistakes or no manipulation in the measurements" (ibid., p. 8).

This view of accounting based on Professor Ueno's philosophy of truthfulness was presented as the fruit of his profound long-term study of the German accounting institution. His opinion was timely, considering that Japan was in a special situation at that time, and that the truthfulness had particular significance in this situation. Even today, his opinion is still significant as a measure against the unreasonable relativization of accounting measurement.

Furthermore, this view of accounting based on Professor Ueno's philosophy of truthfulness, which followed the tradition of the German Balance Sheets Law, is historically significant, especially with regard to the effect on accounting under the Commercial Law. This is because the FASBE was "accounting standards" itself, and was intended to be the principle of guidance for accounting under the Commercial Law, the Securities & Exchange Act, and the Corporate Income Tax Law, in other words, the conceptual framework ("standards" for "accounting standards-setting") at the same time.

Another view attempted to consider the following three principles as the basis of the general principles: the principle of disclosure, the principle of consistency, and the principle of materiality.

This view was basically in accordance with "generally accepted accounting principles" in the United States, and was the accounting thought proposed by Professor Iwao Iwata.

Based on his comprehensive understanding on the content of the accounting principles in the United States and the U.S. experience of setting standards, he had already repeatedly presented the institutional framework developed especially in AIA accounting principles in the United States. It included (1) the approval of the selective application of alternative accounting policies and procedures within a "considerably broad frame (method of unification with big latitude)," (Iwata's speech at round-table discussion, May 15, 1948, p. 74), and (2) the "notes of accounting policies" (ibid., p. 85 ff.). It would be true that his understanding of the accounting principles of the American model, in the aspects of both the accounting measurement structure and the institutional framework of accounting principles, formulated one of the two most authoritative accounting thoughts—the other was Professor Ueno's on the German accounting system—in Japan at that time.

In the meeting of the Investigation Committee on the Business Accounting System on December 2, 1948, the Kurosawa Memorandum that "systematically combined these two accounting thoughts and gave them expression in sentence" was proposed, and caused a lively discussion (Ueno [ICBAS], 1948, pp. 43–70). Here are shown the main points about the "general principles" in the Kurosawa Memorandum which was to shape the original form of the FASBE.

Firstly, "the principle of truthfulness does not mean objective and absolute truthfulness (*Wahrheit*) such as the 'principle of truthfulness' in the German Balance Sheets Law, but [is defined as] 'subjective and relative truthfulness in reports prepared under the sound opinion and judgment of management'" (ibid., p. 47).

With regard to the principle of regular bookkeeping, the following are remarkable: the Kurosawa Memorandum says that with the principles of regular bookkeeping (GoB) in the German Commercial Law as a starting point, "financial statements must be prepared in accordance with not the Inventory method but the Derivative method" (ibid., p. 48); and an attempt was made to interpret and unify the principle of regular bookkeeping in the Ueno Memorandum and the principle of materiality in the Iwata Memorandum and to include the principle of materiality into the principle of regular bookkeeping (ibid., p. 48; Kurosawa, 1979 [7], p. 116).

As to the principle of clearness, how it should be distinguished from the principle of clearness (*Prinzip der Bilanzklarheit*) in the German law was one of the issues. The Kurosawa Memorandum says that "the content of this principle, which consists of the demand for clearness in financial statements and that for publicity, is [eventually] the same as the Doctrine of Disclosure in the United States," and the Memo attempts to unify the opinions of Ueno and Iwata (Stenographic Records, 1948, p. 49).

Furthermore, the Kurosawa Memorandum considers the principle of consistency especially significant, because "the principle of consistency, which is much more important than it looks, ensures the freedom or flexibility of business accounting on the one hand, and maintains the unification on the other" (ibid., p. 50).

Finally, the Kurosawa Memorandum refers to the view which influences the nature of accounting principles: "in the future, it is rather necessary to accept the principle of conservatism as the 'sound accounting' in order to facilitate the self-growth of Japanese companies as long as the principle is not considerably inconsistent with the other principles" (ibid., p. 50).

In the process of the deliberation on the Kurosawa Memorandum in the Investigation Committee, the most controversial issue was "whether the equalization of income should be accepted as a principle" relating to the principle of truthfulness. In conclusion, it was agreed that "the equalization of income should be accepted as a principle within a certain limit, which should be provided also from the viewpoint of Dividend Purpose" (ibid., Iwata's speech, 1948, p. 60).

This means, for example, that "setting secret reserves would not be prohibited, but that it would have to be represented on the balance sheets if set" (ibid., Kurosawa's speech, p. 66). "In short, the meaning of truthfulness here is fair," that is, truthfulness here "should not refer to objective truthfulness but truthfulness in the sense of fair" (ibid., p. 68).

Based on this interpretation of truthfulness, other principles such as consistency, clearness, and conservatism, were of course set almost along with the Kurosawa Memorandum.

This means that the FASBE, since it was set, has had the characteristic of a compromise between two views of accounting principles: (1) the selective broad accounting principles should be accepted and then integrated with disclosure in footnotes, and (2) the accounting principles should be a "compromise between conservatism, and truthfulness and disclosure" based on the very strict principle of truthfulness in which "there has to be no manipulation" (Ueno, 1948, p. 5). In other words, the compromise or "integration" was made between the philosophy of disclosure of the American model and the philosophy of truthfulness of the German model when the FASBE was first set. Consequently "two souls" (*zwei Seelen* in Goethe's *Faust*) existed together. This coexistence has inclined toward the former in the process of development.

THE DEVELOPMENT OF THE "PHILOSOPHY OF DISCLOSURE" IN THE "FINANCIAL ACCOUNTING STANDARDS FOR BUSINESS ENTERPRISES"

As we have discussed, one of the fundamental characteristics of the Japanese financial accounting system after the war, the FASBE above all, is the introduction of the disclosure system of the American model.

But the significance of this system as the embodiment of the philosophy of disclosure was not clearly recognized yet in 1948 when the system was introduced. This is proved by the fact that the gap of recognition concerning the GAAP existed not only between those who set standards and those who would apply the standards but also even among the standard-setters, i.e., the members of the Investigation Committee (Kurosawa, 1979 [4], p. 98).

It was after Kurosawa attempted to systematize the "theoretical and practical structure of accounting principles" in his work *Modern Accounting* (1951), that the significance of the financial disclosure system began to be generally recognized to some extent. However, it took a while until the recognition became commonly shared by the public. At last, this recognition was established in the FASBE, though additional provisions in "Supplement 1: Application of Materiality Concept" and "Supplement 3: Consistency in Financial Accounting" were provided in the amendment in 1974; and furthermore, "Supplement 1–2: Disclosure of Significant Accounting Policies" and "Supplement 1–3: Disclosure of Significant Subsequent Events" were provided in the amendment in 1982.

These amendments of the FASBE were all made for the purpose of adjustment with the revised Commercial Law or Article 3 of the revised Financial Accounts Rules of the Commercial Law, but not for the development of the philosophy of disclosure. However, these two revisions specified: (1) the concrete meaning of "relative truthfulness," i.e., accepted alternative accounting policies to an accounting event, and (2) the scope for the selection of accounting policies; and provided not only (3) the supplementary disclosure concerning the changes of accounting policies but also (4) the supplementary disclosure of important accounting policies selected. As a result, it could be concluded that the FASBE got closer to the accounting system of the American model as the dual system of disclosure.

One of the most interesting movements which symbolized the development of the philosophy of disclosure in the Japanese accounting system at that time was the changes of representation (not revisions of the contents) in the English version of the General Standards of the FASBE, among others, the principle of truthfulness and the principle of disclosure. These reflected the changes of the view of accounting rather than mere changes in translation. This is remarkable because these changes reflect those in recognition of accountants such as CPAs, though the changes of words in the FASBE reflect the further development of the philosophy of disclosure at the level of standard-setters.

That is, "The Tentative Business Accounting Principles" in *An Interim Report on the Conference of the Investigation Committee on the Business Accounting System in Japan*, which was published by the Economic Stabilization Board in 1948, represented the General Standards in English as follows: "Any business accounting should be devised so as to be able to furnish *the true report* on the financial condition and operating results of a given enterprise."

On the other hand, "Financial Accounting Standards for Business Enterprises" (The Business Accounting Deliberation Council, Ministry of Finance, Japan), which was re-translated and published by the International Committee of the Japanese Institute of Certified Public Accountants (JICPA) in 1985, represented the same sentence as follows: "(Principles of *true and fair reporting*) Financial accounting for business enterprises should provide *a true and fair report* of the financial position and of the results of operations of a business enterprise."

It is obvious that there is an important difference between "true report" and "true and fair report," which corresponds to the difference in the views of accounting between the German concept of truthfulness (*die Bilanzwahrheit*) and the Anglo-American concept of "true and fair."

Similar changes are found in the principle of clearness, "General Standard 4."

"The Tentative Business Accounting Principles" was translated when published in 1949 as follows: "Any business accounting should be devised so as to furnish the interested persons with the financial statements of a given enterprise *exhibiting clearly and accurately those financial facts* to them in judging *its true financial condition* quite free from the likelihood of a serious misunderstanding."

These representations in English reflect the fact that when the FASBE was set the principle of clearness was understood as a formalized principle such as the principle of clearness in balance sheets (*der Grundsatz der Bilanzklarheit*) in Germany but was not yet fundamentally understood as the Doctrine of Disclosure by accountants with a few exceptions. This was the prevailing level of recognition at that time.

In the re-translated version in 1985, however, the principle of clearness was understood as the doctrine of disclosure but not only as a formalistic principle;

(*Principle of clear disclosure*) Financial accounting for business enterprise should, through financial statements, present *clearly essential accounting facts* to interested parties and present them in a manner that will not be misleading in their interpretation of the financial status of the business enterprise.

These changes of representations in the translated version of the FASBE show the crucial development of the philosophy of disclosure in the Japanese accounting system during the past 40 years.

The philosophy of disclosure in Japan entered a new phase, as the globalization of economy progressed, with the significant change of foreign exchange environment (BADC, "Setting Accounting Standards for Foreign Currency Transactions") after the late 1970s, and "the international harmonization of accounting standards" became a problem after the late 1980s.

The Interim Report of the BADC on the "improvement of financial information in the disclosure system based on the Securities & Exchange Act" (including consolidated financial statements, fund statements, segment reporting, and quarterly reporting) was issued on October 31, 1986. Subsequently the BADC published its "Opinion on the Reporting Standards of Financial Information by Segment" on May 26, 1988, and the "Consideration of Practical Techniques on the Disclosure of Financial Information by Segment" to the JICPA on August 30 that year. Furthermore, the first section of the BADC published "Opinion on the Accounting Standards for Future and Option Transactions" on May 29, 1990, and the Disclosure Issues Section of the Securities Exchange Council published its report on the "Reform of Disclosure System" on April 26, 1991.

The characteristics of these new movements are that all the movements were initiated by international requirements (pressure from foreign countries) but tried to use the foreign pressure positively as a spring to extend disclosure rather than cope with it negatively, and they aimed at the extension of disclosure in areas where it didn't conflict with the provision of the Commercial Law.

CONCLUSION

As proved above, the history of the development of the thought of disclosure in the Japanese accounting system was, in a sense, the history of the integration or harmonization between the German system and the Anglo-American system.

Some issues which are significant today can be drawn from consideration of the process of the development of the thought of disclosure in Japan.

The first issue is concerning the rationale and significance of the integration or compromise between the philosophy of truthfulness and the philosophy of disclosure in the FASBE.

As already clarified, the financial disclosure system in Japan was, for the first time, formally introduced as an important part of the democratization of the economy after the Second World War. At first, however, this disclosure system embodied in the FASBE was institutionalized only as a compromise between the philosophy of truthfulness of the German model and the philosophy of disclosure of the American model.

Moreover, this was partly because there remained the essentially same economic and political environment as in the prewar days at that time. Among other

Table 5.1
Capital Increase of All Listed Companies in Japan (1949–1963) (¥ 100 mil.)

F.Y.	Issuing for Shareholders		Private Placement		Public Offering		Amount Raised	
	Value	%	Value	%	Value	%	Value	%
1949	328	82.0	27	5.8	57	12.2	466	100
1950	125	75.8	37	22.4	3	1.8	165	100
1951	419	95.3	16	3.7	4	1.0	440	100
1952	971	96.7	19	1.9	15	1.5	1,004	100
1953	994	95.9	26	2.5	17	1.6	1,037	100
1954	804	97.7	14	1.7	5	0.6	823	100
1955	656	95.8	29	4.2	1	0.1	685	100
1956	2,128	95.5	25	1.1	76	3.4	2,228	100
1957	1,775	97.3	6	0.3	44	2.4	1,825	100
1958	1,478	97.0	1	0.1	45	3.0	1,523	100
1959	2,865	91.1	10	0.3	269	8.6	3,144	100
1960	3,968	88.7	6	0.1	502	11.2	4,475	100
1961	6,059	90.2	13	0.2	644	9.6	6,716	100
1962	5,228	96.3	9	3.1	193	3.6	5,430	100
1963	4,275	96.2	73	1.6	97	2.2	4,445	100

Source: Yamaichi Shoken Keizai Kenkyoshu (Y.R.I.), Securities Statistics.

factors, granting at par value to shareholders represents the underdevelopment of the Japanese securities market (Tables 5.1 and 5.2). But these conditions were not the only reason for the compromise between the two philosophies in the FASBE, because such a compromise was also related to the inherited structure of the Japanese accounting system.

The Japanese accounting system consists of the triangular legal system in which the Commercial Law, the Securities & Exchange Act, and the Corporate Income Tax Law are closely tied together with the Commercial Law in the center (Arai & Shiratori, 1991, pp. 2–3). In this system, while the purpose of accounting under the Commercial Law, which has been formulated as a variation of the German model, is the "determination of disposable income to protect creditors," the purpose of accounting under the Securities & Exchange Act which has been formulated based on the American model is the "disclosure of financial information to protect investors."

At first, the FASBE was set as the accounting standard itself in this triangular system and, at the same time, as a conceptual framework for accounting under the Commercial Law and the Securities & Exchange Act. As a result, the FASBE could not help facing the conflict not only between the system of the German model and the American one, but also between the purpose of the determination of disposable income and the purpose of the disclosure of financial information (Iwata's speech at round-table discussion, Oct. 2, 1948, p. 60). The

Table 5.2

Capital Increase of All Listed Companies in the United States (Common Stock) ($ mil.)

F.Y.	Issuing for Shareholders		Private Placement		Public Offering		Amount Raised	
	Value	%	Value	%	Value	%	Value	%
1948	643	40.9	476	30.3	452	28.8	1,571	100
1949	435	47.3	60	6.5	424	46.1	919	100
1950	695	45.1	59	3.8	787	51.1	1,541	100
1951	621	42.3	30	2.0	817	55.7	1,428	100
1952	933	32.9	507	17.8	1,399	49.3	2,839	100
1953	875	31.1	253	9.0	1,680	59.3	2,808	100
1954	626	24.0	332	12.7	1,653	63.3	2,610	100
1955	1,105	28.6	302	7.8	2,457	63.6	3,864	100
1956	857	18.9	474	10.4	3,212	70.7	4,543	100
1957	2,399	41.0	524	8.9	2,934	50.1	5,858	100
1958	1,201	20.0	1,592	26.6	3,205	53.4	5,998	100
1959	893	14.0	736	11.5	4,758	74.5	6,387	100
1960	560	8.7	562	8.7	5,314	82.6	6,435	100
1961	1,671	21.6	870	11.4	5,176	67.0	7,718	100
1962	606	30.6	45	2.4	1,326	67.0	1,978	100
1963	330	38.6	16	2.1	507	59.3	854	100
1964	1,695	69.7	108	4.6	627	25.7	2,431	100

Source: SEC Annual Report.

integration or compromise of the two philosophies in the FASBE represented a way to cope with such conflicts.

This may provide a useful experience for resolving the problem of international harmonization with regard to the relationship both between the German system and the American one and between the purpose of the determination of disposable income in the Commercial Law and the purpose of the disclosure of financial information in the Securities & Exchange Act.

The second issue, relating to the first one directly, concerns conditions which facilitated the development of the thought of disclosure in the Japanese accounting system.

As stated, the structure of integration or compromise between the two philosophies in the FASBE had been gradually modified to become close to the disclosure system of the American model in which the philosophy of disclosure was embodied, and was finally institutionalized as Article 8, clauses 2 and 3, of the Financial Statements Rules of the Securities & Exchange Act, and Article 3, the Financial Accounts Rules of the Commercial Law. This is further in process now in the new situation of the international harmonization of accounting standards.

This development of the philosophy of disclosure has been facilitated in the Japanese accounting system under certain conditions; e.g., the changes in the

Table 5.3
Capital Increase of All Listed Companies in Japan (1970–1991) ((¥ 100 mil.)

F.Y.	Issuing for Shareholders		Private Placement		Public Offering		Amount Raised	
	Value	%	Value	%	Value	%	Value	%
1970	5,289	80.0	63	1.0	1,260	19.1	6,613	100
1971	3,885	71.8	536	9.9	990	18.3	5,411	100
1972	3,457	26.6	915	7.0	8,610	66.3	12,982	100
1973	3,021	41.3	372	5.1	3,921	53.6	7,314	100
1974	3,570	58.3	60	1.0	2,496	40.7	6,126	100
1975	6,493	71.9	96	1.1	2,436	27.0	9,024	100
1976	2,800	34.0	108	1.3	5,326	64.7	6,887	100
1977	2,145	30.2	290	4.1	4,660	65.7	7,094	100
1978	3,079	29.8	629	6.1	6,621	64.1	10,330	100
1979	1,280	19.4	682	10.3	4,643	70.3	6,605	100
1980	1,761	15.2	777	6.7	9,063	78.1	11,601	100
1981	4,807	26.8	326	1.8	12,799	71.4	17,932	100
1982	1,854	18.3	241	2.4	8,059	79.3	10,154	100
1983	1,415	16.7	1,511	17.8	5,569	65.5	8,495	100
1984	696	8.6	345	4.2	7,106	87.2	8,148	100
1985	1,866	28.6	272	4.2	4,375	67.2	6,513	100
1986	1,198	19.0	377	6.0	4,745	75.0	6,317	100
1987	4,780	22.9	1,113	5.4	14,946	71.7	20,839	100
1988	9,958	21.8	1,012	2.2	34,668	76.0	45,638	100
1989	10,386	13.7	2,643	3.5	63,571	82.8	75,600	100
1990	2,793	42.0	1,876	28.3	1,977	29.7	6,646	100
1991	2,108	61.5	988	28.8	331	9.7	3,427	100

Source: Yamaichi Shoken Keizai Kenkyusho (Y.R.I.), Securities Statistics.

securities market after the 1970s, that is, the epoch-making transition of the trend of issuing from granting at par value to shareholders, to the public offering at market price (see Table 5.3); and the development of the consciousness of democracy which has gradually become prevalent after the war. These conditions mean that the economic and political basis for the development of the philosophy of disclosure has been generally formed in Japan. Furthermore, this development was subject to the democratization of economy policy such as the dissolution of *zaibatsu* and land reform just after the war, and to the structural change of the Japanese economy after the 1960s.

However, a direct factor in the development of the philosophy of disclosure in Japan was the change in the power balance in the triangular system; the Commercial Law took over the leadership from the FASBE, especially through revising the Commercial Law and setting the Financial Accounts Rules of the Commercial Law during the period from 1962 to 1963, and this takeover made it "impossible to set accounting standards inconsistent with the regulations in the Commercial Law" (Arai, 1989 [2], p. 32).

As a result, the area in which the FASBE could play a leading role in standard-setting was limited. Therefore, the FASBE was to play only such roles as "setting standards in the areas which the Commercial Law does not cover, for instance, the area of disclosure such as consolidated financial statements and interim financial statements which the Securities & Exchange Act mainly covers," and "setting additional and supplementary standards relating to the areas where the Commercial Law provides nothing or does so ambiguously" ("Accounting Standards for Foreign Currency Transactions," 1979). In other words, the FASBE could not help moving from the area of the determination of distributable income to that of disclosure, and consequently led to the development and establishment of the philosophy of disclosure.

This means that it was attempted, by means of the requirement (pressure) for international harmonization from foreign countries, particularly after the 1970s, to establish the thought of disclosure gradually in the area of the determination of disposable income in the Commercial Law, while the development of the thought of disclosure was quite rapidly set forward in the area in which it didn't conflict with the provisions of the Commercial Law, that is, the area of the disclosure of financial information.

This experience in Japan also might be able to provide some insight to the issue of the international harmonization as well as the first issue.

However, as Shakespeare said, "the course of true love never does run smooth." The experience of Japan shows that a long and difficult process is needed for the financial disclosure system based on the philosophy of disclosure (not merely the disclosure system) to be understood by standard-setters at first, and then to penetrate into the public socially. This indicates that the development of the thought of disclosure in Japan was made, not as the process of the change of each individual person's philosophy inside his/her own consciousness, but as the process of the change of generations, i.e., change from a generation branded by the philosophy of truthfulness to the next generation strongly influenced by the philosophy of disclosure. This is the third issue.

The Japanese accounting system has learned many valuable lessons from the experiences in certain other countries, and will be more modestly learning in the future. However, we believe that it is necessary to discover anything that would be useful for international development from the experiences (failure and success) the Japanese accounting system has accumulated. The research and study of accounting history will be of great help for that purpose.

REFERENCES

Arai, Kiyomitsu, (ed.), *Nihon Kaikei-Kansa Kihan Keisei Shiryo* (Historical Materials on the Formation of Accounting and Auditing Institutions in Japan) (Chuokeizaisha, 1989) (Arai, 1989 [1]).

Arai, Kiyomitsu, (ed.), *Kigyo Kaikeigensoku no Keisei to Tenkai* (Formation and Development of Financial Accounting Standards for Business Enterprises) (Chuokeizaisha, 1989) (Arai, 1989 [2]).

Arai, Kiyomitsu, and Shiratori, Shonosuke, Legal and Conceptual Framework of Accounting in Japan, JICPA, 1991.

The Business Accounting Deliberation Council (Ministry of Finance, Japan) Financial Accounting Standards for Business Enterprises, as amended Apr. 20, 1982 (JICPA, 1985).

Chiba, Junichi, British Company Accounting 1844–1885 and Its Influence on the Modernisation of Japanese Financial Accounting, Keizai to Keizaigaku, no. 60 (October, 1987).

Chiba, Junichi, ''Shokosho Junsoku' kara 'Kikakuin Junsoku (Soan)'' e (From Working Rules of the Ministry of Commerce and Industry to Tentative Standards [drafts] of the Planning Council) (Kurosawa, 1987).

Economic Stabilization Board, An Interim Report on the Conference of the Investigation Committee on the Business Accounting System in Japan: The Tentative Business Accounting Principles & Working Rules for Preparation of Financial Statements, 1948.

GHQ of Allied Powers, Instructions for the Preparation of Financial Statements of Manufacturing and Trading Companies (Arai, 1989 [1], pp. 74–125.)

Hisano, Hideo, *Wagakuni Zaimushohyoseido Seiseisi no Kenkyu* (A Study on the History of Formation of Financial Statements Institutions in Japan) (Gakushuin University, 1987) (Hisano, 1987 [1]).

Hisano, Hideo, *Wagakuni Zaimushohyo Seido no Seisei to Kadai* (Financial Statements Institution, Its Formation and Problems) (Kurosawa, 1987, pp. 1–21.) (Hisano, 1987 [2]).

Iwata, Iwao, Chairman of Convention, Japan Accounting Association, Improvement and Unification of Financial Statements: Stenographic Records of Round-Table Discussion of the 7th Annual Convention, *Kaikei*, vol. 56, no. 2 (May 15, 1948): pp. 65–96.

Izutani, Katsumi, *Hukusikiboki Seiseisi Ron* (A Treatise on the History of Formation of Double Entry Bookkeeping) (Moriyama Shoten, 1980).

Johnson, L. Todd, Research on Disclosure, *Accounting Horizons* (March 1992): pp. 101–103.

Kataoka, Yasuhiko, *Itaria Bokisi Ron* (A Study on the History of Double Entry Bookkeeping in Italy) (Moriyama Shoten, 1988).

Kikakuin (Cabinet Planning House), *Seizo Kogyo Zaimushohyo Junsoku* (Draft Working Rules for Preparation of Financial Statements of Manufacturing Industry) (1941).

Kimura, Wasaburo, *Nihon ni okeru Boki Kaikeigaku no Hatten* (Development of Double Entry Bookkeeping and Accountancy in Japan) (Choryusha, 1950).

Kojima, Osao, *Hukusikiboki Hasseosi no Kenkyu* (A Study on the History of Genesis of Double Entry Bookkeeping, Revised) (Moriyama Shoten, 1965).

Kurosawa, Kiyoshi, *Kindai Kaikeigaku* (Modern Accounting) (Shunjusha, 1951).

Kurosawa, Kiyoshi, *Kindai Kaikei no Riron* (Theory of Modern Accounting) (Hakuto Shobo, 1955).

Kurosawa, Kiyoshi, *Shiryo: Nihon no Kaikeiseido* (Accounting Institutions in Japan: Historical Data), (1)–(16), *Kigyo Kaikei*, vol. 31, no. 1 (January, 1979); vol. 32, no. 4 (April, 1980).

Kurosawa, Kiyoshi, *Nihon Kaikeigaku Hattenshi Josetsu* (A Historical Study of Development of Accountancy in Japan: An Introduction) (Yushodo Shoten, 1982).

Kurosawa, Kiyoshi (ed.), *Wagakuni Zaimushohyo Seido no Ayumi, Senzenhen* (The Course of Development of Financial Statements Institutions in Japan: Prewar Period) (Yushodo Press Co., Ltd., 1987).

Kurosawa, Kiyoshi, *Nihon Kaikei Seido Hattenshi* (A Historical Study on Development of Accounting Institutions) (Zaikeishohosha, 1990).

Littleton, A. C., *Accounting Evolution to 1900* (New York: American Institute Publishing Company, 1933).

May, George O., *Financial Accounting, A Distillation of Experience* (New York: The MacMillan Company 1943).

Previts, J. G., and Merino, B. D., *A History of Accounting in America, An Historical Interpretation of the Cultural Significance of Accounting*, A Ronald Press Publication (New York: John Wiley & Sons, 1979).

Rikugunsho (Ministry of the Army), *Rikugun Gunjuhinkojojigyojo Zaimushohyo Junsoku* (Working Rules for Preparation of Financial Statements of Ministry Munitions Factories and Plants) (1940).

Shokosho Rinjisangyogorikyoku (Temporary Industrial Rationalization Board of the Ministry of Commerce and Industry), Working Rules for Preparation of Financial Statements (1934).

Someya, Kyojiro, *Kikakuin Zaimushohyo Junsoku Soan ni tuite* (On the Tentative Standards [drafts]) (Kurosawa, 1987): pp. 35–40.

Someya, Kyojiro, *Nihon ni okeru Kaikei Kakumei* (Accounting Revolution in Japan), *Kaikei*, vol. 134, no. 1 (July, 1988): pp. 1–15.

Tsumori, Tsunehiro, *Haito Keisangensoku no Shiteki Hatten* (The Historical Development of Dividends Tests) (Yamakawa Shuppansha, 1962).

Tsumori, Tsunehiro, *Kaikei Gensoku Ron* (On the Accounting Principles), *Riron Kaikei gaku* (Theoretical Accounting, edited by Matsuo Kenkitsu) (Chuokeizai sha, 1981).

Tsumori, Tsunehiro, *Kaikeihosin no Kokai to Kaikeikisei* (Disclosure of Accounting Policy and Accounting Regulation), *JICPA News*, no. 312 (August, 1982): pp. 10–11.

Tsumori, Tsunehiro, *Kaikei Kijun Settei no Gendaiteki Tokucho to Hoko* (Recent Tendencies of Accounting Standards Setting and Its Future), (1 × 2), Kaikei, vol. 133, no. 1 (January, 1988): pp. 44–64, and no. 2 (Feburary, 1988): pp. 91–108.

Takatera, Sadao, *Meiji Genkashokyakushi no Kenkyu* (A Treatise on the History of Depreciation Accounting in the Meiji Era) (Miraisha, 1974).

Ueno, Michisuke, Chairman, Conference of the Investigation Committee on the Business Accounting System (ICBAS), Business Accounting Principles, Stenographic Records, Kaikei, vol. 56, no. 5 (October 2, 1948), pp. 43–70.

Ueno, Michisuke, *Wagakuni Keizaisaiken ni okeru Kaikeigaku no Igi* (The Significance of Accounting in Economic Restructure in Japan), *Kaikei*, vol. 56, no. 1 (1948): pp. 1–11.

Yamey, B. S., Aspects of the Law Relating to Company Dividends, in Baxter, W. T. (Ed.), *Studies in Accounting* (London: Sweet & Maxwell, Ltd. 1950).

6

The Development of the Japanese Railway Accounting System: The Japanizing Process of the British System, 1885–1950

Shigeto Sasaki

INTRODUCTION

The *Government Railways of Japan* (GRJ) was founded in 1869 and started service in 1872. It was divided into seven private railway companies (*Japan Railway Companies:* JRs) in 1987 after its 117-year operation under the control of the Japanese government. The main purpose of this reorganization was to improve the flexibility of the railway management to make it easier to serve regional needs through introducing a competitive situation and wiping out past accumulated losses. The accounting systems employed by those seven companies followed almost without change the basic framework of the GRJ accounting system, although the change in owership required some changes in the accounting terms and procedures.

The framework of the GRJ's accounting system just before its division was established under the Japanese National Railways Act, 1948. But this basic framework of the railway accounting system stems originally from the British railway accounting system in the 19th century.

Plan of Study, Time Period, and Summarized Conclusion

We regard the current framework of the Japanese railway accounting system as the effect of Japanization of the British system. When the British railway accounting practices were introduced into Japan, and how they were applied,

changed, or improved according to economic, technological, juridical, or political circumstances will be seen chronologically in this paper. Especially, this
study will focus on accounting practices for fixed assets, because they were
normally most valuable among the various railway assets and the railway management gave top priority to the their maintenance and renewal.

This paper recognizes the following five periods to identify the Japanizing
process of the British railway accounting system:

1. July 1, 1885—March 31, 1907
2. April 1, 1907—January 18, 1927
3. January 19, 1927—March 31, 1947
4. April 1, 1947—March 31, 1950
5. April 1, 1950—March 31, 1951

The first period covers July 1, 1885, to March 31, 1907. In this period, the
British railway accounting ideas were reflected in the GRJ's accounting system
almost completely. This especially applied to the accounting procedures for the
fixed assets.

The second period covers April 1, 1907, to January 18, 1927. In this period,
GRJ as a government enterprise started to design its original accounting system
especially for maintenance, construction, renewal, and improvement of the fixed
assets. Convenience and cost efficiency were the basis underlying this system
design.

The third period covers January 19, 1927, to March 31, 1947. During this
period, the question as to whether the application of the depreciation method to
the fixed assets would be proper for the GRJ accounting or not gave rise to
much controversy. Economic and political conditions were the main factors in
settling this question. The depreciation method was rejected by the Japanese
government because of some additional cost, low benefit, and bothersome work
which would be accompanied by the application. In this regard, it would be
interesting to know the contrast between the accounting policies and thoughts
in the London & North Western Railway Company (LNWR) and GRJ.

The fourth period covers April 1, 1947, to March 31, 1950. In this period,
GRJ tried to catch up with the elaborate theoretical accounting practices which
had been developing in other countries and which had been neglected by GRJ
during the foregoing periods. The inclusion of depreciation expenses among the
expenses for operation was a good example. But the depreciation expenses were
distorted by the book value of the fixed assets, because it appeared far lower
than the current value.

Lastly, the period from April 1, 1950, to March 31, 1951, will be noticed as
the starting point for sound railway accounting practices for fixed assets. The
additional depreciation expenses were calculated to supplement the deficiency
of the depreciation expenses based on the book value, although this procedure

was extraordinary and preparatory for the formal revaluation of fixed assets (1955) which was suggested by the *Report on Japanese Taxation by the Shoup Mission, 1949.*

We conclude that the development of the railway accounting system in Japan has owed much to the British system among others and the Japanese government has made the most of it as the object of Japanization at the same time. The process of Japanization is characterized as policy-making, influenced by other considerations such as convenience, profitability and expediency for example.

INTRODUCTION AND ESTABLISHMENT OF THE BRITISH RAILWAY ACCOUNTING SYSTEM (JULY 1, 1885 TO MARCH 31, 1907)

The first annual report of GRJ was published as of June 25, 1887, although it included the financial data of the periods from its foundation (January, 1869) to March 31, 1887. The financial accounts were prepared under *Tetsudo Kaikei Jorei* (The Railway Accounting Regulation Act) which was promulgated in May 7, 1885, and put in force on July 1, 1885. This act was the first regular railway accounting regulation for GRJ.

Tamiyoshi Zushi, the chief accountant of the Kobe Division of the Superintendent's Office of GRJ, made a large contribution toward promulgating this act. He presented a statement of his views to the director of the Railway Department in 1885 in order to promulgate the accounting regulation specialized for GRJ, because the railway accounting practices were becoming complex and beyond the extent of the existing accounting laws which had been effective until then. Also, in the prospectus based on that statement, he maintained the introduction of the British railway accounting system into GRJ as follows:

I want to establish the railway accounting system for GRJ on the basis of the accounting law which has been applied to the British railway companies, although it must be arranged to be suitable for the present circumstances in Japan. (Japanese National Railways, 1969, vol. 1, p. 365)

The Double Account System prescribed by the 1868 Regulation of Railways Act in Great Britain was a model for the first railway accounting regulation in Japan. The fact that GRJ depended upon Great Britain in the light of the railway technology and finance about the time of its foundation would explain why Mr. Zushi selected the British railway accounting system as a model. In those days, a lot of British railway engineers were engaged by GRJ and the Japanese government financed one million pounds in 1870 through the first issue of foreign bonds in Great Britain partly for the construction of the railway plant and the purchase of the rolling stocks.

How the Regulation of Railways Act was followed by GRJ and arranged for by GRJ can be analysed in the light of two elements, the purposes of railway accounting and the forms of the accounts. The prime purpose of *Tetsudo Kaikei Jorei* was to clarify the differences between capital and revenue receipts and between capital and revenue disbursements through the application of the Capital Account and the Revenue Account, although the GRJ accounting was on the cash basis.

Tetsudo Kaikei Jorei includes the following regulations:

1. Any disbursements for the railway construction should be on the capital account.
2. The means to get the receipts from the operation, like permanent way, rolling stocks, machinery, stations, works, land, and buildings and the funds granted from the Japanese government to get such means are presented in the Capital Account.
3. The receipts from the operation of the capital and the disbursements to operate the capital and keep it in good condition are presented in the Revenue Account.

The Capital Account and the Revenue Account prescribed by *Tetsudo Kaikei Jorei* are derived from the Double Account System under the Regulation of Railways Act. As the amount available for the payment of dividends which is calculated through the revenue account and the net revenue account should be carried to the general balance sheet in this system, the capital assets presented in the receipts and expenditures on capital accounts can be maintained compulsorily and materially without making an appropriation of those assets for dividends.

In order to make use of this characteristic of the double account system, *Tetsudo Kaikei Jorei* adopted this British system for GRJ. In Japan, the capital account seems to be designed as the joint form of the receipts and expenditure on the capital account and the general balance sheet, and the revenue account (Japan) as the joint form of the revenue account (Great Britain) and the net revenue account. But, it doesn't mean that *Tetsudo Kaikei Jorei* decided to adopt the single account system instead of the double account system, because *Tetsudo Kaikei Jorei* recognizes the concepts of consolidated (or fixed) capital and floating (or working) capital in the capital account, and the concept of the operational expenses in the revenue account definitely. Figure 6.1 illustrates how the GRJ's capital was classified in its first annual report, covering the periods from January 1869 to March 31, 1887.

GRJ divided its Aggregate Capital into consolidated capital and the unadjusted funds. Since the unadjusted funds for railway construction could be recognized as future consolidated capital, it may be safely said that GRJ's aggregate capital consists of two elements, that is, the consolidated (or fixed) capital and the floating capital. The consolidated capital is independent of the floating capital so as to keep it in good condition, although GRJ is free from paying dividend because it is a government enterprise. The floating capital consists of cash, accounts receivable, stores, postal stamps and so on.

Kansetsu Tetsudo Kaikei-hoh (The Government Railways Accounting Act) went into effect on April 1, 1890, replacing *Tetsudo Kaikei Jorei*. The clas-

Figure 6.1
Government Railways of Japan's Classification of Its Capital, January 1869–March 31, 1887

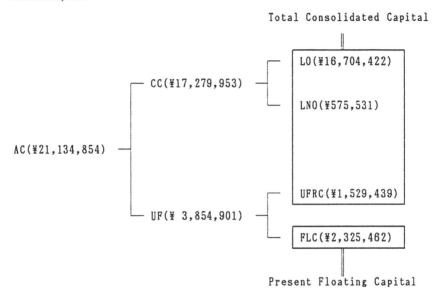

AC= Aggregate Capital for Railway Construction (=the total funds
    granted from the Japanese government)
CC= Consolidated Capital (=the funds which has already been
    expended for the Railway Construction)
LO= Consolidated Capital for the Lines which had already been
    opened.
LNO= Consolidated Capital for the Lines which had not been opened
    then.
UF= Unadjusted Funds
UFRC= Unadjusted Funds for the Railway Construction (=the funds
    which will be expended for the Consolidated Capital in future)
FLC= Floating Capital (Current Assets)

sification of aggregate capital was partly revised in the annual report of GRJ (for the year ending March 31, 1891) as follows:

1. The floating capital was divided into the fixed working capital, the deposit made on construction work, and the value of stores for rail way construction. The last two items were regarded as unproductive capital which could not be transferred to the consolidated capital. Such items as Unproductive Capital were recognized until March 31, 1907.
2. Consolidated capital for the lines which had not been opened then (LNO) was not regarded as consolidated capital but as unproductive capital, and was renamed construction expenses under way, although this part of the revision was cancelled and the former classification was resumed in the annual report of GRJ for the fiscal year ending March 31, 1895.

Also, *Kansetsu Tetsudo Kaikei-hoh* established a supplementary and convenient system to enrich the consolidated capital through the capitalization of the additional work expenses. The additional work expenses are the small expenditures for supplementary construction works which are done with the repair or replacement of property during a period (Nakagawa, 1936, p. 102). Such expenses are primarily totalized at an account in the revenue account and transferred to the capital account to be added to the consolidated capital after the end of the accounting period. When *Kansetsu Tetsudo Yohin Shikin Kaikei-hoh* (The Government Railway Stores Fund Accounting Act) came into effect on April 1, 1894, the store funds of ¥1,800,000 were separated from the fixed working capital.

The Capital Account for the fiscal year ending March 31, 1907, was as follows:

	Yen
1. Consolidated Capital	186,790,595.694
2. Fixed Working Capital	200,000.000
3. Stores Fund	2,050,000.00
4. Unadjusted Value of Stores Included in Construction Expenses, Improvement Expenses and Laying Expenses	925,874.508
Total	189,966,470.202

Classified into productive and unproductive capital, the figures stand:

Consolidated Capital	168,286,895.180	
Fixed Working Capital	200,000.000	170,536,895.180
Stores Fund	2,050,000.000	

Unproductive Capital:

Consolidated Capital	18,503,700.514	
Unadjusted value of Stores included in Construction Expenses, Improvement Expenses and Laying Expenses	925,874.508	19,429,575.022

Figure 6.2
Government Railways of Japan Classification of Its Capital, Fiscal Years Ending March 31, 1887 and March 31, 1907

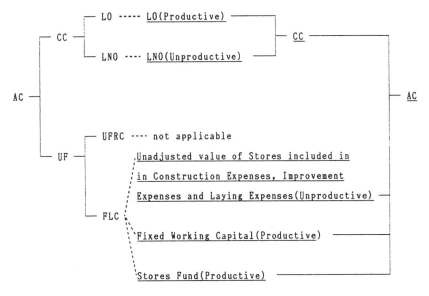

Note: Underscored items are for the fiscal year ending March 31, 1907.

The classifications of the capital in the annual reports for the fiscal years ending March 31, 1887, and March 31, 1907, are on the same principle which recognizes the difference between the consolidated (fixed) capital and the working capital. This correspondence is shown in Figure 6.2.

One may safely say that GRJ studied the principle or the idea of classifing the aggregate capital into the fixed capital and the working capital through the British railway accounting regulation and copied it faithfully during this period (July 1, 1885–March 31, 1907).

START OF JAPANIZING THE BRITISH RAILWAY ACCOUNTING SYSTEM (APRIL 1, 1907 TO JANUARY 18, 1927)

Teikoku Tetsudo Kaikei-hoh (The Imperial Government Railways Accounting Act) came into effect from April 1, 1907, to refine *Kansetsu Tetsudo Kaikei-hoh*. Seventeen private railway companies were nationalized and joined to GRJ during the period from April 1, 1906, to March 31, 1907, and this contributed to the completion of the national network of GRJ, encouraging the new accounting act to cope with a larger amount of capital and a variety of sources of funds. *Teikoku Tetsudo oyobi Doh Yohin Shikin Kaikei-kisoku* (The Imperial

Government Railways and Its Stores Funds Accounting Regulation Act), which is the detailed regulations for the application of *Teikoku Tetsudo Kaikei-hoh,* classified the value of the capital of GRJ into three classes, *Mikan Shihon* (capital borrowed from the Japanese Government), *Kikan Shihon* (GRJ's own capital transferred by refund from capital borrowed from the Japanese Government) and *Tokusetu Shihon* (GRJ's original capital). It should be noticed that the concept of the fixed working capital was abandoned in these acts. This would be the evidence that the capital account of GRJ as the joint form of the capital account and the general balance sheet in the double account system was transformed into the capital account as a single form, that is, the balance sheet in the single account system.

The above two acts were revised soon and replaced by the revised *Teikoku Tetsudo Kaikei-hoh* and *Teikoku Tetsudo Kaikei-Kisoku* (The Imperial Government Railways Accounting Regulation Act) on April 1, 1909, to establish the special account system independent of the government finance and elaborate the structure of the financial accounts. Figure 6.3 illustrates the capital account and the profit and loss account for the year ending March 31, 1910. The various refunds and temporary advances are substracted from the foregoing items of earnings and disbursements, and the balance is further distributed under various headings as shown in Figure 6.4.

The financial accounts consisted of the following three accounts in the revised *Teikoku Tetsudo Kaikei-hoh:* the capital account, the profit and loss account, and the reserve account, which was included in the capital account (Article 5). Net profit in the profit and loss account was transferred to the capital account, not to the National Treasury, after the maximum ten percent of the net profit had been transferred to the reserve account (Articles 8 and 9). *Teikoku Tetsudo Kaikei-Kisoku* classified the total value of the capital of GRJ into special capital and borrowed capital by the source of its funds. Public loans, debenture, and debts devolved from the nationalized railways belonged to borrowed capital, and others to special capital (Article 20).

In order to identify the characteristics of the GRJ's accounting practices for the fixed assets in this period, the accounting practices for the permanent way of GRJ are contrasted with the (1909) practices in the London & North Western Railway Company (LNWR) in Figure 6.5.

In the case of item No. (4), GRJ recognized the difference between the replacement to maintain the present condition of permanent way and the replacement accompanied by improvement of permanent way. The replacement method (a) was applied to the former and the retirement method (b) to the latter. The writing off of property scrapped or transferred was regarded as a capital transaction by *Teikoku Tetsudo Kaikei-Kisoku* (Article 25). The retirement method was supposed to be applied to GRJ independently of the replacement method, at least in 1901.

The GRJ's accounting procedure in the case of item No. (5) is derived from *Teikoku Tetsudo Kaikei-hoh* (Article 7), and *Teikoku Tetsudo Kaikei-Kisoku* (Ar-

Figure 6.3
Capital Account and Profit and Loss Account, Fiscal Year Ending March 31, 1910

CAPITAL ACCOUNT

Assets	yen	Liabilities	yen
Cash............	7,597.538.433	Special Capital......	159,488,826.811
Unsettled Receipts	1,182.590	Borrowed Capital.....	625,474,942.000
Consolidated		Loans..............	591,269,750.000
Capital........	769,624,014.760	Debenture...........	20,136,992.000
Stores Funds	8,506,649.434	Debts devolved from	
Works Account....	494,054.667	the nationalized	
Prepayments......	2,066,508.319	railways...........	14,068,200.000
		Amount payable.......	73,265.269
		Reserve.............	609,310.000
		Accounts beside revenue	
		and expenditure.....	101,377.880
		Temporary Appropria-	
		tion	2,542,226.243
Total.......... 788,289,948.203		Total.............. 788,289,948.203	

PROFIT AND LOSS ACCOUNT

Gross disbursements	yen	Gross earnings	yen
Expenses for		Receipts from	
operation.......	74,795,238.949	operation.........	84,829,293.217
Net profit.......	10,034,054.268		
Transferred to			
reserve fund....	609,310.000		
Transferred to			
capital account.	9,424,744.268		
Total........ 84,829,293.217		Total........ 84,829,293.217	

ticle 21 and Article 22), although it was originally recognized under *Kansetsu Tetsudo Kaikei-hoh*. It was convenient and cost-efficient to apply this procedure to such a case because a number of supplementary works happened during a fiscal year and the expenditure per work was relatively small. The scrapped consolidated capital was offset against special capital by each work.

Figure 6.4
Refunds, Advances, and Balance Distributions

Working receipts	Passenger receipts...............	43,511,990.046
	Goods receipts...................	37,522,659.020
	Sundry receipts..................	1,201,787.191
	Total......................	82,236,436.257
Working expenses	General expenses................	1,089,559.362
	Maintenance of way, etc..........	8,472,835.277
	Transportation expenses..........	19,982,447.787
	Traffic expenses................	10,200,065.883
	Electric expenses...............	1,080,079.525
	Shipping expenses...............	1,236,001.189
	Total......................	42,060,989.023

Administration and inspection expenses for railways

and tramways.......................................   96,595.887

Supplementary expenses(=Additional work expenses)......   2,542,234.649

Interest and charges for loans........................   27,502,562.430

        Grand total.....................................   72,202,381.989

Net profit..   10,034,054.268

During the period from April 1, 1907, to January 18, 1927, the GRJ's accounting followed the British system basically on the one hand, but on the other hand, it started to arrange the British system to be suitable for the GRJ's accounting policies that could be characterized as expedient in a Japanese situation.

THE POLITICAL AND ECONOMIC INFLUENCE ON THE FIXED ASSETS ACCOUNTING OF GRJ (JANUARY 19, 1927 TO MARCH 31, 1947)

The GRJ's accounting, especially its fixed assets accounting, had been in a swirl of controversy under the pressure of the political and economic circumstances during this period. The start of the controversy was the question and answer period between Mr. Muto, a member of the House of Representatives, and Mr. Kataoka, the Minister of Finance in the 52nd Imperial Diet of Japan, on January 19, 1927. Mr. Muto requested to Mr. Kataoka to transfer the net profit of GRJ from GRJ to the public finance to make up for the deficiency of financial funds caused by the depression. But the Minister of Finance refused this request for the reason that the net profit of GRJ should be appropriated for expenditures on the improvement of property and the replacement accompanied

Figure 6.5
Contrasts Between the Permanent Way and the London and North Western
Railway Company

(1) Repairs of Permanent Way during a period

  GRJ   yen

  (Dr.) Maintenance of Way   8,472,835.277 (Cr.) Cash   8,472,835.277

      -Profit and Loss Account- └→(including the renewal cost of

                                     Permanent Way, and so on)

  LNWR   £   s. d.

  (Dr.) Maintenance & Renewal

      of Permanent Way   296,123 0 9 (Cr.) Cash   296,123 0 9

      -Revenue Account-   └→(including the renewal cost of

                                       Permanent Way)

(2) Construction of Lines during a period

  GRJ   yen

  (Dr.) Construction Expenses 20,324,651.348 (Cr.) Cash   20,324,651.348

      (Consolidated Capital)

      -Capital Account-

  LNWR   £   s. d.

  (Dr.) Lines open for Traffic 304,732 12 7 (Cr.) Cash   304,732 12 7

      -Receipts and Expenditure

        on Capital Account-

(3) Improvement of Lines during a period

  GRJ   yen

  (Dr.) Improvement Expenses   5,245,260.452 (Cr.) Cash   5,245,260.452

      (Consolidated Capital) └───→(including improvement of rolling

      -Capital Account-   stocks, the replacement of

                                      Permanent Way and so on)

  LNWR

      It should be included in the case(2), Lines open for Traffic

      £ 304,732 12 7, if any.

Figure 6.5 (continued)

(4) Replacement of Permanent Way during a period

<u>GRJ</u>   yen

(a) Replacement method

(Dr.) Maintenance of Way   8,472,835.277 (Cr.) Cash   8,472,835.277

      -Profit and Loss Account- └→(including the repair cost of

                                        Permanent Way, and so on)

(b) Retirement method

(Dr.) Special Capital   1,269,817.848

      -Capital Account-   (Cr.) Consolidated Capital   1,269,817.848

                            -Capital Account-   ↓

                            (including property scrapped as a

                            result of supplementary

                            construction, land transferred

                            and so on)

(Dr.) Replacement expenses of Permanent Way (included in Improvement

                                  expenses)

      (Consolidated Capital)   5,245,260.452

      -Capital Account-   ↓

                            (including Improvement of rolling

                            stocks and Permanent Way and so

                            on)

                            (Cr.) Cash   5,245,260.452

    <u>LNWR</u>   £   s. d.

(Dr.) Maintenance & Renewal

      of Permanent Way   296,123 0 9 (Cr.) Cash   296,123 0 9

      -Revenue Account-   └────→(including the repair of Permanent

                          Way)

(5) Supplementary Construction of Lines during a period

<u>GRJ</u>   yen

(Dr.) Supplementary Expenses (Additional Work Expenses)   2,542,234.649

      -Profit and Loss Account- └→(It is almost related to the lines)

                            (Cr.) Cash   2,542,234.649

(Dr.) Special Capital   1,269,817.848

      -Capital Account-   (Cr.) Consolidated Capital   1,269,817.848

                            -Capital Account-   ↓

                            (including property scrapped as a

Figure 6.5 (continued)

```
                                result of improvement of Permanent

                                Way, land transferred and so on)

(Dr.) Supplementary expenses (Consolidated Capital)      2,542,234.649

      -Capital Account-        ⌐→(to be transferred from Profit and

                                Loss Account after the end of the

                                fiscal year)

                    (Cr.) Supplementary Expenses 2,542,234.649

                          (Special Capital)

                          -Capital Account-

LNWR

      It should be included in the case(2), Lines open for Traffic

      £304,732 12  7, if any.

   [LNWR: The 127th Report of the Directors and Statement of Accounts

   for the Half Year ending 30th June, 1909.]

   [GRJ: The Annual Report for the Year ending March 31st, 1910]
```

by improvement of property necessary to keep GRJ working well (Official Gazette of Japan, 1927, pp. 71–74).

The above discussion led to the understanding that the expenses for the replacement accompanied by improvement of GRJ's property corresponded to depreciation expenses. The further discussion in the Imperial Diet of Japan came to focus on the question whether the depreciation expenses should be considered or not in the GRJ accounting, although it was on a cash basis. The idea that the balance given by subtracting the depreciation expense from the net profit of GRJ would be regarded as the true net profit which could be transferred to public finance was supported by some powerful Diet members. The grounds for thinking that the depreciation method might be ignored in the GRJ accounting were given originally in its budgetary system (*Teikoku Tetsudo Kaikei-hoh:* Article 2).

Teikoku Tetsudo Kaikei-hoh

Construction expenses and improvement expenses of GRJ should be appropriated by the net profit of GRJ, but in the case of the deficiency of the net profit, GRJ may make up for it through the public loans issued by the government and charged to GRJ or the borrowing from other special accounts and so on. The total amount of the public loans and the borrowed money may not exceed the GRJ's budget for the construction expenses and the improvement expenses.

The more direct grounds for thinking that the depreciation method might be ignored in the GRJ accounting can be clarified by the fact that the annual improvement expenses, including the expenditures for the replacement accompanied by improvement of GRJ's property, had been approximately equal in amount to the net profit for each fiscal year. It is clear that the net profit in itself can be one of the main sources of funds for such a replacement. In other words, the net profit was substituted for the depreciation funds which would be accumulated every year through the application of the depreciation method with a troublesome calculation. As for the funds for the construction, they had been supplied almost entirely through the issue of the public loans.

The comparison of the total improvement expenses of GRJ with its net profit is shown in Table 6.1 to demonstrate the above conditions. It was impossible for us to separate the expenses for the replacement accompanied by improvement of fixed assets precisely from those total improvement expenses because of the limited information given by the annual reports.

The relationship between the net profit as the primary funds for the replacement accompanied by improvement of GRJ's fixed capital and the depreciation expenses was also discussed in the Budget Subcommittee of the House of Representatives, the 67 Imperial Diet, February 7, 1935. Mr. Shimizu, a member of the House of Representatives, asked Mr. Uchida, the Minister of Railways, to comment on whether GRJ should apply the accounting procedure of depreciation to its fixed capital just as in the private companies or not. Mr. Uchida confirmed the theoretical justice of the depreciation practice and suggested the introduction of this practice to the GRJ accounting in the near future. But the Ministry of Railways decided not to apply the depreciation practice to the GRJ accounting on February 17, 1939, due to the result of an inquiry entrusted to the specialists. Professor Ohta (Tokyo University of Commercial Science), who was engaged in this inquiry, summarized the findings of the research in the third meeting of *Teikoku Kaikei Hohki Chosa Iinkai* (the Research Committee on the Imperial Government Railways Accounting Act) on March 18, 1941, as follows:

We have come to the conclusion that it is not only unnecessary but also cost-inefficient to apply the depreciation practice to the accounting system of the Imperial Government Railways (GRJ) as a government enterprise, unlike a profit-making corporation whose purpose is the maintenance of its monetary capital for the following reasons:

(1) The general purpose of depreciation is to recover the money invested originally to the fixed capital. But, the Imperial Government Railways should maintain the rea' capital in itself rather than the monetary capital.

(2, The Imperial Government Railways is not satisfied with the application of the depreciation for the nominal capital maintenance, because it needs to maintain the real capital and improve it. *Improvement* in the Imperial Government Railways is compared with *Depreciation.*

(3) The reinvestment of the depreciation funds to the fixed capital and the reinvestment of the net profit transferred from the Profit and Loss Account to the Capital Account to the fixed capital (the present procedure) are materially indistinguishable.

Table 6.1

Comparison of the Total Improvement Expenses of GRJ with Its Net Profit, 1909–1947

items year	Improvement Expenses(yen)	Net Profit(yen)
1909-1910	5,245,260.452	9,424,744.268
1910-1911	15,678,797.590	12,326,743.497
1911-1912	29,236,812.863	19,752,164.078
1912-1913	31,017,764.976	19,132,058.547
1913-1914	22,591,407.306	19,294,314.869
1914-1915	22,230,486.596	13,752,566.928
1915-1916	20,073,151.893	23,723,217.739
1916-1917	21,578,873.083	34,587,226.266
1917-1918	27,617,674.201	43,085,812.645
1918-1919	54,820,951.381	42,908,040.587
1919-1920	104,230,859.300	59,386,096.258
1920-1921	108,167,264.860	53,837,590.851
1921-1922	124,831,152.537	115,538,022.713
1922-1923	138,512,730.616	131,529,368.448
1923-1924	121,013,097.257	110,264,095.761
1924-1925	132,640,787.430	129,819,334.944
1925-1926	145,409,079.131	143,258,087.016
1926-1927	153,274,028.767	130,907,279.164
1927-1928	156,244,968.585	138,167,619.197
1928-1929	139,634,863.000	135,875,714.000
1929-1930	125,199,688.000	118,989,507.675
1930-1931	76,916,112.086	75,587,460.648
1931-1932	54,714,746.633	68,451,762.001
1932-1933	51,991,054.936	61,079,536.743
1933-1934	56,304,721.496	88,675,257.341
1934-1935	67,662,895.291	100,896,729.539
1935-1936	86,367,948.360	109,986,002.252
1936-1937	89,446,249.538	145,462,029.918

Table 6.1 (continued)

1937-1938	104,152,937.212	166,148,691.602
1938-1939	144,500,774.022	200,443,414.911
1939-1940	189,086,989.196	266,325,952.425
1940-1941	229,946,935.384	277,771,339.317
1941-1942	241,570,846.	243,879,615.
1942-1943	269,955,694.485	429,908,030.148
1943-1944	382,757,000.000	513,264,000.000
1944-1945	575,003,785.28	340,331,395.650
1945-1946	629,440,226.29	− 741,450,681.700
1946-1947	3,508,007,565.57	123,850,255.230

*The accounting period of GRJ is one year, ending March 31.
*The amounts for 1928–1929 and 1943–1944 are approximate.

(4) Setting off the fixed capital against the special capital can be substituted for the depreciation method as a procedure of writing off the fixed capital. Therefore, the depreciation method cannot be regarded as the sole means to enrich the financial situation. (Japanese National Railways, 1956, pp. 1,032–1,033)

The period from January 19, 1927, to February 17, 1939, could be regarded as the process of GRJ's giving up the application of the depreciation practice. It would be interesting to compare this process with the accounting practices in LNWR from April 25, 1849, to December 31, 1864. LNWR decided to adopt the new accounting system for the renewal of Permanent Way from the 7th half-year ending June 30, 1849. This new system was owed to the recommendation given by the report prepared by Captain Mark Huish (General Manager of LNWR), *Report to the General Works Committee, on the Present Condition of the Permanent Way: with Remarks on the Nature and Extent of a fund for Deterioration and on the Principles of Relaying and Maintaining the Road* (April 25, 1849). This report proposed that LNWR should accumulate the renewal funds of permanent way every half year through setting up the Renewal of Rail Account. Also, it suggested that the amount subtracted from the net profit every half year should be calculated on the basis of the sound commercial theory of knowing the amount of liability accruing for the renewal of the permanent way in the future (Huish, 1849, p. 47). The Renewal of Rail Account could be functionally equivalent to the account of the allowance for depreciation, although the Renewal of Rail Account might be a means to equalize the disposable balance because it had been a debtor balance and presented as Advance upon Renewal of Rail Account in the General Balance Sheet of LNWR. LNWR decided to stop such a depreciation practice recommended by the Huish report after the 38 half-year ending December 31, 1864, and substitute the replacement

Table 6.2
Process to Substitute the Replacement Method for the Depreciation Method in LNWR (£ s. d.)

Year	Accounting Periods	Repair Expenses	Depreciation Expenses	Total
1864	37	65,653 3 2	53,333 6 8	118,986 9 10
	38	76,370 10 9	106,666 13 4	183,037 3 13

(substitution)

Year	Accounting Periods	Repair and Renewal Expenses	Depreciation Expenses	Total
1865	39	114,822 17 6	none	114,822 17 6
	40	176,391 6 3	none	176,391 6 3

*"Amount set aside this Half-Year" in *Renewal of Rail Account* was picked up as the depreciation expenses in the above table.

method for it, for the outlay from year to year in renewals of permanent way was found to accord with the amount debited to revenue, through the deterioration (depreciation) allowance, so closely as to render such a process no longer necessary (LNWR, 1865, p. 1).

The process to substitute the replacement method for the depreciation method in LNWR is evidenced in Table 6.2.

LNWR practiced the depreciation method considered ideal to make the future renewal of permanent way smooth from the theoretical viewpoint at first despite its troublesome calculation. The justification for changing the accounting methods was given from the changes in its own actual accounting data. But GRJ had given up the depreciation method without experimenting because it gave priority to cost efficiency and approximation of the results of two accounting procedures, the reinvestment of the net profit to the fixed capital, and the appropriation of the depreciation funds for the fixed capital, over their theoretical desirability. The GRJ's accounting policy which would be based relatively on expediency was easy to be influenced by political and economic circumstances. The fact that a large amount of funds (shown in Table 6.3.) was being transferred from the GRJ accounting to the national finance from the fiscal year ending March

Table 6.3
**The Amount being Transferred from GRJ to the National Finance as of Each
Year (March 31, 1937–March 31, 1947) (yen)**

year	Government funds	War Funds	Total
1936-1937	7,000,000.000	none	7,000,000.000
1937-1938	37,000,000.000	none	37,000,000.000
1938-1939	37,000,000.000	40,000,000.000	77,000,000.000
1939-1940	37,000,000.000	80,000,000.000	117,000,000.000
1940-1941	37,000,000.000	130,000,000.000	167,000,000.000
1941-1942	37,000,000.000	190,000,000.000	227,000,000.000
1942-1943	37,000,000.000	355,000,000.000	392,000,000.000
1943-1944	37,000.000.000	471,000,000.000	508,000,000.000
1944-1945	37,000,000.000	726,000,000.000	763,000,000.000
1945-1946	37,000,000.000	727,000,000.000	764,000,000.000
1946-1947	37,000,000.000	727,000,000.000	764,000,000.000

31, 1937, until the fiscal year ending March 31, 1947, to make up for the
deficiency of the government funds or the war funds will explain such characteristics of the GRJ's accounting policies.

CATCH-UP WITH ELABORATE AND THEORETICAL
ACCOUNTING PRACTICES (APRIL 1, 1947 TO MARCH 31,
1950)

Kokuyuh Tetsudo Jigyo Tokubetsu Kaikei-hoh (Special Accounting Act for
National Railways Operations) was substituted for the *Teikoku Tetsudo Kaikei-
hoh* on March 31, 1947, and applied to GRJ from April 1, 1947. This act
expected GRJ to be more competitive, like private companies (Article 1), and
introducted the accrual basis into GRJ instead of the cash basis (Article 4). Also,
the organization of GRJ was transformed from a government enterprise as a
kind of administrative organ to a public utility corporation by *Nihon Kokuyuh
Tetsudo-hoh* (Japanese National Railways Act) which came into effect from June
1, 1949, instead of *Kokuyuh Tetsudo Jigyo Tokubetsu Kaikei-hoh.*

Kokuyuh Tetsudo Jigyo Tokubetsu Kaikei-rei (Government Ordinance for the
Accounting of National Railways Operations) decided to apply the depreciation
procedure to the depreciable assets of GRJ on December 29, 1947 (Article 10)
to help the rational preparation of financial statements, the proper costing, and
the sound charging of the fares (Japanese National Railways, 1969, vol. 10, p.

Table 6.4
Depreciation Expenses

Year	Depreciation Expenses	Allowances for Depreciation	Fixed Assets (Book Value)
1948-1949	613,000,000.00	613,000,000.00	45,134,500,136.93
1949-1950a	219,814,000.	832,201,000.00	47,006,302,634.84
b	1,099,072,000.	1,830,972,488.09	61,067,376,275.00

Note: 1949–1950 is divided into two periods, a (April 1, 1949–May 31, 1949) and b (June 1, 1949–March 31, 1950).

468). Unfortunately, the depreciation expenses calculated during this period could not reflect the actual depreciation of the fixed assets, for they were calculated on the basis of the book value far lower than the current costs because of the limited national budget (Ishikawa, 1967, p. 96). The depreciation expenses are shown in Table 6.4.

If we consider the fact that GRJ already knew that depreciation based on the book value was insignificant because the current costs of the fixed assets were inflated by the sharp decline in the value of the Japanese currency (Japanese National Railways, vol. 10, 1969, p. 478), one may say safely that the GRJ's accounting policy was still influenced by the sense of values such as expediency and convenience, although it was a good try that GRJ introduced the depreciation method as a means to get the proper periodical profit.

START OF RESTRUCTURING OF THE ACCOUNTING SYSTEM IN GRJ (APRIL 1, 1950 TO MARCH 31, 1951)

The Report on Japanese Taxation by the Shoup Mission (September, 1949) recommended all public corporations and private companies to revaluate their fixed assets and apply the replacement cost depreciation to them (Japanese National Railways, vol. 10, p. 479). Prior to the formal revaluation of the fixed assets prosecuted in 1955, GRJ tried to improve its own depreciation practice through the introduction of the extraordinary or preparatory replacement cost depreciation. Considering that the depreciation expenses for replacement (shown in Table 6.5.) were restricted to a certain amount which was needed for the replacement works (which were accompanied by improvement of the fixed assets) at the moment to supplement the regular depreciation expenses (Kamida, 1950, pp. 131–132) and GRJ didn't need to adjust the original book value of the fixed assets to the revalued figures (GRJ, Annual Report, 1950–1951, p. 25), such practices might be regarded as procedures derived from expediency characteristic of the past GRJ's accounting policies. But, it was also true that GRJ

Table 6.5
Depreciation Expenses and Allowances for Depreciation (1950–1951)

```
Regular Depreciation Expenses ..................¥ 1,767,562,000.00

Special Depreciation Expenses for Replacement ... 18,788,844,000.00

       Total Depreciation Expenses.............. 20,556,406,000.00

(They are presented as the items of the operating expenses)

Regular Allowance for Depreciation .............¥ 3,585,917,745.90

Allowance for Special Depreciation

Expenses for Replacement........................ 18,788,844,000.00

       Total Allowances for Depreciation........ 22,374,761,745.90

(They are presented as the items of the valuation reserve)
```

started the restructuring of its accounting system from the long-term perspective in this period.

CONCLUSION

The railway accounting system of Japan since 1870 has developed mainly as one for the government-managed railways. GRJ acquired the well-organized accounting system of the U.K. automatically when it decided to establish its first regular accounting regulation with reference to the British regulations in 1885.

But the developing process of the GRJ accounting system seems to be in striking contrast with one of the influential British railway companies, i.e., the LNWR, especially in terms of the ways of choosing the accounting procedures. When the accounting practices of LNWR are taken into consideration, one may notice that LNWR is characterized as a company that justified trial and error in experimenting to ascertain the propriety of an accounting procedure considered theoretical or ideal by the result of the voluntary research. For example, although the Huish report in 1849 contributed to the introduction of the depreciation practice to accumulate the funds for the renewal of permanent way, LNWR found some changes in its accounting data to justify the adoption of the replace-ment method instead of the depreciation method in 1864. On the other hand, the GRJ's accounting policy toward the choice of the accounting procedures was much influenced by the kind of worldly values such as expediency, con-venience, result for result's sake and cost-efficiency rather than theoretical pro-priety.

Therefore, the process of arranging the British railway accounting system to be suitable for GRJ through such a worldly sense of value could be termed the Japanizing of the British system, although it does not mean immediately that the Japanese government as an accounting regulator inflicted mischief on the sound development of accounting practices.

REFERENCES

Chiba, J, *A History of British Financial Accounting* (Tokyo: Chuokeizai-sha, 1991).

Edwards, J. R., *British Company Legislation and Company Accounts 1844–1976* (New York: Arno Press, 1980):174–187.

Huish, M., *Report to the General Works Committee, on the Present Condition of the Permanent Way: with Remarks on the Nature and Extent of a fund for Deterioration and on the Principles of Relaying and Maintaining the Road* (Manchester, 1849):47.

Ishikawa, T., *Japanese National Railways—Its Financial Structure,* (Tokyo: Kohtsu Nihon-sha, 1967):93–99.

Japanese National Railways, *The Centenary History of Japanese National Railways,* vol. 1 (Tokyo: 1969):365.

Japanese National Railways, *The Centenary History of Japanese National Railways,* vol. 7 (Tokyo: 1969):454–455.

Japanese National Railways, *The Centenary History of Japanese National Railways,* vol. 10 (Tokyo: 1969): 468, 476, 478, 479.

Japanese National Railways, *The Centenary History of Japanese National Railways,* vol. 12 (Tokyo: 1969):589.

Japanese National Railways, *The Report of the Board of Managerial Investigation of Japanese National Railways,* vol. 1 (Tokyo: 1956):1032–1033.

Kamida, C., *Railway Accounting* (Tokyo: Kotsukeizai-sha, 1950):92–95, 130–132.

London & North Western Railway Company, *Report of the Directors, To Be Submitted to the Proprietors at the Half-Yearly General Meeting,* (18th August, 1865):1.

Nakagawa, S., *The Modern Railway Accounting* (Tokyo: Nihon Kotsu Gakkai, 1936): 102.

Nakamura, M., *A Study on the History of British and American Railway Accounting Systems* (Tokyo: Dohbun-kan, 1991).

Official Gazette of Japan, *The Minute Book of the House of Representatives in the Imperial Diet,* no. 5, (Tokyo: Printing Bureau of the Cabinet, January 20, 1927): 71–74.

Sasaki, S., The Accounting Practices for the Fixed Assets of London & North Western Railway Company in the Middle of the 19th Century, *Japan Industrial Management & Accounting,* vol. 46, no. 4 (Tokyo, 1987):74–83.

Takatera, S., *A study on the Depreciation Practices in the Meiji Era* (Tokyo: Mirai-sha, 1974):67–83.

7

An Introduction to Strategic Management Accounting

Makoto Kawada

ABSTRACT

The machine industry, as the core of any nation's industrial infrastructure, almost decides the industrial strength of the nation despite its relatively small size. Teijin Seiki, a machine manufacturer in Japan, is holding its own in this tough, global competition, with 1,700 employees and some world-class products in the fields of textile machinery, industrial components, and aerospace equipment. The author of this paper is a practitioner, not a scholar. So, the paper starts by describing experiments we ran in our company to coordinate production and accounting in a more functional manner and to raise productivity, such as

- "Quit measuring actual time,"
- "Target burden rate,"
- "Lead time-based costing,"
- "Cash flow and getting along well with financial accounting."

Some of these practical experiments are perhaps unique, and some might be commonplace. However, the assessment of each individual case is not the purpose of this paper. The paper primarily aims to demonstrate an empirical approach whereby a useful theoretical framework is formed via practical experiments and enthusiasm. Thereafter, the conceptual framework of strategic accounting shall be presented, especially from the standpoint of a historical analysis of management accounting theory.

The stance stressed in this article is a wholistic approach. The attitude of viewing accounting from the wider perspectives of total management systems had already been initiated in the 1960s by R. N. Anthony's "Planning and Control Systems." However, actual, in-place managers seem to have pursued production issues and accounting issues in isolation until today. Such a separation does not work any more in the 1990s. A "big plan, small start" attitude is indispensable in designing a total management scheme like CIM (Computer Integrated Management), for example. No matter how difficult it may be, we must have a long-term range of vision, covering at least five years in the whole socioeconomic context, for how the entire management function should be organized and run, while we are allowed to take a short horizon, less ambitious, approach in initiating actual steps.

Addressing this interdisciplinary problem in the age of global turbulence is expected to constitute a significant part of the intellectual aid given to the Eastern Bloc, which is struggling to introduce a market economy.

INTRODUCTION

The conventional cost accounting system, linked to the financial profit and loss statement and based on the principle of matching expenses with revenues, was mostly perfected in the 1910s and elaborated into budgetary control theories by H. W. Quaintance and J. O. McKinsey in the 1920s.[1] The completion of traditional accounting theory was Schmalenbach's "Dynamische Bilanz" in 1939.

Since J. N. Harris indicated in his "What Did We Earn Last Month?" in 1936, however, fictitiousness in indirect cost distribution has become an object of controversy in the field of management accounting. "Full costing versus direct costing" became a most controversial accounting topic in the 1950s. The new production paradigm since the 1980s has made the obsolescence of standard, full absorption costing quite obvious: with drastically lower direct labor content for automated production environments and rising ratios of overhead to total product costs, metamorphoses of conventional accounting, such as ABC (Activity Based Costing), have become inevitable in the 1990s.[2]

Intellectual products reflect the socioeconomic climate of the age. In the 1960s, a paradigm of "economies of scale" dominated production management. The economies of scale paradigm was supported by traditional costing: the larger the production volume, the cheaper the unit cost, no matter whether it sells or not. Keynesians believed that economic growth could be controlled through fiscal and monetary policy on the demand side. In the 1980s, small batch production superseded economies of scale and the emphasis in economics shifted from the demand side on to the supply side. Such changes reflect the current socioeconomic climate in which business is being globalized, competition becoming harsher, markets more volatile, and technology is making rapid progress. Strangely enough, however, financial accounting alone has hardly responded to the changing environment.

In the new manufacturing paradigm, the production processes are viewed as a continuum which is not discrete but continuous and dependent on each other. Instead of men or machine activation, the velocity of material flow is the driver of productivity; and the sum of the local optimums is not equal to the global optimum.

Under the new paradigm, cooperative study between production people and accounting people seems to have just started in the U.S. in the 1980s in order to reclaim American productivity.[3] Japan seems to be following the U.S. in this interdisciplinary field, too.

CASES

Case I—Quit Measuring Actual Time

In 1983, a division in the author's company abolished its long-cherished method of measuring actual time for costing. This plant, then making reduction gears for earth excavators, had languished in red ink since its inception ten years before. As a last resort, the plant manager determined to reform its production systems drastically by introducing JIT (just-in-time) theory, a new production paradigm at that time.

The first step was to quit using the actual times of each individual process as a means of calculating product costs. Daily issuance of efficiency reports involving standard and actual variance of the previous day was also stopped. Asking workers the cause of the efficiency variance was banned. Instead, activities like helping bottleneck work centers digest the overload was encouraged as the top priority in the plant. The rationale for the new behavior was given as follows.

1. The Customer is King! Workloads come as clumps of customer requirements which are not meant to be levelled. Instead, capacity should fluctuate following the fluctuations of customers' orders. That can happen when every worker does not hesitate to help out and move among different workshops. Essential ingredients: teamwork, multiskills, and flexibility.

2. The purpose of setting a standard time is to estimate the product cost in advance and find the "sweet spots" for cost reduction. For this purpose, the standard times need not necessarily be matched with the actual times.

3. Contributions of individual workers are assessed by the frequency of mutual aid among work centers for total efficiency. Whether performing within standard time in each individual process is appreciated or not depends on the situation. At a non-bottleneck work center, such behavior is rather blameworthy.

4. Most of the staff and management activities in such downstream areas such as analyzing or controlling efficiency tend to be a waste of money. Most of the product costs are decided at such upstream areas as design and engineering.

Freed from actual-time bondage, people began to accept flexible job dispatching that changes almost daily according to the workload. The notion of division of labor, in which a chain of work is segmented into small units, the motion is simplified and workers are dedicated to that simple, special job, was thus shattered. The plant soon shifted from being the underdog to being a star in the company, now enjoying the largest world share of the reduction gear market.

Under the old production paradigm initiated by Frederick Taylor's "Scientific Management," deviation from the standard had to be eliminated. In conventional standard full adsorption costing, the gap between the standard and the actual was defined as an "efficiency variance." So, measuring actual time had some significance for both production and accounting. But when the new production paradigm of JIT and OPT (optimized production technology) proclaimed that the sum of the local optimum does not equal to the total optimum any more, recording local, actual times lost relevance.

Case II—Target Burden Rate

A division of the author's company, which makes textile machine plants and components like automatic take-up winders for synthetic fibers, introduced a FMS (Flexible Manufacturing System) into its main factory in 1984, thinking that in-house parts production was necessary for higher quality, lower costs, and quicker delivery. But things were not that easy. Unexpected confusion happened in calculating product costs. Suppose the company has some work to order from the outside and considers shifting a part of the outside work to in-house operation. The work takes twenty hours for outsiders to process, but only ten hours for the company, thanks to the FMS. If the company takes in twenty hours of work from outside suppliers, the comparative processing costs for inside and outside work are calculated as follows:

The old calculation of conversion cost is as follows.

In-house processing cost (conversion cost)
$$= \text{direct labor plus manufacturing overhead}$$
$$= \text{hourly rate} \times \text{processing time}$$
$$= \$80 \times 10 \text{ hours}$$
$$= \$800$$
Outside conversion cost (payment for outside order)
$$= \$35 \times 20 \text{ hours}$$
$$= \$700$$

This shows that farming it out is more economical than making it inside by FMS despite the fact that the machining time with FMS is one half that of outside work with conventional machines. This was the typical case of make-versus-buy confusion caused by the fully burdened hourly rate in full absorption costing. Production people at this plant who introduced FMS got frustrated with this cost report. Fortunately, company accountants were modest enough to re-examine the method of product costing.

One accountant proposed charging variable costs alone as the product cost, in which only direct costs (out-of-pocket costs) are charged to the product so that people will not be deceived by the seemingly higher, in-house product cost. This method, however, did not gain much support from the people who wanted both fixed costs to be recovered in product costs and the cost fluctuation due to make-versus-buy change to be minimized. It seemed impossible at the time. But a breakthrough in thinking occurred: "target burden rate."

The new calculation is as follows.

Target hourly rate ÷ outside manufacturer's level (mandatorily set)
$$= \$35$$
In-house conversion cost = Target Hourly Rate × Processing Time
$$= \$35 \times 10 = \$350$$
    * Allocation residual = (Actual Hourly Rate − Target Hourly Rate)
        × Processing Time
$$= (\$80 - \$35) \times 10 = \$450$$
Outside conversion cost = \$35 × 20 = \$700

Rationale

The burden rate is better charged by external assessment as the yardstick for competitiveness, and not by internal calculation as in the traditional way. When outside suppliers, in the NIES (Newly Industrializing Economies) as well as among domestic competitors, are expected to make some product at an hourly rate of overhead burden at $35/hour on average, then inside work must be done at the same rate in order to be competitive. A $35 hourly rate is to be recognized as the baseline to be attained through either reducing product costs or saving fixed costs.

The conversion cost under the new target costing, $35 × 10 = $350 in this case, can be regarded as variable cost (out-of-pocket costs) so that deceptive cost fluctuations with volume changes can be removed.

The allocation residual of $450, representing the gap between target rate and actual rate, was settled as a variance at the fiscal year end so that the target burden could be recognized as a generally accepted accounting principle by Japan's Taxation Bureau.

It is important to recognize this $450 residual as the "Competitive Variance," that is, a lump of waste to be eliminated (except for depreciation). It shows that activities for reducing waste must promptly be set in motion.

Emancipated from this make-versus-buy confusion, managers' and workers' attention began to be directed outward, toward market and competitors. This division, once forced to lay off employees in the 1980s, resurged as one of the most competitive textile machinery manufacturers at the end of that decade.

Whether a new production system takes hold depends on how the management accounting system makes people in the organization think and act. Accordingly, management accounting should constantly make efforts to contrive

Figure 7.1
Traditional Formula of Standard Time-Based Costing

```
Traditional Formula:

   Product Cost = Material + Conversion Cost

   Conversion Cost = Standard Machine Time X Hourly Burden Rate


 * Hourly Burden Rate =  Total Indirect Expense / ΣStandard Time
      (preset)
```

devices so that the corporate culture can adapt to changing business environments. The business environment, thought to be a constant in the 1960s, has
become a variable since the 1970s. How to build in a market-driven mind-set
across the organization is the key mission for strategic management accounting.

Case III—Lead Time-Based Costing (LTB)

Problem

This case occurred at the same reduction gear plant of the company mentioned
earlier, after signs of recovery gradually began to appear there. Product costs in
this plant had been calculated under the traditional full costing system as shown
in Figure 7.1.

Under this formula, cutting standard machine time at a certain process point
by a drawing change, for example, seemed to realize a lower conversion cost.
Through the plant-wide Quality Control Circle campaign, many improvement
proposals were collected, so managers expected great benefits. The results, however, turned out far from expectations. Where have all the proposals gone?

The plant faced another hitch. In designing its MRP (Material Requirements
Program) system, which was to be guided by the JIT (just-in-time) or OPT (Op-
timized Production Technology) theory, the plant tried to cut the batch size, but
increased frequency of setup times due to smaller lot size led to higher unit cost.
Which was wrong, the traditional cost accounting or the new production theory?
It was confirmed that the solution had to satisfy the following conditions:

1. The goal is to leap into the new paradigm, where the velocity of material flow is
   important.
2. Accounting must serve production, not vice versa.

3. Accounting must be revised to comply with the direction JIT and OPT suggest.

4. Accounting must justify small batch production.

Through joint study by production people and accountants in the company, a breakthrough came out. What they arrived at was the concept of lead time-based costing (Figures 7.2 and 7.3).

Solution

Figure 7.2
Lead Time-Based versus Standard Time-Based Costing

	Part A				Part B			
Process	#1	#2	#3	Total	#1	#2	#3	Total
ST	2	10	3	15min	7	5	8	20
LT	10	10	10	30	8	8	8	24

Question: Part A takes 15 min. in ST and 30 min. in LT.
Part B takes 20 min. in ST and 24 min. in LT.
Which conversion cost is lower, part A or B?

Answer: Part B is lower than Part A.
The sweet spot for cost reduction is Process #2 of Part A and #3 of Part B.

Figure 7.3
New Formula of Lead Time-Based Costing

```
New formula :

   Product Cost = Material + Conversion Cost

   Conversion Cost = Lead Time X Hourly Burden Rate

 * Hourly Burden Rate = Total Indirect Expense / Σ Lead Time (LT)
```

Comments

Lead time (as shown in Figure 7.4) is the elapsed time for material to go through a plant; so that it encompasses the conventional, standard time-man hours, and machine hours, and waiting time.

Figure 7.4
The Concept of Lead Time

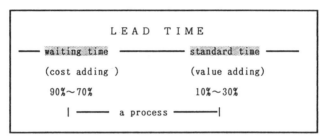

Note the reversal in the conversion cost of Part A and Part B. Under the new production paradigm, the longer the lead time, the more overhead is charged. The degree of contribution towards shorter lead time is the yardstick to evaluate the effectiveness of cost reduction efforts. You can easily identify Process #2 for Part A, and Process #3 for Part B as the most effective object for cost reduction activities.

Saving one minute at Process #2 contributes fully toward the shorter lead time of Part A. Total lead time will be cut by three minutes to twenty-seven minutes, since process #2 is the bottleneck. Whereas, trying to save one minute at Process #1 or at Process #3 just wastes money; that is, there would be an increase in work-in-process inventory, with no increase in the throughput.

So, you can see that LTB costing encourages small batch production. The smaller the batch size, the faster the velocity of material flow. Accordingly, the conversion cost should become lower. Therefore LTB costing perfectly coincides with new production theories like JIT and OPT.

In Frederick Taylor's Scientific Management paradigm, each production process is a discontinuum, that is, discrete. Since each is independent and isolated from the other, activating either workers or machines was always worthwhile. Whereas, under the new paradigm, production processes are recognized as a continuum, that is, continuous and mutually dependent on each other. According to this view, activating the bottleneck process alone accelerates material flow.

Several rules for LTB costing come from OPT, developed by Dr. E. Goldratt, and formulized as an innovative production system:

1. Balance flow, not capacity.
2. An hour saved at a non-bottleneck is a mirage.
3. The bottleneck governs both throughput and inventories.
4. The sum of the local optimums is not equal to the global optimum.

These rules are the linkages for integrating the once-disrupted relationship between production and accounting. Thus, LTB costing can become an integrator of production and accounting as has ABC in the 1990s.

In view of the fact that 10% to 30% of lead time is for value-adding operations, which is the direct conversion of materials, and 90% to 70% is for cost-adding waiting time when the flow is interrupted and costs accumulate, cutting waiting time is easier and more effective than cutting machine time, especially at the early stages of improving productivity. You can see that conventional accounting, nevertheless, focused only on this 10% to 30% part of lead time. Strategic management accounting treats both machining and waiting time equally.

Case IV—Other Devices to Change People's Mind-set about Cash Flow

Financial cost reports do not necessarily reflect a company's virtual profitability or productivity. Under the full cost accounting system, profit is deceptively high when building inventory and deceptively low when reducing inventory. This was indicated by J. N. Harris in 1936 in his "What Did We Earn Last Month?" and evolved into the direct-versus-full controversy in the 1950s. After Just-in-Time production thinking became popular in the 1980s, it became obvious that putting small batch production into actual practice was difficult because reported profit shrank when inventory began to decrease, although it is a fortunate outcome in all its effects. As a result, the direct costing, because of its similarity to cash flow, seems to be reviving as a management tool although, as a financial accounting principle, direct costing was defeated by full costing during the 1950s dispute. Recently, more investors are saying, "it's cashflow that counts."[4]

In the same vein, Teijin Seiki uses the notion of cash flow in evaluating the business performance of its decentralized business units in order to preclude actions to enhance short-term return on investment at the expense of the company's long-term profitability (Figure 7.5). This is not a new idea. The proto-

Figure 7.5
Cash Flow for Company Game

```
Cash flow (for company game)
  = Net profit * 0.5 (tax rate) + Depreciation + R&D expense
```

type of this thought had already been introduced in the 1920s by the Du Pont Company.[5] The difference between Teijin Seiki's usage of cash flow and Du Pont's is in that Teijin Seiki added R&D (research and development) costs to the calculation of return as a company game rule to encourage R&D activities. The rationale is that R&D expense is the future cash-in, because no R&D is done today without the future prospect of cash-in. Validity considerations aside, this company game works.

Getting Along Well with Financial Accounting

It is not an easy job even for insiders to assess business performance objectively. Profit fluctuates in a deceptive manner with fluctuations in inventory, depreciation, and other factors. In addition, there is a familiar "end-of-the-period" effect which the financial accounting system causes: the factory is fairly busy at the end of a month, and tends to be frightfully busy at the end of the fiscal year. A company's performance is assessed by the financial data issued at the end of the fiscal year. Cost variances such as standard, volume, and efficiency variance are figured at the fiscal year end in the financial reports, making virtual profitability all the more obscure.

An idea like "Columbus' Egg" was born to cope with this ambiguity. It is to regard each unit of month as the final month end of the fiscal year, and render a yearly income statement for the past twelve months, such as May–April, June–May, July–June, rolling every month. Then, unwieldy fluctuations due to the "end-of-the-period" effect are levelled by making every month the month of reckoning. Profitability trends are uncovered with a very gentle curve of moving averages.

Despite the obsolescence of traditional financial cost accounting, combining devices such as Columbus' Egg in terms of financial accounting makes it possible to see what lies beyond the horizon of the fiscal year. Detente is possible.

INTRODUCTION TO STRATEGIC MANAGEMENT ACCOUNTING

Wholistic Approach

In 1989, the MIT Commission on Industrial Productivity indicated the importance of the wholistic approach in its *Made in America,* saying that, "everything we have learned from our industry studies in the United States and abroad suggests that individual part of the old patterns can not be replaced piecemeal. It will not do to borrow pieces of the West German or the Japanese system and try to make them fit an American context. Rather, for any of the reforms to survive and flourish, the environment in which it is implanted must be transformed."[6]

Well before that, in 1949, Robert K. Merton used the example of the sea anemone to explain what is meant by "dysfunction" in the introduction to his *Social Theory and Social Structure*. Because of its low degree of organic integration, when a sea anemone tries to move its body, a part of the leg still clings to a rock, so that the leg is torn from the body. This metaphor suggests the difficulty in functionally integrating social systems like management systems, which are far more complex than sea anemones.[7]

Since the turn of the century, the notions of bureaucracy and the division of labor have flourished in harmony with the "atomism" of Newtonian mechanisms. With atomism, not the wholeness or unity of the universe but its separateness was emphasized, and atomistic views dominated the management of manufacturing industries. Despite Einstein's demolishing the notion of time as absolute,[8] Frederick Taylor's Scientific Management, with its time-and-motion study, promoted the penchant for "analysis" rather than "synthesis." In the 1980s, however, a paradigm shift occurred. The manufacturing paradigm shifted from "product-out, make-to-stock, mass production" to "market-in, make-to-order, small-batch production." Innovative production methods like JIT and OPT appreciated synthesis more than analysis, and rejected the atomistic idea that the sum of local optimums is equal to the total optimum.

We should understand, however, that JIT has not been as widely applied in Japan as the media tell us. Despite the JIT fad in the 1970s, it became patent that implementing a Kanban system entails a wholistic approach: it requires penetrating an entire organization with the same rigid principle, including outside suppliers. This remains quite a challenge for the great majority of Japanese manufacturers. In addition, the dissonance between the new production paradigm and the traditional cost accounting has made shifting paradigms all the more difficult. Reported failures in introducing JIT, OPT, MRP II (Material Requirements Program), and CIM in the 1980s are mostly ascribed to a conservative, patchwork-style incrementalism instead of challenging organizations as a whole with "a big plan-yet-small start" approach.

Made in America pointed out recent signs of a U.S. effort to improve relationships in the industry that have traditionally been weak, such as those between assemblers and suppliers, unions and management, and technical specialists and general management.[9] Such an effort suggests the necessity of taking a wholistic approach instead of a parochial one.

In the history of management accounting, wholistic approaches began in the 1960s. R. N. Anthony, in his 1965 "Planning and Control Systems," proposed an analytical framework, in which he regarded management accounting as an integral part of management activities, the part which coordinates the other managerial functions. In 1966, ASOBAT (A Statement of Basic Accounting Theory), issued by the AAA (American Accounting Association), proposed to broaden the commitment of management accounting to decision process, human behavior, and computer technology and systems design. It said that the accounting function is essentially information control, and encompasses "measurement methods for social science in general."

Keys for Strategic Management Accounting

An amplification of R. N. Anthony and the ASOBAT model seems to enable us to construct the architecture of strategic management accounting for the 1990s. The following are keys for workable strategic management accounting:

1. Taking a wholistic approach is essential.
2. Externally oriented processes must be strengthened.
3. Do product planning first.
4. Integrate production and accounting.

Comments

Taking a Wholistic Approach Is Indispensable

In order to achieve management excellence, one must draw, at the start, a thoroughly integrated state of managerial function, regardless of the size of business, in which essential missions of each function must effectively be organized from the viewpoint of global market and competition, balancing and consistency is required in designing relationships between strategy and tactics, between long-term and short-term goal setting.

Made in America reported, to the contrary, that U.S. auto companies have at times been dominated by "bean counters," who looked inward only to the U.S. heartland rather than outward to global markets, and who favored short-term returns over long-term investments. Another contrary example comes from *The Reckoning,* by David Halberstam. He tells how the Ford Motor Co. was embroiled in serious conflicts between the production people and the finance people, in a way that resembled the small-car/big-car struggles of the 1970s. This time the issue was even graver: whether or not Ford would turn over production of all its compact and subcompact lines to Mazda.[10] Fragmented and uncoordinated functional process is the major cause of dragged productivity. In order to avoid the problem of the sea anemone, a wholistic view and total approach is absolutely the first requisite.

Externally-Oriented Processes Must be Amplified

Externally-oriented processes represented only "financial accounting" in R. N. Anthony's model. It can be amplified to mean "environmental information control" at large, through which sensitiveness towards trends in technology, market and competition should be developed in this age of global turbulence. The new set of externally-oriented processes is thus to function as a "dealer with external impact" that gives signals continuously to the internally-oriented processes by gathering, interpreting, and arranging information according to management requirements.

Product Planning should come First

The priority of period profit-planning over product planning seems to be a given in traditional management accounting, and even in Anthony's model. That priority must be reversed in the 1990s, when product life cycle is so short and volatile. In Anthony's "Framework for Analysis," general management duties and tasks such as decisions about financial policy, budgeting, and recruitment planning come, consciously or unconsciously, before production tasks such as choosing new products, rearranging equipment layout, and performance measurement in listing of examples of activities at each phase of the management process.[11] Confidence in American industrial power of the 1960s may have made production seem to be a constant, although in reality it is variable.

Product planning should come first because product and technology are the very substance of industry; and that must be manifested in the architecture of strategic management accounting. Otherwise, the delusion of general management will obscure the core issues, as seen in the history of the American auto industry.

The following developments—MIS (Management Information System, or trying to let computer run the business), OR (Operations Research, or trying to find out solutions mathematically), Keynesian economics (trying to control economic growth through fiscal and monetary adjustment), PPBS (Planning-Programming-Budgeting System), the concept of the multinational corporation, psychological approaches like the Managerial Grid and Theory Y, and the rage of mergers and acquisitions in the 1980s—all reflect a concern for general management, and diversions from the core issues in the U.S. Whereas, Japanese management, due to its concern for execution and how to make things, lacks accountability in more general terms. An alliance, not a confrontation, of the two approaches could form the best guidebook for the Eastern Bloc to follow in accelerating its industrialization from this moment on.

Functional Integration of Production and Accounting

Since the turn of the century, accounting theory has constantly been exposed to conflicts of various kinds. One is the "chasm" between the budget control, which is linked to the double entry bookkeeping system of financial accounting, and the production control, which is based on non-monetary yardsticks linked to each individual task. In the 1970s, Atsuo Tsuji, then Professor of Osaka City University, described the chasm with a model that he called "from the engineer's accounting to the accountant's accounting."[12] *Relevance Lost,* written by Johnson and Kaplan in 1987, pointed out the illogic in two tiers of indirect cost allocation, a single, volume-oriented cost driver, and other factors of obsolescence in the traditional cost accounting systems, eventually leading to the notion of "nonfinancial indicators."

The chasm between production and accounting reaches a point of critical confrontation between them. New production paradigms like JIT or OPT encouraged small batch production. But under the conventional costing systems based on a single, volume-oriented cost driver like direct labor hours, the smaller the batch size, the higher the product cost appears to be because of increased setup times. Eliyahu M. Goldratt, creator of OPT systems, therefore said, "Accounting is one hundred percent the enemy of productivity."[13]

How to Realize Functional Integration

Today, there seem to be two schools of management accounting thought for reestablishing a working relationship between production and accounting. One is the "accuracy school" which tries to improve the accuracy of product cost. Another is the "strategy school," which pursues what may be called "strategic adaptability" rather than accuracy. The notion common between the two is that traditional financial cost accounting undermines productivity unless it is radically revised, and the only way to a workable management accounting is to cut the knot between financial accounting and production control—at least for now.

Advocating the accuracy school, Professor Kaplan of Harvard University insists that indirect cost allocation itself is the cause of distorted product cost; he says that almost all costs, with only a few exceptions like R&D expense, should be regarded as variable costs. Moreover, nonfinancial indicators of performance should be used for improving productivity instead of financial data. This school's stream of thought soon evolved into ABC. In ABC, both the volume-sensitive and non-volume-sensitive, real, overhead cost drivers are identified, and indirect costs are traced to each of them—thus achieving high accuracy of product cost.

In strategic management accounting, cost drivers are not necessarily derived from intra-management calculations. Cost drivers, as determiners of competitive advantage, are chosen from a strategic point of view. The flow of thinking here—from the outside to the inside, that is, from environment to management—presents a striking contrast to the "accuracy school" in which the flow of thinking is from the inside to the outside. As mentioned earlier, Teijin Seiki, the author's company, identified target burden rate as a determiner of competitive advantage, that is, KFS (Key Factor for Success).

Clarifying the role and status of the financial accounting field within the framework of strategic management accounting is an important process for preventing the problem of the sea anemone. Financial accounting information is not irrelevant yet in making strategic decisions if properly used, and obviously, companies must keep financial score and report it to concerned outside parties. So, peaceful coexistence with financial accounting is a must. That means that financial accounting should not be rejected but put in the right place within management systems. We must, without doubt or hesitation, ban the direct commitment of financial accounting to the production sphere. So, the possibility of cohabitation between financial accounting and production must be systematically prohibited in the framework of strategic management accounting. Coexistence without cohabitation can be realized by directing the flow of information unidirectionally from internal to external. For a workable strategic management accounting system, financial accounting should be an information receiver, not a sender to the operational sphere of management.

The Architecture of Strategic Management Accounting

The architecture of strategic management accounting which will work in the 1990s can be drawn as an updated version of R. N. Anthony's framework in Figures 7.6 and 7.7.

Figure 7.6
Architecture of Strategic Management Accounting

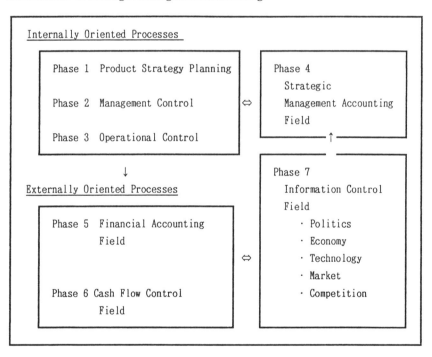

Figure 7.7
Proper Order of Thinking

```
┌─────────────────────────────────────────────────────────┐
│                                                           │
│         Proper order of thinking                          │
│            in strategic management accounting             │
│                                                           │
│                                                           │
│         EXTERNAL  ⇒  INTERNAL                             │
│                                                           │
│                                                           │
│         1  Recognizing environment                        │
│                     ↓                                     │
│         2  Identifying  KFS                               │
│                     ↓                                     │
│         3  Arrange management accounting apparatus        │
│                                                           │
└─────────────────────────────────────────────────────────┘
```

Comments

Definition

Strategic management accounting is a method which creates change in the management scheme by means of accounting devices in order to adapt effectively to the constantly changing external business environment.

Proper Order of Thinking

Strategic management accounting has an ironclad rule to be observed: recognizing the environmental change must come first, the KFS (Key Factors for Success) must be redefined next, then, thirdly, a relevant accounting device must be designed. For example, we can recognize market environment as more "quality-oriented"; the KFS may be "quality through speed" (quality and cycle time is the yin and yang[14]), then a management accounting framework for encouraging to cut cycle time is devised. The order of thinking thus always flows from external to internal, never vice versa.

The Person in Charge of Strategic Management Accounting

Strategic management accounting should be managed by production people, including sales and engineering, not by accounting people.

Phase 1—Product Strategy Planning

"What to make?" instead of "How much to earn?" is the starting point for strategic management accounting. Items for product strategy planning follow. These items shall constitute the conceptual framework of the CIM data base.

Data Base

1. What product to make?
2. Where to sell, how many, with what unit price?
3. How many people are required to make it? (Incremental workforce)
4. What facilities are needed for making the product, as in item 3? (Incremental facilities)
5. Incremental capital needed to fund items 3 and 4.
6. Life-time cash flow of the product throughout its life cycle.
7. Aggregation of each product's lifetime revenue and expense.
8. Period profit (or loss) for each fiscal year drawn from item 7.
9. Then, when fiscal profit is unsatisfactory, return to item 1.

Phase 4—Strategic Management Accounting Field

Strategic Management Accounting Field supports decision making in internally oriented processes. The most important mission at this phase is to plan the cost configuration of the product; that will establish the feasibility of the product strategy planning at Phase 1. Cost planning at the design stage takes top priority.

Notice that the accounting method employed by this field is cash flow accounting. That is, simple "cash in minus cash out" calculations which are closely linked to material flow in the production process—or direct costing. Full costing is not applied here. In addition, note that, using ROI (Return on Investment) or DCF (Discounted Cash Flow) at this phase often undermines a promising product. Be patient and simple in counting your future beans.

Configuration of Values for Cost Management

Different engineers and clerks in different divisions and sections of the company deal with a variety of values related to product cost. Those values need to be integrated into a single database, processed on a real-time basis, and made available to management for any of several purposes, as follows:[15]

Value	Purpose
1. Quoted Value	(to comply with customer's request)
2. Profitable Value	(to secure product profit)
3. Forecast Value	(to forecast future cost trend)
4. Budget Value	(to comply with budgetary request)
5. Bidding Value	(to set bidding price into competition)
6. Idealistic Value	(to set the ultimately possible goal)
7. Standard Value	(conventional one)
8. Actual Value	(ditto)

Note that, although not completely obsolescent, setting standard times is losing justification these days. Standard and actual times have long been standard datums of conventional cost accounting. In the 1990s, the role of standard time dwindled because product life cycles became drastically shorter, and work performance was figured at the design stage. Controlling by variance from standard times can even be harmful in cases where it hampers labor flexibility.

Costing Process Synchronized with Production

Nothing ever really stops, as traditional financial accounting would have us assume. Production is a dynamic, ongoing process of increasing added value. Accounting facts also constantly evolve as time passes. Therefore, production and accounting should be treated as simultaneous and synchronous events, like the head and tail of a coin. So material flows from design, purchasing, machining, and assembly to shipping, and money flows from accounts payable, and accounts receivable to bill collecting should occur in a single business process and be processed in a single database in real time, tracing the value-adding process in production activities at every moment.

The management accounting process should thus be assimilated with production process, each in a symbiosis with the other. Until the 1980s, production had been one thing, and accounting another. Accounting was performed prior to production as budgeting, or after production as variance control, in what we may call a "production-accounting dualism." We can allow financial accounting to stand on a dualistic footing, but not management accounting. Monism or a philosophy of unity is necessary for a workable CIM to materialize. In the 1990s, we need an atavistic development from an "accountant's accounting" to an "engineer's accounting," as Professor Tsuji termed it, and this time supported by computers. Chances are still great.

NOTES

1. For critical analyses on McKinsey and Quaintance, refer to Atsuo Tsuji, *Basic Theory of Management Accounting* (Kanrikaikei no Kiso Riron) (Tokyo: Chuo Keizai Sha, 1985), Chapter 3, "Formation of American Management Accounting," pp. 38–64. Tsuji identifies the chasm between budgetary control, which is general and periodic, and task control, which is individual and objective, concerning which both McKinsey and Quaintance were nonchalant.

As for an analytical introduction to McKinsey, refer to Kengo Kobayashi, *History of Budgetary Control* (Yosan Kanri Hattatsushi) (Tokyo: Soseisha, 1987), Chapters 7 and 8, "Budgetary Control Theory of J. O. McKinsey," pp. 148–197. McKinsey was aware of the necessity of horizontal adjustment of budgeting among different functional departments, but not of vertical adjustment.

2. Currently, direct labor content of product is around 10%, 20% at best, even in a labor-intensive product. According to a joint study by NAA & CAMI, the ratio of manufacturers who use labor hours or labor dollars exceeds 60%, and those who use single overhead rate is 30% in the U.S. (Management Accounting in the New Manufacturing

Environment, NAA, 1987, p. 38, p. 131). See also Robert S. Kaplan, "Yesterday's Accounting Undermines Production," *Harvard Business Review* (July–August, 1984).

Among the recent plethora of information on ABC, see Robert W. Hall, H. Thomas Johnson, and Peter B. B. Turney, *Measuring Up; Charting Pathways to Manufacturing Excellence* (Business One Irwin, 1991), Chapter 4, "Activity Based Costing," pp. 87–111; H. T. Johnson, "Activity-Based Management: Past, Present, and Future," *The Engineering Economist*, vol. 36, no. 3 (Spring 1991): pp. 219–238; and H. Thomas Johnson and Robert S. Kaplan, *Relevance Lost: The Rise and Fall of Management Accounting* (Cambridge, Mass.: Harvard Business School Press, 1987).

3. Refer to *Management Accounting*, May 1988, pp. 78–79, "ASSOCIATION NEWS—Global Solutions to Global Problems," a report on the NAA Conference on Feb. 25–26, 1988; where interdisciplinary problems were actively discussed under the title "Global Solutions to Global Problems." Speakers included T. Johnson, on "The Evolution of Cost Management Systems"; R. Kaplan, "The Need for Multiple Cost Systems"; R. McIlhattan, "The Impact of JIT on the Financial Executive"; M. Kawada, "Integrating Accounting and Production Systems"; R. Fox, "A New Framework: The Theory of Constraints"; and Eli Goldratt, on "Procedures for Applying the Theory of Constraints."

4. See *Business Week,* July 24, 1989, p. 30, "Earnings, Schmernings—Look at the Cash."

5. See H. Thomas Johnson and Robert S. Kaplan, *Relevance Lost: The Rise and Fall of Management Accounting* (Cambridge, Mass.: Harvard Business School Press, 1987): pp. 73–74.

6. Michael L. Detouzos, Richard K. Lester, Robert M. Solow, and the MIT Commission on Industrial Productivity, *Made in America: Regaining the Productive Edge* (Cambridge, Mass.: The MIT Press, 1989), p. 49.

7. Robert K. Merton, *Social Theory and Social Structure,* 1947. The Japanese version was published in 1961 (Tokyo: Misuzu Shobo, 1961). See pp. 22–24, pp. 45–46 of the Japanese edition.

8. Alvin Toffler, *The Third Wave* (Pan Books Ltd., 1980), p. 85, p. 121, p. 128, p. 307, and others.

9. See Detouzos et al., 1989, p. 175.

10. David Halberstam, *The Reckoning* (Tokyo: Avon Books, 1986): p. 722.

11. Refer to "Examples of Activities" in the table presented by R. N. Anthony, *Planning and Control Systems: A Framework for Analysis* (1965), p. 19.

12. Atsuo Tsuji, *Study of Management Accounting Theory* (Kanri Kaikeiron Kenkyu) (Tokyo: Dobunkan, 1977), pp. 97–100, pp. 106–107, and especially p. 98, "Examination of Anthony's Concept of Management Control." Tsuji's perspectives are summarized on pp. 108–109. " 'Control' is an activity closely linked to the implementation of physical control of a specific task which is individualistic, analytical and objective. 'Control' in cost control is of an entirely different nature, which means analyzing the variance between the budget or standard and the results, which is general, monetary, and abstract, and destined to lose linkage to the real control" (author's translation).

See also Atsuo Tsuji, *Basic Theory of Management Accounting* (Kanrikaikei no Kiso Riron) (Tokyo: Chuo Keizai Sha: 1985), particularly Chapter 7, "Development of Modern Management Accounting and Its Problems," pp. 127–149.

13. Eliyahu M. Goldratt and Jeff Cox, *The Goal* (North River Press, Inc., 1984) is a

story of a challenge to the new production paradigm, in which conflicts between production and accounting (a typical case of "sea anemone" problems) are vividly described.

14. See *Business Week,* Dec. 2, 1991, p. 18, "Questing for the Best." This article tells that, currently, there is no perception gap as to manufacturing management between the two countries.

15. Makoto Kawada, "A Study of Combining Production and Accounting Systems" (Seisan Shisutemu to Kanrikaikei no Setten o Saguru), *Accounting* (Kigyo Kaikei), vol. 38 (November, 1986): pp. 91–94.

8

Secret Accounting in New Zealand: P&O and the Union Steam Ship Company, 1917–1936

Christopher J. Napier

The use of secret reserves in order to conceal the financial position and performance of companies from shareholders and other users of accounts appears
to have been widespread in Britain before the Second World War (Edwards,
1989: 137–41). Secret reserves could be achieved through accelerated depreciation or writing off of assets, excessive provisions for liabilities, the retention
of profits in subsidiaries whose accounts were not published, suppression of
income and overstatement of expenditure, and a wide range of other techniques,
the use of which would not be disclosed in the accounts. The overall effect of
secret reserve accounting was to understate the financial position of the company, as the net asset value disclosed in the balance sheet would be lower than
if such accounting techniques had been eschewed. As far as the determination
of profit is concerned, however, the disclosed profit could be understated or
overstated, depending on whether secret reserves were being accumulated or
utilised in a particular period. In any event, the *trend* of profit would tend to be
smoothed by the use of secret reserves.

What were the incentives for company directors to create and maintain secret
reserves? These derived in part from shareholder attitudes to dividend payment.
It appears that shareholders preferred dividends to remain stable from year to
year; they would not object to occasional increases in dividends, so long as they
could expect these to be permanent, but resisted decreases. At the same time,
shareholders were reluctant to permit companies to retain significant amounts
of profit. Directors could normally justify the creation or augmentation of *dis-*

closed reserve accounts only in special circumstances. A regular retention of a significant proportion of disclosed profits would have been objected to. These factors would have encouraged the smoothing of reported profits, and the retention of "excess" profits in secret reserves. Other incentives for the use of secret reserves would have come from the view that the balance sheet in some sense provided a warranty that the financial position of the company was at least as good as disclosed. Directors would have believed that they might be penalised for balance sheets that were not "conservative" while garnering no reward for disclosing the "true" financial position of the company. This view gained judicial approval in the case *Newton v. Birmingham Small Arms Co. Ltd.* ([1906] 2 Ch 378), which was subsequently interpreted as deciding that "secret reserves were perfectly in order provided the directors acted honestly and so long as the auditors were allowed to comment on them if they considered it necessary" (Edwards, 1989: 148). A final incentive for the use of secret reserves was that they gave directors financial slack (Myers & Majluf, 1984)—by retaining resources in the company rather than paying them out as dividends, directors would be able to undertake new investment opportunities without the need for fresh capital issues.

However, the use of secret reserves could have adverse consequences for company shareholders. If company balance sheets are biased downwards, there is the danger that investors will undervalue their shares, and this can be particularly significant in a takeover. On the other hand, if dividends have been maintained at a relatively high level because of the utilisation of secret reserves built up in previous years, investors might be misled into believing that a company on the verge of financial collapse was sound. Allegations involving secret reserves were central to the *Royal Mail* case of 1931 (Edwards, 1989: 148–54).

Analysis of the costs and benefits of secret reserve accounting generally focus on the interests of shareholders.[1] However, in certain cases the use of secret reserves, while entirely in the interests of shareholders, could have adverse social implications, for example where secret reserves were used to conceal wealth transfers from one social group to another. A case in point might be the use of secret reserves to understate profits in order to assert that a company cannot afford to meet a wage claim. Secret reserves might be associated with tax minimisation (if the tax authorities accept the use of accelerated depreciation or excessive liability provision) or even with tax evasion (for example, by applying profits that would otherwise be taxable to undisclosed write-downs of assets). On an international level, secret reserves might permit the extraction of substantial sums from overseas subsidiaries without the knowledge of the local population, providing benefits to the parent company's shareholders that might have led to adverse political repercussions if they had been widely known.

This paper examines how the Peninsular & Oriental Steam Navigation Company (P&O) used its control of the Union Steam Ship Company of New Zealand Limited (Union) to remove over £8 million from Union during the years to 1936, with no public disclosure of these transfers. It is no exaggeration to state that this allowed P&O to survive at a time when rivals such as the Royal Mail Group collapsed.[2]

THE ACQUISITION OF THE UNION STEAM SHIP COMPANY

The rapid expansion of P&O in the 1910s, largely as a result of a series of takeovers of other publicly quoted shipping companies, is a good example of Hannah's argument that "takeover bids contesting the views of incumbent directors were virtually unknown before 1950. The position of directors in potential bid situations was strengthened by the inadequacy of the information possessed by shareholders about the asset and profit position of their companies" (Hannah, 1983: 130). In 1914, P&O had merged with the British India Steam Navigation Company Limited (BI). Although P&O was larger, it was the managers of BI, in particular their chairman Lord Inchcape, who were to gain control of the enlarged group. In 1916, P&O merged with the New Zealand Shipping Company Limited (NZS). This company had been set up in 1873 to operate a service between England and New Zealand and had grown rapidly over the next 40 years. In 1913, NZS had bought the Federal Steam Navigation Company Limited, which itself operated services from England to Australia and New Zealand, via Cape Town (Holman, 1973, 60; Maber, 1967, 121–35, 254– 58). In both the BI and NZS acquisitions, the initiative seems to have come from the management of the acquired companies rather than P&O itself. A similar pattern occurred in the next major acquisition made by P&O—The Union Steam Ship Company of New Zealand Limited.

Union had been formed in Dunedin in 1875 by a group of shipowners and merchants led by James Mills (1847–1936), who was to serve as Managing Director until 1913 and Chairman from 1906 until his death. Mills was knighted in 1907. Although Union initially concentrated on the coastal shipping trade in New Zealand, it quickly expanded (partly through taking over other companies) into the trans-Tasman trade with Australia. By 1885, Union's capital was about £500,000, held not only in New Zealand but also in the United Kingdom. In that year, Union owned a fleet of 28 steamers totalling 28,000 tons, valued at £617,800 (McLauchlan, 1987: 33). By this time, Union had entered the trade between New Zealand and the Pacific Islands, which was to culminate in 1885 with a service from Sydney and Auckland to San Francisco via Honolulu. By the beginning of the First World War, Union had entered the New Zealand- England trade, as well as providing services from Calcutta and Singapore to the east coast of Australia and New Zealand via the Torres Straits. It owned 75 ships representing a total 232,147 tons. Union's capital was by now £2 million, consisting of £1 million of 5½% cumulative preference shares and £1 million of ordinary shares. The latter were mainly held in the United Kingdom, with only about 25% held in New Zealand itself and about 15% in Australia (McLauchlan, 1987: 66). Union dominated the New Zealand shipping industry, crucial for a country "which had a tiny local market and exported half its products, which had the highest *per capita* external trade in the world" (Sinclair, 1959: 253).

During 1916, rumors circulated that Union was being considered as a possible acquisition by several shipping combines (as well as P&O, Lord Kylsant's Royal Mail Group was also growing rapidly through acquisitions at this time—Green and Moss, 1982: 32). Sir James Mills denied these rumors, but he was being disingenuous in this, as he had already entered into discussions with Lord Inchcape of P&O with a view to amalgamating the two businesses. Inchcape was aware that P&O and its affiliates were already working extensively with Union—indeed, the agents for Union in Calcutta were Inchcape's own firm Mackinnon Mackenzie & Co., who managed BI and were P&O's agents in India and the Far East (Jones, 1986, 1989), while Union were BI's agents in New Zealand. In a memorandum to the P&O Board in April 1917, Inchcape reported:

I think probably at the back of the mind of Sir James Mills is also a desire to hide away the profits which have been and are being made by the Union Company of New Zealand from the public in that country, and it may be also the possibility of the P&O and British India Companies getting a footing in the N.Z. Coasting Trade through the entry they have now secured into New Zealand by the absorption of the New Zealand Shipping Company. (P&O/31/6)

Mills appears to have been keen on the merger as a way of protecting Union as a separate entity, within the ambit of a large shipping combine. He was aware that a takeover of a large New Zealand-based company[3] might be unpopular, not only with shareholders but also with the New Zealand government and public, and attempted to pre-empt this through negotiating generous terms. P&O agreed to pay 30/- in cash and 10/- nominal value of P&O Deferred Stock[4] for each £1 ordinary share in Union (the preference shares were not to be acquired). The cash and stock package valued each Union ordinary share at over 60/-, whereas the market quotation before the announcement of P&O's offer was about 45/- per share (McLauchlan, 1987: 67). In addition, as Union had been paying a 10% dividend on its ordinary shares while P&O was paying 18% on its Deferred Stock, Union shareholders could expect a substantial increase in income. P&O announced its offer on 30 May 1917, at which time it provided assurances that there would be no alteration in the management, personnel or operations of Union.

The deal was by no means universally welcomed by Union shareholders in New Zealand, particularly as they were given only ten days in which to make up their minds as to whether or not to accept the P&O offer. Moreover, the Reform/Liberal coalition government led by William Massey also had reservations.

There was no immediate approval by the Treasury in Wellington while both Massey and [Liberal leader Sir Joseph] Ward took time to study the proposals. Mills cabled Massey from London assuring him the interests of New Zealand would "receive the fullest consideration by the company as hitherto." Mills argued that the arrangement was a purely domestic one between shareholders of the two companies, that it had been ratified by the P&O Company and had by this time (27 June 1917) been almost unanimously accepted by Union Company shareholders. . . .

Although Massey was personally in favour, there was strong feeling in Cabinet that the matter should be debated in the House of Representatives. Two cabinet ministers advocated state ownership of the company, one of these being the Minister for Marine, G. W. Russell. . . . Russell argued that the Union Steam Ship Company had been built out of the New Zealand trade, out of government mail subsidies and with New Zealand enterprise. However, by 7 July, government approval was given and the share transfer transactions were proceeded with. (McLauchlan, 1987: 67–8)

If the deal was financially attractive to the Union shareholders, it was even more so for P&O. Union had followed a policy of accelerated depreciation for its ships, and in the years of the First World War had been able to conceal substantial earnings through creating secret reserves. While the disclosed ordinary shareholders' equity in Union was less than £1.3 million in 1917, information provided by Mills to Inchcape enabled the latter to show to the P&O Board that Union's net equity was £5,315,000, basing depreciation on the original cost of ships and using a 5% straight line rate (this was P&O's stated depreciation policy—Napier, 1990: 39). Indeed, Inchcape was able to claim that "at today's values the steamers are worth certainly double the [adjusted written down value of] £2,750,000, namely £5,500,000" (P&O/31/6), which would have given ordinary shareholders' funds for Union of over £8 million.

A more accurate picture of the benefit to P&O of its acquisitions of the NZS and Union companies is given in Figure 8.1, which reproduces a P&O Board memorandum of 5 June 1918 (P&O/31/9). Given that P&O had incorporated the investments in NZS and Union in its own accounts at amounts equal to the cash consideration plus the *nominal* amount of Deferred Stock issued, all of the £8.7 million difference between "cost" of investments and value of net assets acquired could potentially be extracted from the resources of NZS and Union, for the benefit of the P&O stockholders.

Following the Union merger, the operational independence of Union was, as promised, maintained. Management continued to be exercised from Wellington, although a "London Advisory Board" was set up to provide a liaison between P&O and Union. The main personal liaison came through Mills, who lived in London and received regular reports from New Zealand. This function was later taken over by Charles Holdsworth, who had been appointed as Union's Managing Director in 1913, but from the 1920s spent most of his time in Britain. Mills and Holdsworth apparently showed these reports to Inchcape, whose boast it was that he had never been inside any of the offices of the P&O subsidiaries (Annual Meeting, 14 December 1927, P&O/6/23). Union's official historian was to claim:

Figure 8.1
Gain on Acquisition of Certain P&O Subsidiaries

<u>NZ SS Co. & Union SS Co. of New Zealand Amalgamation</u>

<u>Memorandum for Board</u>

I have had a statement drawn up at 31st December 1917, showing the assets of the <u>Union SS Co. of New Zealand</u>, valuing the ships at Cost price and allowing 5% per Annum depreciation. It brings out a surplus over liabilities of <u>£6,387,935</u>.
We paid 30/- per Share in Cash and gave 10/- per Share in P&O Deferred Stock. We have practically got the whole of the shares 1,000,000 of the nominal value of £1 each.
The Cash and the £500,000 nominal P&O deferred Stock made the payment £2,000,000. If the P&O Stock is taken as worth £350 per £100, the Union Coy's shareholders have got

	£1,500,000 in cash	
and	£1,750,000 in stock	
		£3,250,000

whereas the Assets of the USS Co. on the conservative basis mentioned of the discharging all liabilities are worth   6,387,935

showing a gain to the P&O Co.
by the purchase of   £3,137,935

On the same basis the Assets of the <u>New Zealand Shipping Company</u> (which owns the shares of the Federal S N Co.) give the following results at the same date:-

Surplus of assets over liabilities
at 31st Dec '17   5,249,870
Total Share Capital 90,672 shares of £10 each
P&O Stock issued in exchange (dealing with total)
   = 906,720 @ 350 per £100 P&O Stock   3,173,520
Gain to P&O Company   £2,076,350

Total gain to P&O Company by acquisition of
above undertakings   £5,214,285

Put in another way we have secured Assets after
discharging all liabilities worth   £11,637,805

in return for a cash payment of   £1,500,000
and an issue of Deferred P&O Stock
of the nominal value of   1,406,720   2,906,720

or a difference in favour of P&O Co. of   £8,731,085

May 1918

(Reported to the Board 5 June 1918)

Source: P&O/31/9.

The Union Company's policy and conduct of operations has remained entirely at Wellington in the hands of its board of directors. This is clearly a wise policy having regard to the major extent to which the company serves New Zealand and Australia and to there being £1,000,000 of preference capital held by the general public, mostly in these two countries. The association with the Peninsular & Oriental Steam Navigation Company has assisted the maintenance and development of the Union Company's services, and so been advantageous alike to the company and the communities served. (Waters, 1951: 77)

As the next section shows, whatever the truth of this statement as regards Union's operational activities, its major financial decisions were firmly under the control of P&O, which acted to advance the interests of its own shareholders, even at the expense of Union's interests.

EXPLOITING THE UNION STEAM SHIP COMPANY: 1917–1931

The first evidence of the willingness of P&O to use the Union's resources for its own benefit came at the time of the merger. Some 40% of the Union ordinary shareholders lived in Australia and New Zealand, and P&O owed them about £600,000 as the cash element of the cost of their shares. As Union had some £1 million of cash (Inchcape Memorandum, P&O/31/6), it was decided that the Australian and New Zealand shareholders would be paid by Union, who would account for the £600,000 as a loan to P&O (McLauchlan, 1987: 68). Although this arrangement was certainly convenient, it was only the first of many that would increase the amount lent by Union to P&O to a maximum in 1929 of £5.4 million.

In 1932, P&O commissioned a detailed report on the accounts of itself and its principal subsidiaries (including Union) for the ten years 1922–1931 (Napier, 1991: 312). This report, prepared by P&O's newly appointed auditors Deloitte, Plender, Griffiths & Co., reproduces Union's internal profit and loss accounts for those ten years (P&O/36/2: 322–3). During the period under review, Union was one of the most profitable parts of the P&O group. Operating profits, before providing depreciation, averaged nearly £500,000 per annum. A further £320,000 per annum on average came from dividends and interest, while £100,000 per annum came from surpluses on Union's Insurance Fund. Tax averaged £100,000 per annum, so Union was generating net cash flows of about £720,000 per annum to apply in paying dividends and in purchasing ships. Total disclosed dividends in the ten-year period were £1,430,000 (of which P&O received £880,000), while expenditure on new ships aggregated £3,438,000 (P&O/36/2: 320). Thus out of operating cash flows alone, Union was able to generate a cash surplus over the ten years of more than £3.3 million.

As Figure 8.2 shows, however, Union's *disclosed* profits were considerably less than these amounts would imply. The most significant difference came from depreciation. Deloittes found that the ships in the Union fleet were being de-

Figure 8.2
Union Steam Ship Company Profit and Loss Account, 1922–1931

	Union's Accounts	Adjustments	Deloittes' Figures
Profit on voyages, revenue from working accounts and other receipts	£5,406,887	£ 5,068	£5,411,955
Less: Administration expenses	(436,518)	–	(436,518)
	£4,970,369	£ 5,068	£4,975,437
Surplus on Insurance Fund	–	1,040,100	1,040,100
Dividends and interest on investments	1,897,275	678,206	2,575,481
Interest received less paid	651,363	–	651,363
Exchange differences and transfer fees	29,572	–	29,572
Profit/(loss) on sale of investments	(24,044)	116,720	92,676
Ministry of Shipping – adjustment	79,244	(79,244)	–
	£7,603,779	£1,760,850	£9,364,629
Amounts written off properties	(75,000)	–	(75,000)
Amounts written off investments	(143,703)	–	(143,703)
Depreciation of securities	–	(92,030)	(92,030)
Income tax, land tax and other taxes	(1,169,794)	105,224	(1,064,570)
	£6,215,282	£1,774,044	£7,989,326
Depreciation of fleet	(4,483,452)	1,418,427	(3,065,025)
Profit on sale of steamers	–	153,588	153,588
Special allowances to P&O	(1,284,442)	–	(1,284,442)
	£ 447,388	£3,346,059	£3,793,447
Transfers from reserves	951,252	(951,252)	–
Net profit	£1,398,640	£2,394,807	£3,793,447
Year ended 30 September			
1922	£ 56,267	£ 519,054	£ 575,321
1923	62,050	596,021	658,071
1924	112,181	407,911	520,092
1925	142,242	313,716	455,958
1926	144,889	303,090	447,979
1927	138,520	268,572	407,092
1928	199,878	435,033	634,911
1929	195,528	354,638	550,166
1930	195,857	(323,395)	(127,538)
1931	151,228	(479,833)	(328,605)
	£1,398,640	£2,394,807	£3,793,447

Source: P&O/36/2: 322–3, 328–9 (adapted).

preciated on a wide range of bases, all of which resulted in amounts of depreciation being provided well in excess of 5% straight line on original cost. Indeed, many ships in the fleet had been fully written off, although they were still in service and were not expected to be scrapped in the foreseeable future. Deloittes estimated that the Union fleet at 30 September 1921, the starting date for their investigation, would have had a written down value of £3,917,503 on a strict 5% depreciation basis, whereas the book value in the Union accounts was £3,142,453, representing "excess" depreciation of £775,050 (P&O/36/1: 117–18). Such "excess" provision might have been justifiable on the basis that some of the ships owned in 1921 were expensive purchases immediately after the end of the War, which were unlikely to cover their cost in future revenues. However, Union had in its accounts a secret "Reserve for Replacement and Special Depreciation of Assets," which was greater than the written-down value of the fleet (P&O/36/1: 116). Between 1922 and 1931, Union debited a total of £4,483,452 of depreciation to profit and loss account, including "special depreciation" of £1,613,853 in 1923. The latter debit was intended to write down those ships whose cost was excessive in relation to the market for replacement ships after the collapse of the post-war boom. An amount equal to the special depreciation was credited to profit and loss account by transfer from the Reserve for Replacement and Special Depreciation of Assets. After 1923, depreciation provided by debit to the profit and loss account each year was rather less than a strict 5% charge, reflecting the impact of accelerated depreciation. Nonetheless, Deloittes calculated that by 30 September 1931 the Union fleet would have had a written down value on a strict 5% depreciation basis of £3,246,211, against the actual book value of £1,684,437. "Excess" depreciation had therefore doubled over the decade to £1,561,774 (P&O/36/1: 118).

Union was able to create and increase its secret reserves during the period before 1931 because the New Zealand law relating to company accounts (the Companies Act 1908) was in all material particulars identical to the British Companies (Consolidation) Act 1908 (Waddy, 1928: 502). As Edey observes:

[This Act] left much latitude to those who wished the balance sheets of their companies to give little information away. Quite apart from the absence of a profit and loss account, there were the generally accepted practices which allowed the deliberate creation of secret reserves and which permitted the grouping of the balance sheet in one aggregate figure of diverse types of asset. (Edey, 1956: 127)

Attitudes within New Zealand in favor of the maintenance of secret reserves were long-lasting. As late as 1968, a leading company law textbook was to cite the *Newton v. Birmingham Small Arms* case approvingly as authority for the proposition that the balance sheet could legitimately understate a company's financial position (Northey, 1968: 300), while New Zealand company legislation after 1908 tended to lag behind its British equivalent.

Union fully exploited the flexibility of New Zealand's Companies Act 1908, as illustrated in Figure 8.3. This shows Union's published balance sheet at 30 September 1931, together with analyses (which were not disclosed) of the main balance sheet items. The most significant feature of this balance sheet is the portmanteau amount shown for "Shipping Property, payments on account of New Steamers, Investments in Securities, etc." of £4,857,022. As the analysis

Figure 8.3
Union Steam Ship Company Balance Sheet, September 30, 1931

LIABILITIES

	Note		
Capital			£ 3,000,000
Divided into			
1,000,000 Cumulative 5½ per cent Preference Shares of £1		£ 1,000,000	
1,000,000 Cumulative 5½ per cent "B" Preference Shares of £1		1,000,000	
1,000,000 Ordinary Shares of £1		1,000,000	
			£ 3,000,000
Reserves			
Insurance Fund			150,000
Voyages Pending (Freights and Passages, less Disbursements)			890,123
Bills Payable			136,091
Sundry Creditors			226,250
Sundry Accounts	1		1,269,811
Balance – Profit and Loss	2		129,206
			£ 5,801,481

ASSETS

	Note	
Shipping Property, payments on account of New Steamers, Investments in Securities, etc.	3	£ 4,857,022
Hulks, Lighters, Launches, etc.		42,666
Coal, Stores, etc. in Stock	4	220,232
Freehold and Leasehold Land, Buildings, etc.	5	367,542
Sundry Debtors – Agents, Trade Debts, etc.		256,181
Cash at Bank and on hand at Head Office and Branches		57,838
		£ 5,801,481

Audited and compared with the Company's Books and Vouchers and found correct.

Dunedin, 2nd December, 1931

GEO. M. MACLEAN F.P.A.N.Z
J. S. HISLOP F.P.A.N.Z } Auditors

Notes (not disclosed)

1. Sundry Accounts

Trade creditors	£	546,233
Taxation reserve		545,759
Miscellaneous other reserves		177,829
	£	1,269,811

2. Balance – Profit and Loss Account

Proposed dividends	£	95,000
Balance carried forward		34,206
	£	129,206

3. Shipping Property, etc.

Steamers: cost	£	6,248,564
Less amounts written off		4,564,127
	£	1,684,437
Payments on account of new steamers		497,417
	£	2,181,854
Investments: Subsidiary, Associated and Other Companies		2,702,728
New Zealand Government and Other Securities		1,488,846
Loan to P&O		3,528,569
Fixed Deposits in Australia and New Zealand		518,000
	£	10,419,997
Less: Reserves		5,562,975
	£	4,857,022

4. Coal, Stores, etc. In Stock

Gross balance	£	320,863
Less: Reserve		100,631
	£	220,232

5. Freehold and Leasehold Land, Buildings, etc.

Gross balance	£	432,542
Less: Reserve		65,000
	£	367,542

Source: P&O/36/1: 120; P&O/36/2: 316–8 (adapted).

shows, this total consisted of the Union fleet, at a heavily written down value of £1.7 million, payments on account of £0.5 million, and cash deposits and other investments aggregating a massive £8.2 million. The latter amount included a loan to P&O of about £3.5 million. Deducted from the total assets were reserves aggregating £5.6 million, the major item being the "Reserve for Replacement and Special Depreciation of Assets," amounting to £4.8 million.

As well as the reserves deducted from assets, a large part of the liability balance "Sundry Accounts" could be considered to represent reserves. In addition to a "taxation reserve" of £545,759 (as noted above, Union's average annual tax bill was only about £100,000), there were assorted balances aggregating £177,829. Overall, as Figure 8.4 shows, Deloittes calculated Union's reserves at 30 September 1931 to be £7,621,523, of which £6,452,194 was undisclosed (P&O/36/2: 318).

Some caution must be exercised in analyzing the amounts treated as reserves by Deloittes. The distinction later drawn by the British Companies Act 1948[5] between "provisions," representing estimates of losses, liabilities and diminutions in value, and "reserves," representing components of shareholders' equity, was rarely enunciated in the inter-war years. Thus the term "secret reserve" may often be a misnomer. As Arnold notes for the Royal Mail Steam Packet Company, "There were eight accounts described in the internal records as 'reserves' which were not disclosed on the company's balance sheets but . . . most of these accounts would now be described as 'provisions' " (Arnold, 1991: 213). The same phenomenon has been observed for P&O (Napier, 1991: 330–1). In the case of Union's reserves listed in Figure 8.4, some of the smaller amounts (such as the Staff Bonus Reserve) could be interpreted as provisions, while part of the Reserve for Depreciation relating to investments could also be regarded as a provision for diminution in value of certain securities (for example, Union owned £625,000 preference stock in the Canadian Pacific Railway, which had a book value of £500,000 but a market value at 30 September 1931 of only £375,000—P&O/36/2: 321). It is, however, reasonable to identify most of the total as genuine secret reserves. Including the Insurance Fund of £890,123,[6] Union's net asset value in 1931 was roughly £8 per ordinary share.

Among Union's assets was a loan to P&O. As already noted, this loan originated with Union's meeting P&O's liability for cash payments on its acquisition of Union ordinary shares from Australian and New Zealand shareholders. The balance due by P&O to Union grew from £967,875 in 1921 to a maximum of £5,394,873 in 1929, falling to £3,528,569 by 1931. Although surviving records do not permit a detailed analysis of the loan, it appears that P&O acted as "banker" to Union, collecting and disbursing both regular revenue receipts and payments and exceptional receipts and payments on Union's behalf. A large part of Union's revenues passed through the hands of P&O, its subsidiaries, and related concerns such as Mackinnon Mackenzie & Co., so it was easy for P&O to hold on to cash that was surplus to Union's immediate requirements.

Figure 8.4
Union Steam Ship Company Reserve Movements, 1921–1931

Balance at credit 30 September 1921		£ 7,406,104
Additions to Reserves during the ten years:–		
Dividends on shares in other companies and ventures	£ 400,316	
Surplus proceeds of steamers sold	606,859	
Profit on realisation of investments	116,720	
Vancouver service sale account	358,632	
Proceeds of inventories, etc.	102,671	
Stores, etc.	5,068	
Surplus on properties	34,275	
Surplus on hulks	1,013	
Recovered from Imperial Government re *Armagh*	48,278	
Adjustment of repairs and inventories of steamers		
taken as transports	37,022	
Miscellaneous credits	38,310	1,749,164
		£ 9,155,268
Amounts debited to Reserves:–		
Transfers to Profit and Loss Account	£ 951,252	
Bonus Dividend in respect of year 1927	1,000,000	
Transferred to Insurance Fund	400,000	
Amounts written off:–		
Special expenditure, *Tahiti*	56,070	
Coal and Bunkering Company	50,000	
Opua	8,660	
Shipping and Trading Agency	58	
Interests in other companies	55,834	
Estimated liability for Income Tax at 30 September 1931	31,200	2,553,074
Balance at credit 30 September 1931		£ 6,602,194

List of Reserves 30 September 1931

Deducted from Shipping Property, etc.		
Reserve for Replacement and Special Depreciation of Assets	£ 4,753,632	
Reserve for Contingencies	58,000	
Surplus proceeds of steamers	189,796	
Proceeds of inventories and allowances for repair	64,867	
Reserve for Depreciation and Loss on Sale:		
Interest in Other Companies and Ventures	496,680	£ 5,562,975
Deducted from Coal, Stores, etc. in Stock		100,631
Deducted from Freehold and Leasehold Land, Buildings, etc.		65,000
Included in Sundry Accounts		
Works and stores surplus	£ 83,507	
Surplus on properties	34,275	
Surplus on hulks	1,013	
Reserve for undetermined liabilities	6,074	
Overhaul account	30,000	
Staff bonus reserve	20,544	
Interest reserve	2,416	
	£ 177,829	
Reserve for Taxes	545,759	723,588
		£ 6,452,194
Disclosed Reserve		150,000
		£ 6,602,194
Insurance Fund		890,123
Profit and Loss Account – Credit Balance		129,206
		£ 7,621,523

Source: P&O/36/1: 116; P&O/36/2: 318.

Until 30 September 1926, Union was credited with interest on the loan, but much of this interest was rebated to P&O. As Deloittes note:

In 1922, 1923 and 1924 [P&O's] Profit and Loss Account was credited with rebates of £80,000, £60,000 and £30,000 respectively, which were debited to the Union Company. We are given to understand that the latter Company allowed these rebates of interest in lieu of declaring dividends on the shares held by [P&O], and that the arrangement was influenced by political and taxation considerations. (P&O/36/1: 16)

Union allowed P&O further rebates in 1926 and 1927, giving a total over the ten-year period of £284,442. In both 1930 and 1931, Union credited P&O with £500,000, the credit being accounted for by a reduction of the loan from Union to P&O. These credits were crucial in enabling P&O to report a profit for those years large enough to cover its interest and dividend payments. As Figure 8.2 shows, the effect of these credits was that Union showed a loss in each of the two years on Deloittes' adjusted figures. In P&O's accounts, these credits were described as being "for services rendered"; Deloittes noted that "No explanation has been given to us of the particular services for which [Union] paid [P&O] £500,000 in each of the years 1930 and 1931" (P&O/36/1: 39). The rebates and special credits totalled £1,284,442 over the ten-year period—none of this was disclosed in the Union accounts.

P&O received further undisclosed benefits from Union in the form of bonus dividends. Deloittes explained these as follows:

With regard to the special bonus dividends paid in respect of 1924, 1925 and 1927, we notice that they were not referred to in any way on the Balance Sheets and Profit and Loss Accounts of the Company for those years. The bonuses of £250,000 and £1,000,000 in respect of 1924 and 1925 were charged against the Insurance Fund, while the bonus of £1,000,000 in respect of 1927 was charged against various Reserve Accounts. . . . The bonus of £1,000,000 in respect of the year 1925 was paid in cash by the Union Company in six instalments of £150,000 each and one instalment of £100,000. (P&O/36/1: 122)

In respect of the year 1927 the Union Company declared a bonus of £1,000,000 on its Ordinary Shares, and [this] was duly brought into the books of [P&O] and credited to Interest and Dividends Account. The amount was not received in cash but was debited to the Loan Account of the Union Company. In 1928 the Union Company issued 1,000,000 5½ per cent. "B" Preference Shares of £1 each which were applied for by [P&O] and the amount of £1,000,000 payable on the shares was credited to the loan of the Union Company. We are informed that the two transactions had no relation to each other but the effect was that no cash passed between the two Companies. (P&O/36/1: 32)

The decline in the balance due by P&O to Union between 1929 and 1931 came about partly through the credits "for services rendered" and partly through Union's purchase in 1930 of the *Razmak,* which P&O had been using to run a shuttle service between Aden and Bombay.[7] Following a reorganization of services, this ship became surplus to P&O, and Union bought it for £665,000, renamed it the *Monowai* and used it on the trans-Pacific service (Maber, 1967: 213). The *Monowai* was Union's largest and most expensive ship of the interwar years.

The effect of these undisclosed transactions was that Union transferred a total of over £3.5 million to P&O between 1922 and 1931. Had these transfers been disclosed at the time, it is likely that Union would have come under pressure within New Zealand to reduce its freight rates. This would have been difficult, given the existence of the Conference System (McLachlan, 1961), which set agreed rates applying to the principal shipping lines operating particular services and aimed to discourage price cutting. The P&O connection was unpopular enough, with the New Zealand government "reluctant to consider any form of assistance to the Union Company that would ultimately be of benefit to the P&O interests" (McLauchlan, 1987: 69). It is small comfort that Union appears to have paid New Zealand income tax on most (but as we shall see below, not all) of the profits out of which these undisclosed transfers were made.

CLEARING THE DEBT: 1932–1936

The early months of 1932 were a time of crisis for P&O. Lord Inchcape's illness and death, the succession to the Chairmanship of his son-in-law, the Hon. Alexander Shaw, and the appointment of Lord Plender and James Kilpatrick of Deloittes as P&O's auditors, were simply external signs of the culmination of problems building up in P&O over the previous decade (Napier, 1991). The most urgent of these were the large net current liabilities disclosed in P&O's 1931 balance sheet (which reflected the more stringent disclosure requirements of the British Companies Act 1929—Napier, 1991: 325), and its inability to generate sufficient profits to allow it to pay a dividend on its Deferred Stock, even utilising distributions from subsidiaries and past secret reserves. Yet the Deloittes Report had revealed substantial resources in the subsidiaries. If P&O could in some way capture these, its balance sheet would be reshaped and its ability to report profits enhanced.

In December 1932, Kilpatrick of Deloittes prepared a secret memorandum for the P&O Board (P&O/3/38), pointing out that P&O's own balance sheet at 30 September 1932 showed an excess of current liabilities over current assets of £1.4 million. The excess would have been considerably greater if Kilpatrick had not disregarded loans from subsidiaries aggregating £6.9 million. These loans were in principle repayable by P&O on demand. In the ordinary course of affairs, readers of the P&O accounts might treat these loans as equivalent to capital, but experience of the Royal Mail collapse had shown that inter-company loans could lead to major problems if some companies in a group became insolvent. It was therefore desirable to clear these loans. Kilpatrick recommended winding up the P&O subsidiaries, with P&O taking over the interests of outside shareholders and debenture holders in exchange for new issues of its own fixed-interest securities. This would enable P&O not only to cancel out the inter-company indebtedness but to get its hands on the net liquid assets of its subsidiaries, which totalled some £4.7 million. Kilpatrick had to concede that liquidating Union could have adverse effects on public opinion in New Zealand, and specifically advised that the P&O Board consult Charles Cowan (managing director of NZS) and David Aiken (managing director of Union in succession to Holdsworth). Shaw noted that "this would probably raise fierce local diffi-culties. Aiken very doubtful." Kilpatrick's plan proved too ambitious for the P&O Board, and it was not pursued.

A less dramatic scheme was for P&O to be paid special bonus dividends by those subsidiaries which had the largest surplus reserves. In practice this meant NZS and Union. However, Kilpatrick was again to raise a warning note, this time in a report prepared by Deloittes in May 1933 on P&O's income tax position:

In any fiscal year for which the Company has paid United Kingdom Income Tax on Dividends received on its holding of Ordinary Shares of the Union Steam Ship Company of New Zealand Limited it is entitled to claim Dominion Income Tax Relief to the extent that the Dividends have been paid out of profits subject to Income Tax in the Domin-ions. . . . Your Company has, in fact, only paid United Kingdom Income Tax for the fiscal years 1928/29 and 1929/30, and we observe from the correspondence that for these fiscal years, claims for Relief are before H.M. Inspector of Taxes.

We understand that H.M. Inspector is only prepared to grant relief on the normal dividends received by your Company from this source and not upon the extraordinary distribution of £1,000,000 which was included in the United Kingdom Assessment for the year 1928/29, on the grounds that the Union Company are not prepared to give a certificate that this dividend was paid out of profits taxed in the Dominion. We think there is no doubt that the decision given by H.M. Inspector is correct and unless the certificate can be produced, no relief is due in this country on the £1,000,000. (P&O/2/7: 82–3)

The dividend in question had been debited to Union's secret reserves, and had not actually been paid in cash, so these factors might have dissuaded Union from giving the required certificate. Should P&O procure a bonus dividend from Union representing the bulk of its secret reserves, it might have to pay as much as £1 million in income tax (at 5/- in the pound), and this would absorb most of any cash element of such a dividend.

During 1933, the attentions of the P&O management were given to reorgan-izing their mail services, saving costs of about £300,000 per annum, and to restructuring P&O's fixed-interest debt, reducing annual debt service by £180,000 (Napier, 1991: 329). The Deferred dividend, which had been passed in 1932, was again not paid in 1933, and the P&O management came under some pressure at that year's Annual General Meeting (6 December 1933) to remedy the situation. The idea of a reorganisation involving certain P&O subsidiaries, more particularly NZS and Union, was revived, and P&O's solicitors Freshfields gave instructions to barrister J. H. Stamp to advise on the problems involved. Stamp was outspoken:

In my opinion, a comparison between the Union Company's published Balance Sheet for the 30th September 1932 with the "Balance Sheet 30th September 1933 (drawn up in more detail)" discloses a position which, under a statute resembling in essentials the English Companies Act 1929 (see particularly sec. 123), would expose all the officers of the Company to the risk of prosecution and imprisonment, the published Balance Sheet being clearly designed to suppress the true position of the Company. (Opinion dated 18 December 1933, P&O/3/47: 1)

This was a realistic possibility, as New Zealand had adopted, in its Companies Act 1933, the relevant accounting provisions of the British Companies Act 1929, and Union's 1934 accounts would have to be drawn up under the new disclosure provisions.

Stamp recommended remedying the position by bringing Union's assets in line with the figures disclosed in the accounts, but noted that payment of a bonus dividend would result in a heavy liability to income tax. He suggested that Union's fleet and other operating assets, together with a sufficient amount of cash to provide working capital, should be transferred to a new company, with the existing company being wound up. P&O would thereby receive the surplus assets of Union, including the inter-company debt. It was estimated that these assets would be worth some £5.8 million to P&O. Shaw welcomed Stamp's reconstruction scheme, but to the P&O Board he was less confident of how it would be greeted in New Zealand:

In spite of the encouragement Cowan and you all have given I feel that there will be a great deal of difficulty with the Board in New Zealand, and may say that [Sir Robert] Horne[8] takes the same view. He was amazed at the scheme when I first revealed it to him, but after discussion became a warm adherent to it. (P&O/3/47: 4)

Shaw concluded that the only way in which he could persuade the Union Board was by visiting them in person, and at the end of January 1934 he sailed for New Zealand.

While Shaw was *en route*, P&O's professional advisers considered the details of the reconstruction. One problem that emerged was that P&O would need the consent of Union's "A" preference shareholders to any scheme. This was necessary as a minimum of 75% of the share capital had to agree to a winding up, but P&O's shares in Union (the "B" preference and ordinary shares) represented only 67%. Stamp suggested that the "A" preference shareholders, who were almost entirely in New Zealand and Australia, could be "bought off" by giving them a small cash premium in addition to the nominal value of their shares, the maximum to which they were entitled on a winding up. A further problem was that, although Union would not have to reveal the value of assets it retained when the reconstruction took place, it would be necessary for the liquidator to file a report with the Registrar of Companies when Union was wound up, and it was considered that this would inevitably become public knowledge.

Shaw arranged to be met in Sydney by Charles White, who was a director of Union and the company's legal adviser, and they sailed to Wellington on the *Monowai*. Shaw revealed the proposed reconstruction to White, who recoiled in shock, telling Shaw that the Union board "regarded the money lent to the P&O Company as a nest egg available for future ship building" ("Report by A. Shaw of Visit to New Zealand in 1934" in P&O/3/47). White advised Shaw that the P&O connection was very unpopular in New Zealand, and any hint that P&O was raiding Union's balance sheet would be disastrous. As Shaw was to report:

New Zealand in general, and Wellington in particular, is a small community. The affairs of the Union Company are keenly canvassed and scrutinised, and every movement in connection with it is a subject of comment and debate. Further, the Government of New Zealand watch the position closely. The close connection between the Union Company and the P&O Company is generally known, and is not popular. I had not realised that this feeling existed until I was on the spot. The position was therefore delicate and it was essential to avoid any action which would cause a rupture on the Board and provoke inevitable comment and possible Government intervention. ("Shaw Report" in P&O/3/47)

White made it clear that the proposed reorganisation was a non-starter, as it would be impossible to keep details of any assets passed to P&O from the New Zealand public.

Fortunately, Stamp had provided an alternative scheme. This involved interposing a new holding company between P&O and Union. If the new company were domiciled in New Zealand, any dividends from Union would have no adverse tax implications. Union would pay an undisclosed bonus dividend to the new company, debiting this to its secret reserves. The new company would then be liquidated, and its assets distributed to P&O. As this would represent a capital distribution on liquidation, there would be no United Kingdom tax to pay. White agreed that this scheme was more likely to be successful, but by the end of their voyage, Shaw was conscious that gaining the consent (and the silence) of the Union Board was "the key to the position."

Shaw lost no time after his arrival in New Zealand before he met Union's full board of directors on 7 February 1934. As he was to describe the meeting:

I was welcomed with courtesy. Mr Aiken [Union's managing director] had made some preliminary reference to the situation, and on my arrival in the room the atmosphere, though polite, was strained to the point of embarrassment. The only possible course appeared to be to tell the Directors frankly that payment of the debt due by the P&O Company was not a practical matter; that the P&O Company regarded this debt as their own money; and that (subject to the payment off at par of the "A" Preference Shares) the legal position was that the P&O Company owned the Union Company lock, stock and barrel. Mr [Charles] Rattray, of Dunedin, who was very unhappy throughout the proceedings then asked me point blank what the proposal was. I told him that by one means or another the Union Company's accounts and those of the P&O Company would have to be cleared of the debt, and that the P&O Company desired in addition to add, from the Union Company's resources to its own, liquid funds in the shape of Government securities to the extent of about £1,000,000 sterling. Mr Rattray then exclaimed "But that means that you want to take about £5,000,000 from us." (The amount is considerably over £5,000,000 in New Zealand currency.) I replied "Yes, and in all the circumstances that appears to me a very moderate demand." There was some amusement at this. ("Shaw Report" in P&O/3/47)

Shaw emphasised that there was no intention of using the Union resources to pay P&O's dividends, the plan being to conserve them "for the benefit of the Company whose strong financial standing was of great importance to the whole Group both as a matter of prestige and as a matter of practice" ("Shaw Report" in P&O/3/47). Ultimately, the Union Board saw no alternative to acceding to the P&O proposals, and it was agreed that White would sail to London in order to make the necessary arrangements with P&O's Board and advisers.

The next few months saw the details of the scheme being put into place, so as to enable Union to pay its secret dividend before 30 September 1934, and therefore avoid disclosing the P&O loan in its balance sheet. White happened to control an inactive company, Land & Mortgage Securities Limited (L&MS), which would serve as a convenient holding company. So as not to alert any possible member of the New Zealand public, P&O's ordinary shares in Union continued to be registered in the names of their existing nominees (P&O Directors Sir Montagu Turner and the Earl of Cromer, together with the Union directors and certain employees), but beneficial ownership was transferred to L&MS, in exchange for 100,000 ordinary shares in the latter company. White, Colonel Norris Falla (who had succeeded Aiken as Union's managing director in May 1934 when Aiken died suddenly) and Union director Walter Green held between them 1,000 preference shares in L&MS, which had votes enabling them to block any winding up of that company. This had been recommended by Stamp to prevent the British tax authorities from imputing L&MS's profits to P&O. On 26 September 1934, Union paid a secret dividend of £4,500,000 to L&MS, made up of £3,500,000 of its loan to P&O and £1,000,000 in New Zealand Government securities. The published Union accounts for 1934 showed little change from those of the previous year (investments in and loans to subsidiaries were disclosed separately, but other investments were still aggregated with ships and shown net of reserves), but the balance sheet figure was closer to a realistic measure of Union's assets.

The P&O plan required L&MS to function "normally" as an intermediate holding company throughout the 1935 financial year, and White ensured that this was achieved. White was able to use his close relations with officials of the New Zealand Government to ensure that no one had the full picture of what was going on. In negotiating with the Stamp Duty Commissioner over the value of the Union ordinary shares transferred beneficially from P&O to L&MS, he was able, by conceding that the "Sundry Accounts" in Union's balance sheet contained inner reserves but remaining silent about the much more substantial reserves set off against the ships and investments, to misdirect the Commissioner into valuing the Union shares at £4 each instead of a more realistic £8. The saving in Stamp Duty was more than enough to cover the costs of the whole scheme. Similarly, White persuaded the Commissioner for Income Tax that L&MS's income tax returns need not disclose the amount of any dividend received from Union (letter from White to Shaw, 18 September 1934, P&O/3/47: 25). Otherwise, there was no way in which the New Zealand public could receive any inkling of what had happened, particularly as L&MS, as a private company, was not obliged to file accounts. Probably fewer than a dozen people in New Zealand, all Union insiders, were aware of the full arrangements, while in the United Kingdom details of the scheme were kept just as confidential.

Shaw continued to come under pressure about the non-payment of P&O's Deferred dividend. At the 1934 Annual General Meeting, L. C. Urling-Clark, a stockbroker who specialised in shipping securities, commented that the reason why P&O was unable to pay a Deferred dividend was the high level of depreciation required, and recommended a once-and-for-all write-down of the P&O fleet out of reserves. Sir William Currie, P&O's managing director (deputizing for Shaw), replied that the reserve figure quoted by Urling-Clark represented the aggregate *group* reserves, and that much of the amount was not available to P&O. He hinted, however, that the P&O Board would "give the matter every consideration" (Annual Meeting, 5 December 1934, P&O/6/28). Two days later, Currie met Urling-Clark and Charles Whittington, another stockbroker, who stated that, if P&O did not resume Deferred dividends, he would arrange for a resolution to be put forward at the 1935 General Meeting for the winding up of P&O. In a subsequent memorandum for the P&O Board, Shaw commented:

It is, of course, not known to Mr Whittington and his friends that the Board have in prospect a very large diminution of the book indebtedness of the Company, and also an accretion to its liquid resources which, though of much smaller amount, will yet be considerable. The knowledge of this would, of course, augment the pressure for Deferred Stock dividends by Mr Whittington and others of his way of thinking. ("Memorandum by the Chairman put before the Board 1st May 1935," P&O/2/7: 212)

Shaw convinced his colleagues that it would not be appropriate to pay a Deferred dividend until the Union transactions were completed, and Whittington must have been placated, as he and Urling-Clark both spoke in defence of the continued policy of non-payment at the P&O Annual General Meeting on 11 December 1935.

In New Zealand, the election in December 1935 of a Labor Government under Michael Savage, following several years of a disastrous Reform/United Party coalition in which the New Zealand economy was brought close to bankruptcy, caused the Union directors to become jittery. The new government "offered state intervention; they promised to intervene where New Zealanders had been hardest hit. . . . Labour promised immediate state control of the entire banking system" (Barber, 1989: 135–6). Falla telegraphed Shaw recommending the expeditious winding up of L&MS, fearing that the Labor Government would have a confrontational attitude to limited companies in general and Union in particular. Kilpatrick of Deloittes advised P&O that it would be dangerous to provide White with a detailed programme of instructions, in case the British tax authorities decided that L&MS was a sham and taxed P&O on the bonus dividend from Union. The first four months of 1936 were a period of mounting frustration at what was seen as White's procrastination ("The winding up would seem to be a particularly simple matter, and I really cannot understand how a man of Mr White's legal ability can find any difficulty"—letter from Shaw to Currie, 9 January 1936, P&O/3/47: 51). Eventually, White set matters in motion, and the meeting to put L&MS into liquidation was held on 1 July 1936. The formalities were performed rapidly, and White was able to ensure that the liquidator's report was suitably obscure about the assets transferred to P&O, particularly the £3,500,000 loan. Everything was complete by 11 September 1936, in time for P&O to reflect the effect of the scheme in its 1936 accounts.

The liquidation of L&MS created a surplus in P&O's accounts of £4.29 million (because of the depreciation of the New Zealand currency relative to sterling, the government securities taken over by L&MS were sold for only £780,000 in sterling). P&O had also been able to procure special dividends from NZS. As this was a British company, the tax problems arising from such dividends were much less severe than on those from New Zealand, so there was no need for subterfuge in obtaining these dividends. P&O received £2,000,000 from NZS, together with a tax credit of £191,000. In total, therefore, the rearrangement of the NZS and Union finances generated a "Special Reserve" of £6,481,000, of which £300,000 was credited to P&O's disclosed Reserve Account, £250,000 applied in writing down the investment in a subsidiary company, and the balance of £5,931,000 in special depreciation of the P&O fleet. The effect of this special depreciation was to reduce P&O's required annual charge from about £1.4 million to under £900,000, and the consequent improvement in P&O's profit and loss account permitted the resumption of the Deferred dividend. The arrangement was described in very vague terms in the P&O accounts and in Shaw's speech at the Annual General Meeting on 9 December 1936, and passed with remarkably little comment at the meeting and in the press. P&O Deferred stockholders were not about to look the gift horse of a resumed dividend in the mouth.

CONCLUSIONS

Over the period from 1917 to 1936, P&O withdrew from Union at least £8 million in ways that concealed the transactions from the preference shareholders of Union and the New Zealand public. These withdrawals were vital in allowing P&O to survive the difficult period of 1930–31, when financial collapse was imminent, and in letting P&O restructure its balance sheet in 1936. To what extent were they harmful to Union, and to the New Zealand economy in general? In the 1920s and 1930s, the proposition that the interests of equity shareholders in companies were paramount was scarcely questioned, and Shaw's comment to the Union directors that "the P&O Company owned the Union Company lock, stock and barrel" went unchallenged. It is questionable whether Union could have found profitable alternative uses of the resources extracted by P&O, without diversifying from shipping into other businesses. Union might have cross-subsidized otherwise unprofitable shipping activities, but such behavior was generally anathema to the Union Board.[9] Opportunities for active diversification were few—although Union became heavily involved in promoting early New Zealand air services (McLauchlan, 1987: 85–9), the sums involved were small. Even portfolio investment in the largest New Zealand enterprises was shunned. Whatever Union's protestations that the loan to P&O represented a ship replacement fund, the fact is that expenditure on replacement was financed entirely out of revenues during the period under review, and continued to be so in the remaining years before the Second World War. There was no incentive to spend on greatly improved ships if the Conference system, and the general state of world trade, meant that Union could not increase its revenues commensurately.

The impact on the New Zealand economy, however, was more serious. Resources that could have been invested within that economy were repatriated to Britain, where they were, in one way or another, ploughed into P&O's less profitable fleet or dissipated in dividends. The £8 million extracted by P&O may appear to be relatively small in comparison with New Zealand's Gross Domestic Product for the period to 1936 (estimated as £2,817 million for the years 1918–1936 by Lineham, 1968), but would have amounted to as much as 5% of gross capital formation during that period. The suspicions in which the P&O connection was held were more than justified.

P&O was assisted in grabbing Union's surplus resources by the flexibility of accounting regulation at the time. The maintenance of secret reserves was encouraged by lax laws and judicial approval. New Zealand took a long time to keep pace with developments in accounting law and practice in Britain—the innovations of the British Companies Act 1948 were not to reach New Zealand until 1955. While it is dangerous to generalise from one case to claim that secret reserve accounting permeated New Zealand in the first half of the twentieth century—to maintain secret reserves, there had to be surplus profits in the first place—the Union Steam Ship Company was, at its peak, the largest private commercial organisation in New Zealand (Arbon, 1973: 1), and therefore significant in its own right as a major user of secret reserves.

NOTES

1. A partial exception to this is banks, where the interests of depositors might be considered to be protected by the existence of undisclosed resources.

2. Thanks are due to the staff of the National Maritime Museum, Greenwich, where the P&O archives are deposited, for their assistance in the preparation of this paper. References of the style ''P&O/X/X'' are to documents in the P&O archives at the National Maritime Museum. The financial years of P&O, Union, and other group companies ended in general on 30 September: references to the accounts for a given year are to the accounts for the financial year ended 30 September.

3. Unlike NZS, which though incorporated in New Zealand was managed from London, Union was managed from Dunedin and later Wellington.

4. P&O's share capital was divided into 5% Preferred Stock and Deferred Stock, the latter equivalent to the ordinary shares of other companies.

5. Following the Institute of Chartered Accountants in England and Wales' Recommendation on Accounting Principles No. 6, ''Reserves and Provisions'' (1943). This Recommendation was reprinted in New Zealand by the New Zealand Society of Accountants in May 1946 (Zeff, 1979).

6. Union credited this with premiums calculated at 4% of the insurance value of steamers (and debited the notional premiums to the appropriate voyage accounts). The Insurance Fund was debited with premiums paid to P&O (which for much of the period acted as underwriters for the fleets of all its subsidiaries) and with claims not recoverable from the underwriters. Between 1922 and 1931, the amount by which notional insurance premiums exceeded actual premiums and unrecoverable losses was £1,040,100. Union was able to use this surplus, together with an undisclosed transfer of £400,000 from secret reserves, to pay P&O undisclosed bonus dividends of £250,000 in 1924 and £1,000,000 in 1925 (P&O/36/1: 117).

7. The main P&O mail service to Australia ran in alternate fortnights from Aden direct or via Bombay. The *Razmak* provided a service from Aden to Bombay in the fortnights when the mail service ran direct from Aden to Australia.

8. Horne, a former British Chancellor of the Exchequer, was an important P&O director.

9. An exception was Union's joint venture with the Canadian Pacific Railway in the trans-Pacific trade, the Canadian-Australasian Line (Maber, 1967: 240–8). Although the setting up of this service in 1930 had accounting benefits, as Union was able to transfer two of its ships and record a book profit of £358,000, it soon proved a millstone round the necks of the Union directors. They believed (quite rightly) that Inchcape had dragooned them into the deal, and the Canadian-Australasian Line was a constant drain of cash from Union during the 1930s.

REFERENCES

Arbon, A. L., *A History of the Union Steam Ship Co. of New Zealand, 1875–1971* (Lobethal, S. Aust.: Ronald H. Parsons, 1973).

Arnold, A. J., Secret Reserves or Special Credits? A Reappraisal of the Reserve and Provision Accounting Policies of the Royal Mail Steam Packet Company, 1915–27, *Accounting and Business Research* (Summer, 1991): 203–14.

Barber, Laurie, *New Zealand: A Short-History* (Auckland: Century Hutchinson New Zealand, 1989).

Edey, H. C., Company Accounting in the Nineteenth and Twentieth Centuries, *The Accountants' Journal* (April and May, 1956): 95–6, 127–9.

Edwards, John Richard, *A History of Financial Accounting* (London: Routledge, 1989).

Green, Edwin, and Michael Moss, *A Business of National Importance: The Royal Mail Shipping Group, 1902–1937* (London: Methuen, 1982).

Hannah, Leslie, *The Rise of The Corporate Economy,* second edition (London: Methuen, 1983).

Holman, Gordon, *In the Wake of Endeavour: The History of the New Zealand Shipping Company and Federal Steam Navigation Company* (London: Charles Knight, 1973).

Jones, Stephanie, *Two Centuries of Overseas Trading: The Origins and Growth of the Inchcape Group* (London: Macmillan, 1986).

Jones, Stephanie, *Trade and Shipping: Lord Inchcape 1852–1932* (Manchester: Manchester University Press, 1989).

Lineham, B. T., New Zealand's Gross Domestic Product, 1918–38, *New Zealand Economic Papers,* vol. 2, no. 2 (1968): 15–26.

Maber, John M., *North Star to Southern Cross* (Prescot, Lancs.: T. Stephenson & Sons, 1967).

McLachlan, D. L., The Conference System since 1919, *Business History* (1961): 54–63.

McLauchlan, Gordon, *The Line That Dared: A History of the Union Steam Ship Company 1875–1975* (Mission Bay, NZ: Four Star Books, 1987).

Myers, S. C., and N. S. Majluf, Corporate Financing and Investment Decisions When Firms Have Information Investors Do Not Have, *Journal of Financial Economics* (June, 1984): 187–222.

Napier, Christopher J., Fixed Asset Accounting in the Shipping Industry: P&O 1840–1914, *Accounting, Business and Financial History* (October, 1990): 21–48.

Napier, Christopher J., Secret Accounting: The P&O Group in the Inter-War Years, *Accounting, Business and Financial History* (September, 1991): 303–33.

Northey, J. F., *Introduction to Company Law in New Zealand,* sixth edition (Wellington: Butterworths, 1968).

Sinclair, Keith, *A History of New Zealand* (Harmondsworth: Penguin, 1959).

Waddy, Percival R., *A Summary of the Mercantile Law of New Zealand* (Auckland: Whitcombe and Tombs, 1928).

Waters, Sydney D., *Union Line: A Short History of the Union Steam Ship Company of New Zealand Limited 1875–1951* (Wellington: Union Company, 1951).

Zeff, Stephen A., *Forging Accounting Principles in New Zealand* (Wellington: Victoria University Press, 1979).

9

The Relationship between the Bookkeeping Systems of Pacioli and Schweicker

Yasuhiko Kataoka

INTRODUCTION

The strongest country in the Italian Peninsula at the end of the 14th century was the Venetian Republic. Venice, which secured a good share of the trade between East and West, held the dominant position as supreme ruler of the Mediterranean Sea after its victory over Genoa in the War of Chioggia. The Venice Republic flourished politically, economically and culturally during the golden age from the late 14th to 15th centuries.

One of the major reasons for economic prosperity in Venice was constant trading with southern Germany, which was carried on in Venice at the Fondaco dei Tedeschi (German house) which dates back to 1228. The Venetian merchants, who placed much importance on profitability and were the main supporters of the Venetian economic system, adopted double entry bookkeeping as a new commercial art and made use of it for their commercial transactions.

The old valuable books of account of the Venetian merchants that are kept in the Venetian State Archives, are the ledgers of the Soranzo Fraternity, the account books of Andrea Barbarigo, and the ledger of Giacomo Badoer.

The journal and the ledger of Andrea Barbarigo began on 2 January 1430 and ended on 30 August 1440. These two account books are the first books of a long series of journals and ledgers of the Barbarigo family from 1430 to 1582. The account books such as Grimani, Soranzo, and Badoer are only ledgers and do not have a journal. It is clear that the account books of Andrea Barbarigo were recorded according to the rules of double entry bookkeeping in Venice. The journal and the ledger of Andrea Barbarigo which is very important in the history of accounting in the middle ages is useful in examining the double entry bookkeeping system in Venice that Pacioli described.

THE BOOKKEEPING METHOD OF LUCA PACIOLI

The first printed treatise of bookkeeping in the world is the *Summa de Arithmetica, Geometria, Proportioni et Proportionalita* of Luca Pacioli. *Summa* was published in Venice in 1494, and was reprinted at Toscolano in 1523. This book is one of the most important books on mathematics. The Treatise 11 of Section 9 of this book—that is, *"particularis de Coputis et Scripturis,"* is a treatise about double entry bookkeeping.

The system of bookkeeping that Luca Pacioli described introduced the practice and theory which had developed in commercial cities in Italy, especially in Venice. He wrote in the first chapter of his treatise, "We will here adopt the method employed in Venice which among others is certainly to be recommended, for with it one can carry with any other method."

Pacioli, who was born in Borgo San Sepolcro, stayed in Venice and became the tutor of three sons of a rich merchant, Antonio de Rompiasi. It seems that he could have had a chance to see the account books of the Venetian merchants and to study the method of double entry bookkeeping in Venice. We don't believe that Pacioli appropriated the part of bookkeeping from the work of an unknown author, and we have to deny the question of the act of plagiarism. The bookkeeping method of Luca Pacioli has several characteristics.

1. Pacioli wrote that there are three things needed by one who wished to carry on business diligently. The most important of these is cash or any other substantial power (*altra faculta substantiale*). The second is a good accountant (*buon ragioneri*) and a sharp bookkeeper. The third is good order in order to arrange all business to debit (*debito*) and credit (*credito*).

2. Pacioli explained the opening inventory (*inventario*), but he did not describe the closing inventory.

3. Pacioli's account book system is three account books—that is, a day book (*memoriale, vachetta o sqrtafoglio*), a journal (*giornale*) and a ledger (*qderno*). The day book is the first book, the journal is the second book and the ledger is the third book. Pacioli thought of the day book as the formal account book, because he wrote that the day book must be presented to a certain mercantile office (*certo officio de mercatāti*).

4. All things pertaining to a transaction must be written in the day book, without omission. Pacioli wrote that no point must be omitted in the day book (*memoriale ño si converria lassare pōto alcuno*).

5. Pacioli described debit and credit—that is, *"per"* and *"A"* in the journal, and *"die dare"* and *"die havere"* in the ledger.

6. Pacioli adopted the higher price, if there were two market prices. He wrote, "make the prices rather higher than low, that is, if it seems that they are worth 20, put them down at 24."

7. Pacioli adopted the word, "capital (*Cavedale*)" that Andrea Barbarigo, Donado Soranzo, and Giacomo Badoer did not use.

8. Pacioli explained the profit and loss (*pro e dāno*) account or profit and deficit (*avanzi e desavanzi*) account, and profit and loss calculation of each item of merchandise (*robba*).

9. Pacioli wrote, "but it is always good to close them each year" (*Ma sēmpre e buono de saldare ogni anno,* Ca. 29), therefore Pacioli knew that the ledger is closed every year.

10. Pacioli described a method to correct some errors of bookkeeping.

11. Although Pacioli explained the trial balance of totals, he did not write out the balance sheet and the profit and loss statement.

12. Pacioli described the manner of keeping accounts with the public office (*li officii publici*), the account of partnership (*Compagnia*), the account of the shop (*bottega*) and the account of entries of trip (*le partite de li viaggi*).

Pacioli's theory is very clear, but it is difficult for the beginner to understand. Pacioli did not make, in particular, a detailed specimen set of bookkeeping except the example given at the end of Chapter 36 that is a very difficult part in his treatise. We therefore must examine and study the account books of Venice, and some of the works on bookkeeping that were published at Venice after Pacioli, in order to understand the practice and theory of bookkeeping which Pacioli explained.

The account books of Andrea Barbarigo are samples of excellent double entry bookkeeping, that is those which were developed and used in Venice. There are some points of similarity and differences between Barbarigo's practice and Pacioli's theory.

Points of similarity are the use of journal and ledger, the form of two account books, the use of the words debit and credit (for example *per* and *A, de dar* and *de aver*), the method of posting from journal to ledger, the method of closing the ledger, the method of transferring from the profit and loss account to the capital account, and the debtor and creditor account in Barbarigo and the balance account of Pacioli. Barbarigo did not employ a day book nor an inventory, and he did not use the word "capital" nor the method of closing the ledger each year that Pacioli described.

Manzoni's work, *Quaderno Doppio* that was published in Venice in 1534, 1540, and 1554 is very important in order to comprehend the bookkeeping method of Luca Pacioli. Although Manzoni described the day book, the inventory, the journal and the ledger, he did not give an illustration of the day book. Manzoni had a theory of closing the ledger yearly that Pacioli described. I don't agree with the opinion that Manzoni's treatise is an accurate copy of Pacioli. It seems that Manzoni's treatise was original. Manzoni succeeded in illustrating the theory of Pacioli, but he failed in the method to close the ledger because he did not understand the last checking of the balances that Pacioli explained.

THE BEGINNING OF ITALIAN BOOKKEEPING IN GERMANY BEFORE SCHWEICKER

The beginning of double entry bookkeeping in Germany was carried out by the merchants of Nürnberg in the 15th century.

Stromer von Reinchenbach investigated many account books of the 14th and 15th centuries of Nürnberg merchants, for example, the "long book" (*lange puch*) of Hilpolt Kress, *Buch der Hantierung* by Marquart Mendels, 1425–1438, and the inventory and balance sheet of the Lang-Hans-Tuchers of 1484. Stromer confirmed that the Nürnberg merchants introduced the double entry bookkeeping from Venice into Nürnberg for the first time in the 15th centry. Nürnberg merchants went to Fondaco dei Tedeschi in Venice and learned the Italian bookkeeping system, and this Italian bookkeeping system was spread from Venice to Nürnberg.

The earliest book on bookkeeping in Germany is Schreiber's work, *Eïn neu kunstlick Buech,* which was published in Nürnberg in 1518. This book is the second work on bookkeeping in the world after Pacioli. Gottlieb's works, *Ein Teutsch verstendig Buchhalten* (1531) and *Buchhalten zwey kunstliche* (1546) were published in Nürnberg, too. The works of Schreiber and Gottlieb are representative of that time and famous books on bookkeeping in Germany in the 16th century.

Though these books were published in the same city and around the same time, they have their individual characteristics, and they were not influenced by the method of bookkeeping of Luca Pacioli. Schreiber and Gottlieb described the system of bookkeeping which requires three main books, a journal (*Zornal*), a debt book (*Schuldbuch*) and a goods book (*Kaps*), but the contents of the two works are not the same. Although the journal of Schreiber is not recorded as a double entry system, the debts book and the goods book are recorded in the double entry system. The accounts of the journal are posted in two account books.

Schreiber did not use a contra account of right and left. Although the verification of Schreiber is based on the fact that the profit made on goods is same as the profit of the same period, he did not show the verification by a table, but only in writing.

Although Gottlieb wrote only a journal, a debt book, and a goods book in his first work (1531), he showed how to write about closing the books, profit and loss, the balance sheet and verification in his second work (1546). The journal of Gottlieb is recorded in a double entry system, and the accounts in the journal are posted in two books according to the double entry bookkeeping method. Gottlieb calculated profit and loss by a specific cost method and derivative method, and he tested the verification of the two methods.

I think that Gottlieb's bookkeeping system is certainly based on double entry bookkeeping. Gottlieb was not influenced by Schreiber, and Gottlieb had much effect upon later works on bookkeeping in Germany. We can say that the double entry bookkeeping system which the Merchants of Nürnberg introduced was accomplished in Nürnberg in the first half of the 16th century by Gottlieb. But Gottlieb's account book system was not influenced by Pacioli.

Matthäus Schwarz, who studied bookkeeping in Venice, became the Fugger's head bookkeeper and wrote a manuscript on bookkeeping in the years 1516, 1518, and 1550. Although the original of this manuscript has not been discovered, three copies of this manuscript have survived. Schwarz wrote about two important bookkeeping methods in his book. He showed an example of agency bookkeeping and gave an example of the two methods of the calculation of the profit for a period, that is, the inventory method, and profit and loss method.

THE BOOKKEEPING SYSTEM IN SCHWEICKER'S WORK

The first work on bookkeeping in Germany which was influenced by the method of Luca Pacioli was Wolfgang Schweicker's *Zweifach Buchhalten,* which was published in Nürnberg in 1549. Schweicker, who came from Nürnberg, had stayed in Venice and had studied double entry bookkeeping there.

Historians of accounting have given different assessments or interpretations of Schweicker's work. Fogo wrote ''it is a translation of Manzoni's *Quaderno doppio.*'' Penndorf believed that Pacioli's treatise was imitated by Manzoni in 1534, and Schweicker depended on Manzoni's treatise completely. Yamey said, ''Schweicker was not a slavish translator of Manzoni.'' It is true that Schweicker is the first exponent of Pacioli's treatise in Germany and he referred to Manzoni's work.

Schweicker's bookkeeping system has several special features.

1. Schweicker explained and illustrated the opening inventory which Pacioli and Manzoni described and illustrated.

2. Schweicker adopted the three-account book system, that is, a day book, a journal, and a ledger, but he thought that the journal is the first book and the ledger is the second main book (*Hauptpuch*).

3. Schweicker used two vertical parallel lines (||) to differentiate between debit and credit in the journal, which Pacioli and Gottlieb also showed. Manzoni used two slanting lines (//).

4. In the journal Schweicker used the words, "*Für*" and "*An,*" translated from the Italian "*per* (p)" and "*A*" that Pacioli and Manzoni showed, but Schweicker adopted in the ledger the words, "*soll*" and "*soll haben*" that were not the same as the Italian, "*die dare*" and "*die havere*" that Pacioli and Manzoni used.

5. Although Pacioli wrote that it is always good to close the ledger each year and

Manzoni illustrates an account example of one year, Schweicker adopted the account example of two months and four days.

6. Although Manzoni did not have the bill of exchange account that Pacioli explained, Schweicker showed a ledger account for the bill of exchange, both for bills receivable and bills payable.

7. Schweicker had fifteen chapters for explanation of regulation of the journal and eight chapters for explanation of regulation of the ledger. Pacioli explained the double entry bookkeeping system in thirty-six chapters and Manzoni had fifteen chapters about the journal and twelve chapters about the ledger.

8. Schweicker adopted ninety-two accounts in the ledger and used the profit and loss (*Nuβ und schaden*) account, capital (*Cavedal Hanptgut*) account, debtor (*Schuldner*) account and closing (*Zubeschliessen diβ Buch oder dise rechnung*) account. Schweicker did not adopt the "*Bilanz*" account.

9. Although Pacioli explained about the account that was submitted to the public office (*gli uffici publici*), the account of partnership (*compagnia*), the account of the shop (*bottega*), and the account of entries of trips, Schweicker did not give any explanation concerning these accounts.

10. The accounts in the journal were posted in the ledger according to the Pacioli's method.

11. The explanation and illustration of the journal had many likenesses to Manzoni. The first five transactions in particular were almost the same as Manzoni.

The connection between Schweicker and Manzoni is closest in the form of the bookkeeping system and a part of the journal. We can say that Schweicker imitated Manzoni's work concerning the journal, but Schweicker did not choose the same way as Manzoni in the explanation and illustration of the ledger. Schweicker tried to improve the method of the total balance sheet that was used to close the ledger by Pacioli's method. The profit and loss calculation that he endeavored to show is not based on Manzoni, but based on Pacioli's theory.

But Schweicker made five mistakes in posting from journal to ledger, and then he committed various errors in the ledger. Consequently, the profit and loss calculation in his closing of the ledger is not correct, and he wrote a mistaken amount. The opinion that Schweicker is only the translator of Manzoni is not correct. Schweicker's work is based on Manzoni's work and Pacioli's theory. Many errors which he made in his illustrations of the ledger decreased the estimation of Schweicker's work. Although Schweicker introduced Pacioli's bookkeeping system to Germany for the first time, he could not get the honor as the first and greatest introducer of Pacioli's theory of double entry bookkeeping. But the seed of the Venetian bookkeeping method that Schweicker sowed in Germany has been nourished by his many successors.

The work *Buchhalten durch zwey bücher* of Sebastian Gammersfelder of Passaw, who was schoolmaster in Danzig, was published in Danzig in 1570. This work is the most important book of double entry bookkeeping in northern Germany in the 16th century. Penndorf wrote, "I have confidence that it is the oldest valuable work on bookkeeping." Kellenbenz wrote, "according to Penndorf, the best German description of Italian bookkeeping was given by Gammersfelder." Gammersfelder prescribed and illustrated the bookkeeping of a journal and ledger. Although he discussed the subsidiary records, the memorial or the day book, the bill book and expense book in his work, he did not illustrate them.

Gammersfelder's bookkeeping system is based on the Italian double entry bookkeeping system of Luca Pacioli. Gammersfelder was affected by Schweicker. And Gammersfelder succeeded in showing the balance account according to the method of Pacioli. We can say that Gammersfelder succeeded in introducing the double entry bookkeeping of Pacioli to northern Germany.

CONCLUSION

Italy is loaded with honors in the history of accounting as the country of the birthplace of double entry bookkeeping and the cradle of Luca Pacioli—father of modern accounting. Although Luca Pacioli played an important role in spreading double entry bookkeeping from Italy to Germany, the Nürnberg merchants introduced the double entry bookkeeping method from Venice to Nürnberg in the 15th century before Pacioli's work was published.

After the Nürnberg merchant Jacob Fugger went to Fondaco dei Tedeschi in Venice (in 1437), he introduced the accounting system of Venice to Fuggers in Augsburg. And the House of Fugger made their Balance Sheet in 1527, 1533, 1546 and 1553, and showed the inventory method to calculate profit and loss. But most German authors of bookkeeping, except Matthäus Schwarz, did not know the inventory method of the House of Fugger. Schwarz's agency bookkeeping method, though not affected by Pacioli, had many points of similarity to Valentin Mennher's Italian bookkeeping method (1550). The cash account and the master account are very important, and profit and loss calculation and the capital account are not necessary in the case of agency bookkeeping. According to the opinion of some professors, agency bookkeeping had its origin in ancient Roman bookkeeping.

The bookkeeping system of Schreiber and Gottlieb, who were not influenced by Pacioli, had much effect upon later works on bookkeeping in Germany, for example Woolf (1610) and Schurtz (1662). The Venetian bookkeeping system of Luca Pacioli was introduced to Germany by Schweicker in 1549. But there are points of both similarity and difference between Pacioli's theory and Schweicker's method. Gammerfelder adopted the method of bookkeeping of Pacioli in 1570 in Danzig.

The bookkeeping method of Pacioli was spread not only in south Germany but also in north Germany in the 17th century. For example, Schurtz published two works on bookkeeping (1662, 1695). Schurtz adopted the traditional account book system of Schreiber and Gottlieb in southern Germany in his first work, but he adopted the Pacioli's account book system in his second book. Schurtz proved that Pacioli's bookkeeping system replaced the traditional German bookkeeping method in the 17th century.

We cannot explain all German works on double entry bookkeeping only by the theory of Luca Pacioli. There were many kinds of bookkeeping systems in Germany. But the theory and method of Luca Pacioli that was introduced by Schweicker had great influence in many German works on double entry bookkeeping for a long time.

REFERENCES

Bariola, Plinio, *Storia della Ragioneria Italiana* (Milano: 1897).

Besta, Fabio, *La Ragioneria* (Milano: Ragioneria Generale, 1922–1929).

Brown and Johnston, *Paciolo on Accounting* (New York: 1963).

Brown, Richard, ed., *A History of Accounting and Accountants* (Edinburgh: 1905).

Bywater and Yamey, *Historic Accounting Literature, a Companion Guide* (London: 1982).

Casanova, Alvise, *Specchio Lucidissimo, nel quale si vedeno essere diffinito tutti i modi* (Venetia: 1558).

Castellani, Arrigo, *Nuovi Testi Fiorentini del Dugento, con Introduzione, Trattazione, Linguistica e Glossario* (Firenze: 1952).

Chatfield, Michael, *A History of Accounting Thought* (Illinois: 1974).

Contrugli, Benedetto, *Della Mercatura et del mercante perfetto* (Venetia: 1573).

Crivelli, Pietro, An Original Translation of the Treatise on Double Entry Bookkeeping by Frater Lucas Pacioli (London: 1924).

De Roover, Raymond, The Development of Accounting Prior to Luca Pacioli According to the Account-books of Medieval Merchants, in Littleton and Yamey, eds., *Studies in the History of Accounting* (London: 1956).

De Waal, P. G. A., *Van Paciolo tot Stevin* (Roermond: 1927).

Gammersfelder, Sebastian, *Buchhalten durch zwey bücher nach Italianischer art und weise* (Danzig: 1570).

Geijsbeek, John B., *Ancient Duble-Entry Bookkeeping,* Lucas Pacioli's Treatise (Denver: 1914).

Gitti, Vincenzo, *Fra Luca Paciolo, Tractatus de Computis et scripturis* (Torino: 1878).

Gottlieb, Johann, *Ein Teutsch Verstendig Buchhalten für Herren oder Geselschaffter* (Nürnberg: 1531).

Green, Wilmer L., *History and Survey of Accountancy* (New York: 1930).

Haulotte et Stevelinck, *Luca Pacioli Sa vie Son oeuvre* (Brussels: 1975).

Kataoka, Yasuhiko, *The Theory of the History of Double Entry Bookkeeping in Italy* (Tokyo: 1988).

Kataoka, Yasuhiko, The Comparative Study of the Consolidated Financial Statements of the House of Mitsui and The House of Fugger, in *Collected Papers of the Fifth World Congress of Accounting Historians,* edited by Craswell (The University of Sydney: 1988).

Kats, P., A Surmise regarding the Origin of Bookkeeping by Double Entry, *Accounting Review,* vol. 5, no. 4 (1930).

Kellenbenz, Hermann, *Der Stand der Buchhaltung in Oberdeutschland zur Zeit der Fugger und Welser, Die Wirtschaftsprüfung, Heft,* no V. (1970).

Kheil, Karel Petr, *Luca Pacioli, Traktát o účentnictivi z roku 1494* (Prague: 1894).

Kheil, Carl Peter, *Benedetto Cotrugli Raugeo* (Wien: 1906).

Littleton, A. C., Accounting Evolution to 1900 (New York: 1966).

Manzoni, Domenico, *Quaderno doppio col suo giornale, novamente Composto* (Venezia: 1540).

Massa, G., *Trattato completo di ragioneria* (Milano: 1912).

Melis, Federigo, *Storia della Ragioneria* (Bologna: 1950).

Mennher, Valentin, *Practique brifue pour cyfrer et tenir livres de compte* . . . (Anvers: 1550).

Moschetti, Giovanni Antonio, *Dell' universal trattato di libri doppii* (Venetia: 1610).

Pacioli, Luca, *Summa de Arithmetica Geometria Proportioni et Proportionalita Venezia, Paganino de Paganini* (Venice: 1494; Toscolano: 1523).

Penndorf, Balduin, *Geschichte der Buchhalten in Deutschland* (Leipzig: 1913).

Penndorf, Balduin, *Luca Pacioli, Abhandlung über die Buchhaltung 1494* (Stuttgart: 1933).

Schreiber, Heinrich, *Ayn new Kunstlich Buech welches gar gewiss* (Nürnberg: 1518).

Schweicker, Wolfgang, *Zweifack Buchhalten, sampt seinē Giornal des selben Beschlus* (Nürnberg: 1549).

Schurtz, Georg Nicolaus, *General Instruction, Der Arithmetischen und Politischen Kunst, Der hochlöblichen Wissenschäfft der Kauff und Handelsleuth des Buchhaltens* (Nürnberg: 1662).

Schurtz, Georg Nicolaus, *Nutzbare Richtschnur der löblichen Kauffmannschaft. Das ist:* neuvermehrt-volkommenes buchhalten (Nürnberg: 1695).

Stevin, Simon, *Memoires Mathmatiques* (A. Leyde: 1608).

Strieder, Jacob, *Die Inventur der Firma Fugger aus dem Jahre 1527* (Tübingen: 1905).

Stromer von Reichenbach, *Die Nürnberger Handelsgesellschaft Gruber-Podmer-Stromer im 15. Jahrhundert* (1963).

Stromer von Reichenbach, *Das Schriftwesen der Nürnberger im 14. und 16 Jahrhundert,* in Beiträge zur Wirtschaftsgeschichte Nürnbergers II (1967).

Taylor, Emmett, *No Royal Road, Luca Pacioli and His Times* (North Carolina: 1942).

Taylor, Emmett, Luca Pacioli, in Littleton and Yamey eds., *Studies in the History of Accounting* (London: 1956).

Weitnauer, Alfred, *Venezianischer Handel der Fugger, Nach der Musterbuchhaltung des Matthäus Schwarz* (München und Leipzig: 1931).

Woolf, Arthur H., *A Short History of Accountants and Accountancy* (London: 1912).

Yamey, Basil S., *Accounting Literature 1494–1800: A Survey* (Tokyo: Yushodo, 1990).

10

Accounting Change and the Emergence of Management Accounting

C. S. McWatters

SECTION I: INTRODUCTION

Accounting change has been characterised as the tendency of the accounting craft to become what it was not (Hopwood, 1987, pp. 207, 225). This paper briefly examines this proposition in the context of a 19th-century organization— The Calvin Company (TCC). Specifically, the emergence of management accounting information within TCC is analysed. Factors which predispose accounting to change and parallels with current accounting developments are suggested. The research seeks to improve our understanding of the phenomenon of accounting change, especially the underlying factors and pre-conditions for its occurrence.

The remainder of this paper is organized as follows: Section II provides a brief introduction to The Calvin Company. Section III outlines the data sources and research propositions. Section IV presents the analysis with the results in Section V. Concluding comments are provided in Section VI.

SECTION II: THE EVOLUTION OF THE CALVIN COMPANY

TCC's[1] history has been divided into two phases. The first phase covers the period from 1839 to 1869. The second phase, which is the focus of the present paper, examines the period from 1870 to 1915. The two periods correspond to those used by D. D. Calvin (1945) in his study of the company. Moreover, the initial analysis of the accounting records led to this partition due to changes in TCC's accounting system; specifically, the introduction of management accounting information in TCC's second phase. TCC is a generic term to designate the multiple co-partnerships of D. D. Calvin in Upper and Lower Canada. Except for the period from 1886 to 1915, the company operated through a series of partnerships (as was the 19th-century norm), where owners and managers were one and the same.

The company began operations in the 1830s as a maker and forwarder of timber and staves, with the first formal co-partnership established in December 1839. TCC grew in both size and scope throughout the 19th century to include shipbuilding, wrecking operations, and towing services (amongst others). Yet, it did not survive the technological changes and advances which had served initially to enhance its operations. TCC's business enterprises encompassed the several stages along the supply chain to meet the demand of the timber market for primarily oak timber, and, to a lesser extent, staves. Given the varied operations undertaken, the firm's information requirements would differ at alternate points along the supply chain.

TCC's operations moved further from its head office at Garden Island, near Kingston, Upper Canada, as proximate sources of merchantable timber began to disappear. First, timber-making moved along the Great Lakes basin, but eventually most timber originated in the United States. As its supply sources became more distant, TCC's activities expanded, including the use of joint accounts to share the risk of far-flung operations, a larger fleet of vessels, and greater capacity of individual ships.

At the supply end, TCC had certain information needs. These were related to the decision to buy or to make its timber, to act solely as a forwarder or also on its own account, the quantity targets and administrative arrangements for its joint accounts, and the financing of its timber operations overall. In all of its ventures, the extensive records kept of each transaction underscored the stewardship of partnership, and of creditor resources.

On the demand side, TCC also had particular information needs. For example, the firm had the option to sell its timber at Quebec, or, to ship it directly to Great Britain (it pursued both courses after 1868). TCC also served as a commission agent for timber rafted to Quebec at the risk of other owners. Thus, it often had to decide when best to sell, taking into consideration market conditions, its own possible commission, and the potential competition created by its own timber. Additionally, TCC had to evaluate the alternate strategies to contract for the sale of its production in the upcoming season, or, to take its chances on the open market. These various decisions hinged upon the actual information received about market prospects, along with the partners' and agents' evaluation of this data. These choices also implied the consideration of the firm's responsibilities towards the partnership and its various clients and creditors.

Three aspects of TCC's operations deserve special emphasis. First, TCC dealt primarily in oak timber. This fact distinguishes it from others involved in the industry, who concentrated upon the exploitation of pine (Lower, 1973, pp. 160–180).

Second, TCC was oriented much more closely towards the economy at Quebec, and to the demands of the timber interests represented there, rather than to the agricultural community of Upper Canada. TCC engaged its labor force for its rafting and winter timber-making operations in Quebec, and not locally. Moreover, business associates at Quebec were personal friends, such that social and business ties reinforced each other.

Third, TCC's diversification efforts were ancillary to its main operations as a merchandiser and forwarder of timber. The firm's shipbuilding, wreckage, and salvage activities at Garden Island began initially to meet its own internal needs. The extension of services to others, when favorable opportunities arose, contributed to the utilization of existing capacity. Similarly, the proposal for and the operation of a government tug line service met TCC's own need for towing from Kingston to Montreal. These ventures, however, did not constitute the core of the business operations. Except for the tug line, which provided a valuable subsidy (often used for credit collateral) they did not generate large profits for the firm.

Phase Two: 1870–1915

The 1860s had been the busiest years in terms of the company's operations. TCC's efforts were broad in scope, including the forwarding of other commodities such as flour, salt and cheese. Yet, all was not smooth sailing. Credit concerns were always prevalent, given the long operating cycle required for timber production and the need to finance the downstream operations. This often was done via advances on subsequent deliveries to timber merchants at Quebec, and, if necessary, via advances secured by the tug line contract proceeds.

Overall, the decade had been a prosperous one, with TCC experiencing rising profits. By the end of 1869, the capital of the two partners, D. D. Calvin and I. A. Breck, had grown to more than $360,000, from $160,724 in 1862. The optimistic note which ended the first phase of TCC would be tested during the next period, as the firm moved from a time of growth and rising profits to that of depressed markets and heavy losses.

The 1870s ushered in a period of depression within the British and American timber markets. TCC was the industry leader in terms of bulk of oak timber passed through Quebec, due to its own operations as a timber-maker, and also as a rafting enterprise and exporter (QUA, Box 117, Folder 1). With TCC's decision to ship its timber to Britain on its own account, a great deal of correspondence consisted of reports to and from its agent in Glasgow, Edmiston & Mitchell. For most of the 1870s, the latter had little good news to convey (QUA, Boxes 9 to 14). In 1874, TCC's agent wrote that trade was "paralyzed," the market was "overdone," and sales were being made only at "sacrifice prices."

This same prognosis continued throughout the decade. While there were no prospects for sales, except for a few made at auction, TCC did not experience low years until 1874. As noted by McInnis (1982, pp. 23–24), "[t]he collapse after 1874 was profound. The Great Depression of the 1870s has a role of prominence in Canadian economic history. The wood products sector was especially severely affected by that depression. Its unusually rapid growth in the years immediately preceding the depression accentuated the situation." This downturn was confirmed by TCC's own situation. The business had had its largest profits (in current dollars) in 1871 and 1873, only to see its return drop by more than 85 per cent in 1874, followed in 1875 by the firm's first loss since 1859. TCC managed to break even in 1876, with additional losses in the last three years of the decade. TCC's situation did not mirror that of aggregate timber exports to Great Britain, which did not decline until 1876, and with the major collapse (especially in the pine market) not occurring until 1879 (McInnis, 1982).

While the timber industry "broke," TCC persisted in the making of timber, pointing to its concern for the workers employed. This resulted in considerable amounts of unsold inventory both at Garden Island and at the Quebec timber coves. TCC continued to expand—especially in the United States—in its pursuit of timber resources.[2]

TCC's losses were not all due to the depressed export market. The company concentrated to a greater degree upon timber cutting in the United States, as far away as Kentucky, Missouri, and Tennessee. Concurrent with the increased geographical distance involved, the quality of the timber was decreasing. The American operations generally did not prove profitable, with TCC left with the risk of holding real estate in the United States, and writing off considerable sums due to the poor quality of both the oak and the board pine produced. TCC had sought to reduce its exposure in the oak market by increasing its production of pine. This did not prove viable, and the firm sold its Michigan properties in 1882 (MMA, Timber and Stave Book 1882–1913).

TCC had continued to operate the government tug line, but, much to its surprise and dismay, the contract was cancelled in 1874. The government decision to end the service probably was related to the expense of the subsidy ("bonus"). Over the course of the operation of the service, the total bonus payments made to TCC amounted to $346,820. Moreover, the bonus represented from forty-four to more than one thousand per cent of the profit declared on the service in a single year [Average = 240.46 per cent; σ = 272.40]. Despite lobbying, especially after a change in government in 1878, the service was not resumed.

In the midst of the depressed market, Calvin's son Hiram entered into the partnership in 1871, purchasing a twenty-five per cent interest in 1873. The market downturn made the situation difficult for Hiram, as the latter had arranged to pay for his share with yearly payments plus interest. In 1877, H. Calvin transferred his share back to his father. Thus, it was D. D. Calvin and I. A. Breck whose capital bore the impact of the major losses.

At the beginning of 1879, I. A. Breck sent D. D. Calvin an estimate of TCC's affairs for the forthcoming year (QUA, Volume 20, pp. 128–130). The balance sheet at January 1, 1880, confirmed Breck's estimate with respect to bills payable, which were indeed nil at the end of 1879. However, it is not certain whether Breck had estimated that 1879 also would see a net loss of over $91,000.[3] At the beginning of 1880, partners' capital was $316,133.82, compared to $389,479.23 in 1870. This was a drop of 18.83 per cent, and a notable decrease from the years 1873 to 1876, in which their capital had been reported at over $500,000.

The decline in the timber industry was mirrored by that of TCC. In 1880, Breck retired and the firm continued as Calvin & Son. D. D. Calvin's death in 1884 signalled the wane and cessation of the business itself. The estate was divided amongst his heirs who began to limit its operations, including the sell-off of timber properties. TCC's final years were incorporated within that of the end of the square-timber trade in general. Increasingly, trade was focussed upon sawn lumber to both the British and the American market. Technological changes, with the rise of railways, and iron ships reduced the viability of TCC's shipbuilding activities.

In June 1886, TCC was reorganized as a limited liability company (49 Victoria, Chapter 107), with the first annual meeting held October 15, 1887. Especially as competitors turned to other interests, TCC's operations were concentrated increasingly upon the forwarding of timber and other commodities. Despite the change in organizational form, TCC remained a family firm. This factor appeared to constrain its flexibility, such that it did not shift successfully from a family business to a business enterprise.

Other factors contributed to TCC's decline: the loss of its labor force, as the younger generation sought alternate occupations to timber work; improvements to the canal system meant that TCC's towing capacity was not utilized to the same extent; the shorter season as the amount of timber to be carried fell. These factors all reinforced TCC's declining profitability, as its facilities and ships were ill-suited for alternate uses. The firm launched its last ship in 1903, and the final raft left Garden Island in 1914. Operations ceased at the outbreak of World War I.

This overview has presented events both within TCC, and within its external environment which influenced its operations and activities. In Section IV, these events are examined in terms of TCC's accounting system, and how the latter reflected changes in the firm's environment.

SECTION III: HISTORICAL RESEARCH METHODOLOGY AND DATA SOURCES

Fundamental differences exist between the methodology of historical research and that employed in other empirical research. Firstly, historical study does not commence with a theory or hypothesis to be tested. Data are gathered, and then major propositions are formulated. A preliminary study resulted in the partition of the company's history, and in the formulation of the research propositions reported here.

Secondly, historical research usually employs archival documents, the latter being primary (or unpublished) documents of the subject under study. In the case of TCC, these records are of interest in terms of charting its evolution from a partnership to a limited liability company in 19th-century Canada. The records identify the choices made by TCC's management in terms of which timber market opportunities to exploit, and the success or failure of these ventures. Importantly from an accounting perspective, the records also chart the changes in the accounting system as TCC sought ways to record, and to account for its various business ventures. Brooks (1969, pp. 11–12) summarises the major characteristics of unpublished sources as: (a) uniqueness; (b) purposeful creation; (c) representation of a person/organization; and (d) specific location within a collection.

Thirdly, the selection and compilation of the data seeks to avoid a selection bias in support of predetermined conclusions. The examination of TCC's records begins with external criticism of the documents (who, what, when, where), followed by an evaluation of their content (why). The paper seeks to assess the "why" of company decisions within their historical context, and not merely to record their occurrence.

This approach to archival research is in keeping with the philosophy of R. G. Collingwood (1961, pp. 9–10), who made the following observation: "History proceeds by the interpretation of evidence: where evidence is a collective name for things which singly are called documents, and a document is a thing existing here and now, of such a kind that the historian, by thinking about it, can get answers to the questions he asks about past events." These answers increase our understanding of the present in relation to the development of society and of its institutions.

Data Sources

The research has utilized a variety of source materials as outlined below.

The Calvin Company Records contained at the Queen's University Archives, Kingston, Ontario, comprise the primary research data. These documents encompass records of the company's timber, shipbuilding, salvage, and towing operations along with records pertaining to family and personal legal matters. The collection includes many items, such as cancelled cheques, receipts, and telegrams, which generally are not retained by the archivist.

Specifically, the catalogue for the collection lists 256 bound volumes and 136 boxes. All materials have been arranged according to the main group or category, as well as chronologically. Although the records are not complete, they are considered to be one of the finest collections of extant business records in Canada for the period under study.

The Queen's University collection is strengthened by its smaller counterpart,

The Calvin Collection, archived at The Marine Museum of The Great Lakes, Kingston, Ontario. This collection contains nine boxes of chronologically-ordered records of a personal and business nature, as well as a large number of bound volumes of company and personal records. Since the Marine Museum collection primarily contains records of the Garden Island branch, it eliminates significant gaps within the Queen's University collection.

Published material dealing with TCC's history has been employed with caution. Since much of this has been written by family members, it must be evaluated for potential bias. A wide spectrum of published materials in both accounting and Canadian economic history has been consulted to provide the necessary background for the major determinants of each phase in the company's development. A list of these sources is included in the references.

Data Analysis and Research Propositions

The data analysis examines the rise of management accounting information in the company's later years, and its relationship to the accounting records. The research propositions are described more completely below:

1. Changes in the external environment led to changes in the accounting information required. External changes resulted in different criteria with which management evaluated its operations.

2. TCC's need for management accounting arose, in part, from the greater number of transactions, increased geographic scope, and the shorter operating cycle.

3. The decline of the timber staple with the increased exploitation of pulp and paper, mineral resources, and grain was reflected in TCC's internal analyses of its operations as a forwarder in these alternate markets.

4. The shift in role from owner-manager in a partnership to salaried manager-shareholder in a limited liability company had a negative impact upon TCC's decision-making ability and assessment of possible options for its continued survival. This drawback of corporate status was related to the heterogeneous interests of shareholders.

This section has outlined the framework for the data analysis, along with the research propositions which form the basis for the following analysis.

SECTION IV: THE EMERGENCE OF MANAGEMENT ACCOUNTING INFORMATION (MAI)

In the later stages of the 19th century, alterations in TCC's environment suggested different criteria were required to assess the firms's operations, as well as its means to account for them. Technological advances, such as the use of steam power and iron vessels, intensified competition including that of the railways, and shifts within the timber market motivated TCC to reexamine its operations. Not surprisingly, this reassessment began concurrent with the experience of heavy losses. TCC was not immune to the depression of the 1870s. The impact of the depression probably was compounded by the onset of heavy losses subsequent to a period of high profits.

TCC was also confronting changes in its internal organization. During the 1870s, D. D. Calvin's son Hiram entered the business. In 1880, Calvin's brother-in-law and partner of thirty years, I. A. Breck, retired from the firm. Additionally, TCC had been expanding its operations into the United States in the quest for timber sources. However, as it moved further afield, the quality of timber continued to decline. Lastly, the death of D. D. Calvin in 1884 brought the reorganisation of the business in 1886, and a change in TCC's leadership. H. A. Calvin assumed the position of manager in the newly-created corporation.

Importantly, some environmental changes, such as the timber market shifts and increased competition, were not subject to TCC's control. This did not eliminate the need for new information with which to assess these situations, but it did require that the former be directed outward. For example, to mitigate the impact of increased competition, TCC entered into a pooling arrangement with its major competitor, Collins Bay Rafting & Forwarding. This relationship led to the subsequent demand for reports to monitor this market-sharing contract. In terms of the timber market at large, TCC began to compile two new types of information: (1) detailed reports about the yearly earnings of its vessels; and (2) the breakdown of its operations in terms of timber freighting, and what TCC called "outside" freighting; primarily commodities other than timber, but including sawn lumber destined for the United States.

While TCC was a price-taker in the external market, it could effect changes in its internal processes. This required totally different information focussed inwards upon the efficiency of the company's operations, and which was concerned with the operating cost of the firm's fleet. The increased use of steam power and a shift to iron ships and to railways had reduced the competitiveness and the profitability of TCC's vessels. Thus, a void existed in terms of criteria to assess its internal operations. MAI emerged to fill this breach in the wake of alterations in TCC's internal and external environment. This MAI can be divided into two categories: (1) reports which focussed upon internal processes and "the impact of the organization's separate parts on its total financial performance" (Johnson & Kaplan, 1987, p. 37); and (2) memoranda which dealt with market prices and transactions for which the "market price supplied every conceivable bit of information for decision making and control." Internal information relied upon data about the firm's operating expenses. The market-oriented reports dealt with TCC's freighting and rafting operations, especially the need to monitor its competitor's conduct in accordance with their market-pooling arrangement.

The Question of Efficiency

While TCC had been expanding and its profits growing, there appears to have been scant attention paid to the efficiency[4] of its operations. This situation changed abruptly in the late 1870's, when TCC experienced major losses. These losses likely motivated the partners to reevaluate their operations, and to direct attention to the question of internal costs. Since TCC could not hope to influence the market at large, it could hope to improve its position by more efficient use of its internal resources.

Other issues probably would have contributed to the attention now directed to efficiency. The switch from wood to coal as a source of fuel for its vessels and Garden Island facilities, altered the firm's outlook. While the cost of wood had been charged to the vessels, wood (like the timber forest) had been considered a never-ending resource. Also, TCC was able to provide for much of its own wood supplies. The switch to coal required TCC to purchase its fuel on the open market, and the cost of fuel now assumed a higher profile. Secondly, the shift to steam power and iron vessels had now reduced the competitiveness of its fleet. As TCC turned to alternate markets, such as the shipment of grain and minerals, it also sought to determine the viability of its efforts in these new areas. The emergence of MAI, as a consequence of the new focus upon cost and operating expense, was not unique to TCC. A similar development took place within the Wedgwood enterprise of the late 18th century. Hopwood's (1987, p. 215) description of Wedgwood's situation could be that of TCC one hundred years later:

Initially, Wedgwood made little use of accounting, particularly for what would now be seen as management purposes. Accounting information did not inform his product and pricing decisions or the selection of his methods of work. . . . This situation was to change however. In 1772 the expansion came to an abrupt end. The pottery industry was caught in a major economic recession. . . . In times of such crisis business methods often are reexamined. With such an aim in mind, Wedgwood started to turn his attention to the level of his production expenses. And it was in this context that his cost accounts were born.

The MAI, which was prepared by TCC, dealt specifically with the cost of its fleet, both for individual ships, and for its fleet as a whole. Two items, board expenses and fuel costs, became the prime target for analysis. Individual ships were evaluated in terms of their operating ratio, i.e., the relationship of expenses to revenues. The current paper examines the reports related to one ship, the steamer *India*.

Operating Ratios

The question of efficiency had directed TCC's attention to the cost of its internal operations, in contrast with its previous reliance upon (primarily) external, market prices with which to evaluate the profitability of its ventures. The calculation of operating ratios as a part of TCC's MAI would have permitted management to assess the contribution of each vessel to the firm's overall profits. As TCC expanded its operating scale and geographic scope, it had to deal with a greater number of, and variety of, business activities. In terms of TCC's reporting system, the latter implied an increased number of transactions to allocate to the ledger accounts. The operating ratio condensed the year-end result of these transactions into a single figure.

In many ways, TCC's demand for new criteria to account for its operations parallelled the situation faced by the management of the railways. While TCC was affected increasingly by the entry of the railways into its market, TCC also adopted methods similar to those utilized by its competitors. The comments of Chandler (1977, p. 110) concerning the American railroads are equally applicable to TCC: "Profit and loss were not enough. Earnings had to be related to the volume of business. A better test was the ratio between a road's operating revenues and its expenditures or, more precisely, the percentage of gross revenue that had been needed to meet operating costs."

The last reports for the steamer *India* (MMA, Letter Book 23, pp. 134–135) covered the period from 1899 to 1912.[5] One statement dealt with coal consumption. For each year, the total usage in tons and in dollar cost were reported. Also provided were the average number of tons per year, the average total cost, and the average cost per ton. As the data were prepared annually, changes in the year to year average reflected the impact of the most recent season. For the years 1899 to 1912, the average cost of coal per ton rose from $2.10 to $3.02— an increase of 43.81 per cent. This compared quite favourably with the total rise in the WPI of 42.44 per cent during the same period. In eleven of thirteen years, TCC's cost of coal (for the steamer *India*) moved in the same direction as the WPI.[6]

While TCC prepared a report specific to coal consumption, a second memorandum examined gross earnings. This statement summarized yearly information about gross earnings and gain or loss in the year, along with the vessel's capital value at year end. The statement also would have permitted the determination of return on its capital investment, as both the yearly gain and capital value were recorded. However, there was no indication that this additional analysis was performed. TCC's treatment of capital assets would suggest that TCC's accounting was lacking in this respect, but not unlike that of most businesses of this period (Brief, 1976; Johnson & Kaplan, 1987).

While the average gain on earnings from 1899 to 1912 was reported as 14.32 per cent, TCC did not provide for any depreciation on the vessel in 1906, or from 1908 to 1910. The failure to provide for any depreciation would have overstated the average gain (operating margin). The loss of more than fourteen thousand dollars in 1914, when the *India* was sold, reinforces this argument. Thus, the average reported gain of 14.32 per cent tended to mask the decline in profitability of the *India*, and the variability in this return from year to year. The yearly gain declined by 50 per cent from 1907 to 1908, and continued to fall thereafter.

The President's report for 1903 (QUA, Volume 80, p. 84) offered several reasons for the poor result: "First the Engine House fire; the bulk of the expense for the renewing of which fell on this year. The buying out of the Collins Bay Rafting Company.... Then freights were not so good as last season and the boats all around did not do as well. Besides this in common with others we had to pay higher wages to our men.'' Not surprisingly, the explanation relied more upon external forces, than upon the efficiency of its own efforts. Despite the regular preparation of MAI during TCC's second phase, MAI did not appear to have been used frequently in a proactive fashion.

SECTION V: RESULTS OF ANALYSIS

The foregoing analysis suggests that changes in TCC's environmental context demanded concomitant changes in its own operations. In turn, new criteria to account for the latter were required. The analysis is the basis for the following conclusions in terms of the research propositions of Section III.

The second phase of TCC's business was marked by rapid technological advances and major shifts in the forest industry, combined with the increased exploitation of new staple products. These external factors, in turn, had an impact upon TCC's internal operations. The firm initially had relied upon market indicators to assess its operations. TCC utilized information about the state of the timber market and its clients and competitors, which was oriented externally. Since the market was growing, and the firm was operating on a small scale relative to the aggregate market, TCC did not appear to consider the need to examine its internal processes. Environmental changes led to the recognition of its internal costs, especially as competition intensified, the firm's operating scale increased, and the market declined. These factors all contributed to the reduction in TCC's competitive advantage. The question of efficiency demanded new information which reported upon the cost to generate the revenues received in TCC's various business ventures.

Additionally, heightened competition within the forwarding market called for better means to evaluate the revenues generated in this sector. Thus, attention was directed to the effectiveness of the firm's operations in terms of its ability to secure contracts. Beginning in 1886, this analysis included the division of operations into outside and timber freighting, along with the reporting of revenues generated in each sector. This change was coincident with TCC's incorporation. The need to report operating results annually to the Board of Directors and to shareholders possibly motivated TCC to establish better records for the assessment of its operations. Since TCC was a price-taker in the market, efforts to evaluate its efficiency and effectiveness contributed to TCC's potential for informed decision-making in terms of which market opportunities to exploit.

As TCC's operations expanded, the number of transactions also increased. The larger number of transactions, coupled with a broader geographic scope, stimulated the analysis of costs, such that the profitability of these operations could be assessed more readily. MAI, including improved cost analysis, provided a more systematic means to monitor TCC's ventures *versus* the reliance upon the aggregate information within the financial records. For example, the cost to maintain its fleet and its fuel expenses were analysed in order that TCC could make decisions about resource allocation. Geographic expansion focused attention upon costs, since it was the ability to control internal expenditures which would allow TCC to remain viable in the face of declining freight rates and intensified competition. Importantly, cost information had a disciplinary potential. It allowed for the assignment of responsibility for costs, such as the relative ratings made of each captain's operating expenditures, and the ratio of expenditures to revenues of individual ships.

The improved efficiency of transportation and the introduction of telegraph and telephone services shortened TCC's operating cycle. The timber itself was moved more quickly, and technological advances reduced the credit term. Moreover, TCC's own shift to a corporate enterprise increased the focus upon the short term. The need for more timely MAI was created, in order that policy decisions could take into account the trends of both expenses and revenues. As well, the annual reporting of its financial position to shareholders and creditors motivated the preparation of MAI, since the year-end profit figure reflected TCC's ability to control internal costs, and to operate effectively in the market at large.

TCC was not immune to the economic shifts of the late 19th and early 20th centuries. These shifts, which led to the greater exploitation of staple products such as grain and minerals, along with the expansion of the forest industry to include pulp and paper, had additional consequences for TCC's internal reporting system. After 1886, TCC became more involved in markets other than square timber. This required different information with which to assess the profitability of these various market segments. TCC's division of its freight operations between timber and outside freighting was a logical decision, given the different rate structures in these markets. Yet, this initial decision had the additional consequence of allowing TCC to analyse readily each of these businesses, and the relative profitability of each sector.

The assumption of corporate status had some consequences beyond the more obvious legal rights and duties of limited liability. TCC's shift to a limited-liability company with authorized capital meant that the firm now had to deal with shareholder interests, which did not have to coincide necessarily with those of management. H. A. Calvin, who had entered TCC while the firm operated as a partnership, assumed the position of salaried manager in the new corporation. The role of manager, rather than that of sole proprietor (as he had considered), brought with it the requirement that policies be approved by shareholders or the Board of Directors. As well, H. A. Calvin's remuneration was contingent upon the firm's results, as a bonus was paid when TCC's return on capital exceeded ten per cent. Decisions taken, their rationale, and the results thereof were subject to shareholder evaluation. While H. A. Calvin had stated that he would operate the firm without interference, this did not eliminate the need to take the interests of shareholders into account, or, the questioning of his actions at annual meetings. This would have been all the more expected, as the shareholders were family members, or business associates.

In summary, the research conclusions suggest a number of contextual factors which had an impact upon the firm's activities, and upon its internal accounting system:

1. The greater scope of the business, including the geographic dispersion of the co-partners, and of their agents;
2. Heightened competition, especially from global competitors and the introduction of new products;
3. Technological changes in the timber industry which fed back into the company's operations, and influenced its methods to account for them;
4. The role of financial credit, especially due to the nature of the operating cycle in the timber industry;
5. The internal organisation of the firm, including a change in organizational form.

These variables are readily translated to our current situation in which the trend to global markets, rapid technological change, and new corporate financial and organizational arrangements have led to concomitant changes in accounting practice and theory. However, it is possible that accounting innovations are circumscribed by accounting's proclivity for tradition. The conclusion of the paper offers some speculative comments in this regard.

SECTION VI: CONCLUDING COMMENTS

TCC's operating environment had certain distinctive social, technological, and cultural features. This contextual framework both constrained and enabled TCC's conduct. It also influenced the nature of the accounting system which evolved throughout the firm's history.

TCC was a product of the Western society of the 19th century. Its operating style and conduct emphasised the concepts of trust, stewardship, and accountability which were part of this world view (Bliss, 1987; McCalla, 1979). These features were reaffirmed in TCC's intensive record-keeping of transactions undertaken on behalf of the firm and its clients. An additional manifestation of these cultural qualities was TCC's approach to its business dealings with clients. Compromise and negotiation were underscored, along with the importance of honor and honesty. Appeal to the courts was seen as a costly and less desirable alternative. Although the partnerships did not operate without friction, these dominant cultural norms provided for established mechanisms to deal with these disputes.

Economically, TCC operated within a market framework oriented towards Great Britain, which was the chief destination of its exports. The timber merchants with which it dealt generally were branches of established British firms.

TCC's decline was exacerbated by its attachment to timber rafting and forwarding. The narrow definition of its market reduced its ability to shift its strategic direction, to redefine itself, and subsequently to fund diversification into alternate market sectors as the trade in square timber declined.

TCC's technological framework altered rapidly throughout the 19th and 20th centuries. The company had begun operations when the pace of business was slower, as reflected in its technological base—the use of wooden sailing vessels. Yet technological changes were rampant in the 19th century. TCC was required to adapt to the growing utilization of steam power and to the shift from wood to coal. This had implications for its accounting, as the cost of coal became a focus of concern. Expenses for wood simply had been recorded, the shift to steam and then to coal-fired steamers led to the additional analysis of its cost in relation to operating revenues. New modes of transport, including more efficient vessels of larger capacity, resulted in a shorter operating cycle. This was a mixed blessing for TCC, as it increased the prospect of idle capacity. TCC's switch to steam power was slow, and it continued to construct smaller, wooden vessels despite their growing inability to compete.

The economic and technological changes of the era left their imprint upon TCC's operations and those of its accounting and information system. The firm was forced to adapt to, and to adopt new technologies, such as steam power, railways, and communication by telephone, to remain competitive. It also had to confront changes in the economic and business environment. The timber industry continued to grow, but it was dominated by products other than square (oak) timber. Other resources, such as grain and minerals, were expanding the economic base. Additionally, the business world experienced changes, as the corporate enterprise became more prevalent due to the concurrent need for greater capital investment. In TCC's early years, the focus had been on individual ventures. During the second period, the dynamic economic and technological environment contributed to heightened consideration of the business entity as a going concern *versus* a series of ventures.

TCC's internal operations began to receive more attention, as it confronted the growing losses of the late 1870s. Not surprisingly, market changes required different information to evaluate TCC's operations. MAI emerged to fill this void in terms of the efficiency and the effectiveness of TCC. The rise in board costs, revealed by its MAI analyses, appeared to confirm that TCC's policy to purchase and to allocate provisions via its company store was inefficient—an overhead cost which was being absorbed unnecessarily by its fleet operations. The report would direct attention to these costs, which might have been neglected when only the net profit of individual vessels had been reported. Yet, TCC did not appear to adopt a more proactive strategy in the face of its declining profitability. This inadequate response may have been affected additionally by TCC's position as a price-taker in the forwarding market, with no ability to influence significantly the price for its services. This was evidenced in 1881 and 1898, when it attempted to increase rates (QUA, Volume 80, p. 65).

MAI dealing with individual ships would have allowed TCC to determine the operating margin of its fleet. Instead, it appeared that MAI was utilized to confirm TCC's predicament, rather than to alert the firm to potential opportunities to alleviate its weakened situation. The reports had been prepared on a regular basis, yet the information therein did not result in the adoption of, or the confirmation of, alternate strategies to remain in business. Instead, MAI reaffirmed TCC's decision to withdraw from the market altogether. The reports also allowed TCC to focus upon external factors, such as lower freight rates, rather than to reexamine internal factors, such as its capital accounting and dividend policy, which reduced TCC's ability to manoeuvre and to remain a competitor in the forwarding industry.

However, external and internal factors jointly contributed to the company's failure. At the end of 1915, this failure had resulted in a deficit which represented 92.02 per cent of its issued capital. TCC's experience lends support to Chandler's (1977) proposition that firms which did not create a managerial hierarchy better equipped to deal with the corporate enterprise did not survive the rapid changes of the late 19th and early 20th centuries. The comments of Bliss (1987, pp. 352–353) are applicable as well:

The secret of making the transition from builder-promoter-entrepreneur was to find ways of bringing the business under accounting control, if only by hiring people who could ... not just to produce a clear sense of where each department was going, but to use the accounts to unleash the energies of managers and employees whose responsibility for their performance could be clearly traced and measured, no matter how big the organization.

The new competitive environment of the 20th century required the ability to control its ventures, but also the accounting of these ventures to control those responsible for them.

The objective of this paper has been to improve our understanding of accounting change, especially the underlying factors and conditions for its occurrence. An important facet of the analysis is the role of alterations in the accounting system. In short, did the accounting system operate and change to assist TCC in the conduct of its business, or, did the system hinder the firm in the pursuit of its goals? The system's (assumed) contingent relationship with its environment has implied that different accounting concepts and practices resulted from events in TCC's operating context, and motivated further changes. For example, in its reporting of profits and operating costs, the accounting system increased the attention paid to these issues.

In TCC's early years, the accounting system primarily served a stewardship function. It was not a decision-making tool, as the information therein was recorded too late to be of relevance. The system did come to be relied upon increasingly for decision making, as the partnership evolved into a larger entity with the geographic dispersion of partners and resources.

A significant development in TCC was the emergence of MAI. As the firm experienced several years of losses in the 1870s, it began to reexamine its operations and to seek different information. MAI also was stimulated by internal events, such as the reorganization of the 1880s, and possibly by the entry of H. A. Calvin. Additionally, TCC received numerous scientific and engineering journals through which many of these analyses first were popularised. The legal requirement to report its financial position annually to shareholders would reaffirm TCC's continued need for information about the timber market at large. Moreover, it contributed to the new focus upon its internal operations.

While the preparation of MAI appeared to be undertaken initially to improve the efficiency and the effectiveness of its operations, MAI was not utilized to its potential. MAI could direct management's attention, but its preparation alone could not ensure that TCC would deal effectively with these altered circumstances in the long run. Rather, MAI often served to confirm past results. Instead of exploiting new opportunities in the forwarding market, TCC attempted to garner better control of a shrinking market. This choice, in combination with TCC's financial policies, culminated in the ultimate decision to wind up the firm. While the accounting and MAI systems emerged to enable TCC to operate more efficiently and effectively, it did not seem that management was sensitive to the information.

The lack of strategic planning and policies, either *ex ante* or *ex post*, coupled with TCC's dividend pay-out policy, further weakened the firm's position in the forwarding market. This suggests that the preparation of MAI had assumed greater importance than the information which was incorporated therein—the means had become the ends. TCC did not seem to adapt its operations in light of the information revealed by these analyses.

Further, while the calculation of profit brought together the related concepts of efficiency and effectiveness, it increasingly shifted TCC's attention to the short-term profit number. This neglected the firm's economic viability in the long run. For example, while TCC's management had sought to change the firm's course via greater investment in more efficient equipment, this option was delayed and later poorly implemented due to TCC's concurrent policy of paying out the major share of its earnings as dividends.

The analysis of accounting change within TCC has affirmed that accounting is embedded within its organizational context, and is not derived from a preordained essence. The emergence and evolution of accounting are the consequence of specific organizational needs and circumstances. In the second phase of TCC, the recognition of internal costs, to mitigate the impact of heightened competition, resulted in the demand for MAI about these internal processes. This emphasis upon cost required a shift in the accounting system from an outward orientation to incorporate an inward focus. Cost as a concept had to be transformed into a discursive category (Hopwood, 1987, p. 216), which was enabled by the creation of MAI to fill the void in TCC's reporting system. The shift from outward-directed to inward-directed information perhaps contributed to TCC's ineffective response to shifts in its operating environment.

Notwithstanding the importance of TCC's exposure to the timber industry, the results of this paper suggest the need to consider additional circumstances which also had an impact upon the firm's survival. Among others, two factors are noteworthy: technological change, and the family style of business.

TCC's failure to remain a viable enterprise can be explained, in part, by its inability to adapt to the technological advances of the late 19th and early 20th centuries. Secondly, its inefficacious shift from a family business to a business enterprise, including the development of an independent managerial hierarchy, contributed to its decline. By negative example, the case of TCC affirms Chandler's (1977, pp. 11, 194) propositions with respect to the economic impact of improved administrative co-ordination, and a shorter business cycle. The latter resulted from the adoption of technological innovations and from market growth. In certain industrial sectors, such as the forwarding trade, the adoption of administrative and technological advances improved the flow of goods and services to the market. Additionally, the managerial hierarchy (as described by Chandler) emerged to dominate the industry. It was not that TCC did not attempt to establish these linkages, primarily through the use of joint ventures; but rather that it did not develop, in parallel, adequate administrative capabilities and human resources to handle these new businesses. TCC required accounting to control its operations, but also to control those responsible for them.

The two factors noted above were not independent. The fiscal policies of the family business, for example, inadequate reinvestment in capital assets, and the high dividend pay-out rate after incorporation, left the firm without the necessary resources to move forward technologically. Accounting was implicated in these circumstances, since the reporting of capital assets helped to sustain the view of dispensable assets. Moreover, in the second phase of TCC, the profit concept was instilled with an importance such that the yearly income number came to dominate survival in the long term. The focus upon costs was oriented to the past, and appeared to influence planning for the firm's continued viability. In short, the accounting and information system reinforced management's traditional tendency to be passive *versus* pro-active.

These examples indicate that the significance of accounting information results from the context in which it is created and utilised. TCC's operations were the basis for the information generated by the reporting system. Yet, this reporting was selective, and its subsequent utilization was influenced by the means of presentation. The preparation of specific reports increased the saliency of the information contained therein. In turn, this emphasis had an impact upon the perception of the firm's management with regard to its alternatives. The failure of TCC to move from a 19th-century partnership to a 20th-century corporation was not distinct from the reporting system which sought to account for this transformation.

The evolution of the accounting system, and the emergence of MAI did not proceed without possibly unanticipated consequences. During TCC's second phase, the accounting and information system appeared to contribute to the firm's inability to forge new strategies and policies. This was a consequence of the system's inherent biases towards the short term and past results, and of its inflexibility. As the accounting became more systematic, it reinforced the perception of TCC's management that its options to innovate were limited at best.

The concept of accounting change is in its early stages of development. The objective of this paper has been to contribute to its elaboration through the delineation of factors which potentially motivate changes in accounting systems. Many of the factors which affected TCC are prevalent in our present global economy. The emergence of activity-based costing (amongst other new measures which attempt to account for technological change and market globalization) has a striking familiarity when considered from an historical perspective. The example of TCC suggests that the examination of these new developments in light of historical experience may be fruitful. In addition, the case of TCC underscores the requirement of future theory development to consider the accounting system not merely as a chronicler of organizational activity, but also as an active participant in its creation.

NOTES

1. The name "The Calvin Company" has been adopted to avoid confusion. The Calvin name was ever-present, although the other partners changed during the company's life.
2. Operations in the United States generally were conducted as joint accounts with individual company agents.
3. This was the largest loss in the firm's history (in current dollars).
4. "Efficiency" refers to the ratio of inputs to outputs, or the amount of output per unit of input. Efficiency is distinct from "effectiveness," which is the relationship between the organization's outputs and its objectives (Anthony et al., 1984, pp. 196–197).
5. The *India* has been selected because the MAI for this ship covers the longest time period (fourteen years). TCC prepared similar information for the other vessels in its fleet.
6. The figures for the Wholesale Price Index (WPI) have been taken from Series J of *Historical Statistics of Canada*, 1965.

REFERENCES

Aitken, H. G. J., "Myth and Measurement: The Innis Tradition in Economic History," *Journal of Canadian Studies*, volume 12, number 5 (Winter 1977).
American Accounting Association, *A Statement of Basic Accounting Theory* (Chicago: 1966).
Anthony, R. N., Dearden, J., & Bedford, N. M., *Management Control Systems*, Fifth Edition (Homewood, Ill.: Richard D. Irwin, Inc., 1984).
Baladouni, V., "The Study of Accounting History," *The Academy of Accounting Historians Working Paper Series*, volume I (1979).

Beatty, S. G., & Clare, S., *Book-keeping by Single and Double Entry* (Toronto: W. J. Gage & Co., 1882).

Beatty, S. G., & Johnson, J. W., *The Canadian Accountant: A Practical System of Book-keeping,* Fifth Edition (Belleville, Canada: The Ontario Business College, 1882).

Bliss, M., *Northern Enterprise: Five Centuries of Canadian Business* (Toronto: Mc-Clelland and Stewart, 1987).

Boyd, M. C., *The Story of Garden Island* (Kingston: Brown & Martin Limited, 1983).

Brief, R. P., *Nineteenth Century Capital Accounting and Business Investment* (New York: Arno Press, 1976).

Brooks, P. C., *Research in Archives* (Chicago: The University of Chicago Press, 1969).

Buckley, K., ''The Role of Staple Industries in Canada's Economic Development,'' *The Journal of Economic History,* volume XVIII (1958).

Burchell, S., Clubb, C., Hopwood, A., Hughes, J., & Nahapiet, J., ''The Roles of Accounting in Organisations and Society,'' *Accounting, Organizations and Society,* volume 5, number 1 (1980).

Calvin, D. D., *A Saga of the St. Lawrence* (Toronto: The Ryerson Press, 1945).

The Calvin Collection, The Marine Museum of the Great Lakes (MMA), Kingston, Ontario.

The Calvin Company Papers, Queen's University Archives (QUA), Kingston, Ontario.

Chandler, A. D., *The Visible Hand: The Managerial Revolution in American Business* (Cambridge, Mass.: The Belknap Press, 1977).

Chatfield, M. (ed.), *Contemporary Studies in the Evolution of Accounting Thought* (Belmont, Cal.: Dickenson Publishing Company, 1968).

Collingwood, R. G., *The Idea of History* (Oxford: Oxford University Press, 1961).

Easterbrook, W., & Aitken, H., *Canadian Economic History* (Toronto: The Macmillan Company 1963).

Edwards, J. R., ''Industrial Cost Accounting Developments in Britain to 1830: A Review Article,'' *Accounting and Business Research* (Autumn 1989).

Edwards, J. R., Hammersley, G., & Newell, E., ''Cost Accounting at Keswick, England, c. 1598–1615: The German Connection,'' *The Accounting Historians Journal,* volume 17, number 1 (June, 1990).

Flamholtz, D. T., ''The Markets and Hierarchies Framework: A Critique of the Model's Applicability to Accounting and Economic Development,'' *Accounting, Organizations and Society,* volume 8, number 2/3 (1983).

Fleishman, R. K., & Parker, L. D., ''British Entrepreneurs and Pre-Industrial Revolution Evidence of Cost Management,'' *The Accounting Review,* volume 66, number 2 (April, 1991).

Hopwood, A., ''The Archaeology of Accounting Systems,'' *Accounting, Organizations and Society,* volume 12, number 3 (1987).

Hoskin, K., & Macve, R., ''Accounting and the Examination: A Geneology of Disciplinary Power,'' *Accounting, Organizations and Society,* volume 11, number 2 (1986).

Hoskin, K., & Macve, R., ''The Genesis of Accountability: The West Point Connection,'' *Accounting, Organizations and Society,* volume 13, number 1 (1988).

Johnson, H. T., & Kaplan, R. S., *Relevance Lost: The Rise and Fall of Management Accounting* (Boston, Mass.: Harvard Business School Press, 1987).

Lisle, G., *Accounting in Theory and Practice,* Revised Edition (Edinburgh: William Green & Sons, 1909).

Littleton, A. C., *Accounting Evolution to 1900* (reissue) (New York: Atheneum, 1966).

Littleton, A. C., & Yamey, B. S. (editors), *Studies in the History of Accounting* (Homewood, Ill.: Richard D. Irwin, Inc., 1956).

Loft, A., "Towards a Critical Understanding of Accounting: The Case of Cost Accounting in the U.K., 1914–1925," *Accounting, Organizations and Society,* volume 11, number 2 (1986).

Lower, A. R. M., *Great Britain's Woodyard* (Toronto: McGill-Queen's University Press, 1973).

Lower, A. R. M., *North American Assault on the Canadian Forest* (Toronto: The Ryerson Press, 1938).

Lower, A. R. M., *Settlement and the Forest Frontier* (Toronto: The Macmillan Company, 1936).

Lower, A. R. M., "The Trade in Square Timber" [1933], in Easterbrook, W. T., & Watkins, M. H., (editors), *Approaches to Canadian Economic History* (Ottawa: Carleton University Press, 1984).

Mann, H., *The Evolution of Accounting in Canada* (Montreal: Touche Ross & Company, 1972).

McCalla, D., *The Upper Canada Trade: A Study of the Buchanan's Business* (Toronto: Univ. of Toronto Press, 1979).

McCalla, D., "An Introduction to the Nineteenth-Century Business World," in Traves, T., (editor), *Essays In Canadian History* (Toronto: McClelland & Stewart Limited, 1984).

McCalla, D., "Forest Products and Upper Canadian Development," *Canadian Historial Review* (April, 1987).

McInnis, R. M., "From Hewn Timber to Sawn Lumber," paper presented at the Eighth International Economic History Congress, August 1982.

McInnis, R. M., "The Competition for the British Timber Market, 1850–1895," unpublished paper, Queen's University, Kingston, Ontario (June, 1989).

Miller, P., & O'Leary, T., "Accounting and the Construction of the Governable Person," *Accounting, Organizations and Society,* volume 12, number 3 (1987).

Miller, P., & O'Leary, T., "Hierarchies and American Ideals," *Academy of Management Review,* volume 14 (1989).

Mintzberg, H., & Waters, J. A., "Of Strategies, Deliberate and Emergent," *Strategic Management Journal,* volume 6 (1985).

Mintzberg, H., "Opening Up the Definition of Strategy" in Quinn, J. B, Mintzberg, H., & Jones, R. M., *The Strategy Process: Concepts, Contexts, and Cases* (Englewood Cliffs, N.J.: Prentice-Hall, 1988).

Murphy, G., "The Evolution of Corporate Reporting Practices in Canada," *The Academy of Accounting Historians Working Paper Series,* volume I (1976).

Murphy, G., "Early Canadian Financial Statement Disclosure Legislation," *The Accounting Historians Journal,* volume 11, number 2 (Fall 1984).

Murphy, G., "A Chronology of the Development of Corporate Financial Reporting in Canada: 1850 to 1983," *The Accounting Historians Journal,* volume 13, number 1, (Spring 1986).

Murphy, G., "Some Eighteenth Century Accounting Treatises," *The Accounting Historians Journal,* volume 12, number 2 (Fall 1987).

Nikitin, M., "Setting up an Industrial Accounting System at Saint-Gobain (1820–1880)," *The Accounting Historians Journal,* volume 17, number 2 (December, 1990).

Norman, C., "A Company Community: Garden Island, Upper Canada at Mid-Century," in Akenson, D., (editor), *Canadian Papers in Rural History,* volume 2 (Gananoque, Canada: Langdale Press, 1980).

Osborne, B., "Kingston in the Nineteenth Century" in Wood, J. D., (ed.), *Perspectives On Landscape and Settlement in Nineteenth Century Canada* (Toronto: McClelland & Stewart, 1975).

Swainson, D., "Garden Island and the Calvin Company," in *Historic Kingston,* volume 28 (1980).

Swainson, D., *Garden Island: A Shipping Empire* (Kingston, Canada: Marine Museum of the Great Lakes, 1984).

Urquhart, M. C., & Buckley, K. A. H., *Historical Statistics of Canada* (Toronto: The MacMillan Co., 1965).

11

Public Sector Accounting in Australia

Robert Gibson

INTRODUCTION

The history of accounting in the public sector in Australia extends over the full two centuries of European settlement but has been a largely neglected field. This is, therefore, an attempt to paint a broad canvas and provide a framework for subsequent, more detailed studies. The term public sector encompasses all activities which involve some form of community accountability. It includes the three tiers of government, federal, state and local government, business enterprises, and a range of quasi-autonomous government organizations (quangos).

For the benefit of foreign readers it is necessary to provide a brief geographical-political outline of Australia. In the 19th century British settlement created six autonomous colonies occupying the continent and Tasmania. Each of these developed a responsible system of government with a governor as representative of the constitutional monarchy and a bicameral legislature. In 1901 the Commonwealth of Australia was created, with powers defined in the constitution. All residual powers remained with the former colonies, which became states of the Commonwealth. The structure of responsible government at commonwealth level is a Governor General representing the constitutional monarchy, a senate elected on a states franchise, and a house of representatives with a universal adult franchise. More recently two territories controlled by the Commonwealth have acquired their own legislatures. There are thus nine governments (excluding municipal authorities) for a nation of 16.8 million people. It is necessary to understand the autonomous constitutional status of the states to comprehend the differences in accounting and audit practice which persist in the country.

For nearly two hundred years there has been little concern shown by politicians, accountants or the community in the state of public sector accounting. This may have been due to the fact that until World War II the tax-financed part of the public sector was relatively small. The development of the welfare state in the postwar years was accompanied by economic growth and full employment. The community had little reason to complain. However, the eighties produced a quite different story. This chapter is intended to outline the accounting developments and then to canvas some propositions as to why a period of little more than a decade produced so different a scene.

COLONIAL PERIOD

There is no doubt that the first accounting in Australia was government accounting, because the first colony of New South Wales was settled as a penal colony. The oldest extant accounting records are those maintained by John McCarthur as paymaster to the New South Wales Corps which administered the colony. These are held in the Mitchell Library in Sydney. For the first forty years the accounts of the colony were part of the records of the British Treasury to whom the local officials were accountable.

When free settlers arrived and some convicts were released (the emancipists) to live freely in the colony there was a pressing need for a monetary system to facilitate dealings between colonists. This was initially resolved by the issue of a form of promissory note by the Storekeeper of the Government Commissariat. Other early examples of how the community overcame these problems are identified by Parker in his account of early trading in New South Wales (NSW). Parker has argued that bookkeeping barter played an essential role in the economic life of early New South Wales until more sophisticated financial systems developed (Parker, 1982). It became a pressing matter to establish the colony's own financial system. It is a measure of the capability of Governor Macquarie that he dismissed the view that he did not have delegated authority from London and in 1817 granted a charter to the Bank of New South Wales. The legality of his action ceased to be of such concern when the bank was incorporated by the Colonial legislature. On the other hand, when the Queensland government was effectively out of cash, Governor Bowen stuck to the letter of the law and refused to sanction the issue of legal tender notes (Sykes, 1988, Chaps. 1 and 5). Associated events provided early evidence of the need for sound financial controls. The first Colonial Treasurer in NSW, William Balcombe, was charged by Governor Darling with depositing public moneys into the Bank of New South Wales when he should have known it was unsafe to do so. Balcombe got off with a caution and instructions to share the deposits equally between the two banks then operating (*Australian Encyclopaedia*, vol. 1, p. 394). Accounting developments may have been retarded because public scrutiny of government finances did not necessarily rest on the evidence of government accounting records. The first major outlay of the Commonwealth was to build the transcontinental railway promised to ensure the participation in the federation of Western Australia. Public debate concerning contracts and preference for using contractors over the use of day labor by the new Cook administration were quite sufficient means to ensure the departure of Dean, the engineer in chief. This was not based on a detailed examination of the railway's accounting records or reports (Burke, 1991, Ch. 6).

ACCOUNTING PERIOD

Most of the government and commercial practices of colonial Australia were transplanted from Britain whence the settlers came. The annual cycle of accounting, however, did not suit the climatic cycle of the antipodes. Professor Arndt provided a colorful insight into how this dilemma was resolved. He has also pointed out how the selection of Canberra as the national capital on the Southern Tablelands of New South Wales where the winters are very cold, in Australian terms, meant that government accounting practices had to change to accommodate the 30 June financial year-end to the rigours of travelling to and living in Canberra (Arndt, 1963).

COMPLIANCE AUDITING

The first hundred and fifty years of government accounting in Australia was undoubtedly dominated by the compliance requirements of the various audit acts. The dominating influence was the provision of adequate documentation and confirmation that all expenditure had been properly appropriated by Parliament. While government was confined to law and order, records of land tenure, and similar activities, this may have been an adequate objective. The growth of other services and the transfer of wealth through taxation and government benefits would mean that in due course the community would expect much better performance from public sector financial managers.

The development of the audit function in New South Wales (NSW) through the period of colonial records maintained for authorities in London, the linking of the colonial office of auditor with membership of the appointed legislature, and the 20th century view of an independent party expressing an opinion on accounts has been well documented (New South Wales, 1963). Perhaps the most famous of early NSW Auditor Generals was William Lithgow who held the post in NSW from the inception of the Treasury Department in 1824 until 1852. During most of this period he was also a member of the appointed Legislative Council. He left politics on the introduction of responsible government. The modern concept of auditor independence was not considered essential at that time (*Australian Encyclopaedia*, vol. 5, p. 340). Similar studies of the other five states and the Commonwealth Auditor General's office so far as we are aware have yet to be documented.

BUDGETS AND APPROPRIATIONS

The emphasis on appropriation and neglect of justification and management of expense with assessment of outcomes persisted until the last two or three decades. As recently as 1964 it was possible to say that the Commonwealth budget papers fell short of the objective of "ensuring an optimum allocation of resources for the overall social benefit and the maximisation of the return or benefit to the object of each item of expenditure" (Gibson, 1964, p. 57).

As recently as 1982 it was possible for Shand to recite this litany of deficiencies in statutory accounts.

Many used only cash-flow accounting, instead of accrual-cost accounting, that all of the authorities dealt with different items in different ways, and that generally there was a strange sort of jam-jar system of funds with no indication of what they were for. (Shand, quoted by Kohler, 1982, p. 60).

In recent years there has been great improvement at the Commonwealth level, but there are still instances where state government budget papers are alleged to be even deliberately misleading. In 1991 the NSW budget papers were changed to show the results for the budget sector rather than just for the consolidated fund. The budget papers explained the previous method used was "misleading." Walker demonstrated how this was closer to the practice of other states, showed a larger deficit but still omitted many liabilities and commitments (Walker, 1991a, p. 16). The failure to reveal the full extent of state liabilities has become a recurring theme of the nineties. In Victoria the Auditor General took up the cudgels against the government (Walker, 1991b, p. 9).

A traditional control device used by Australian governments is the fixed personnel establishment. Changing employment conditions have almost relegated this control to oblivion. In its place is a direct financial appropriation limit. The widespread use of consultants has rendered the control ineffective. For example, in NSW the government employed 4000 consultants over an eight-month period at a cost of $100 million (Cooper, 1989). In one glaring case in Victoria individuals paid out on early retirement were rehired as consultants to maintain the authorities' services.

GOVERNMENT BUSINESS ENTERPRISES

The public sector in Australia developed an unusual characteristic for what is essentially a private enterprise economy. The problems of geography and small population made it inevitable that most public utility functions developed either as government departments or government business enterprises (GBEs).

This included railways, telephones, electricity generation and distribution, water supply, streetcars, tramways, buses, grain elevators, and a host of minor enterprises even including brick kilns and nurseries. Other activities conducted in open competition with private enterprise include banking, insurance, shipping and airlines. The government acquisition of the fledgling railways, all of which failed financially, in the mid-19th century, marked the beginning of this. Many others such as electricity and telephones arose with the advance of twentieth century technology. A desire to provide competitive market forces replaced geography as a motivating force with the entry into banking, insurance, shipping, and airlines in the mid-20th century. Those activities conducted in a competitive role, and some monopolies like electricity, adopted commercial forms of accounting. In some cases they were even subject to normal corporation taxes.

Telephone services were for many years conducted as a department within the annual appropriations. A landmark enquiry in 1961 investigated the accounts of the then Postmaster General's Department and recommended the adoption of commercial accounting treatments of depreciation and interest for what was undoubtedly the largest capitalised service providing activity in the public sector (Australia, *AD Hoc Committee of Enquiry*, 1961). An entirely fresh approach to accounting for GBEs would be initiated by the Victorian Government in the eighties. This is discussed later.

GRANTS COMMISSION

In the 1930s the foundations were laid for a remarkable application of cost accounting concepts in the public sector. The three states of South Australia, Western Australia, and Tasmania faced special financial problems. While the Commonwealth had made ad hoc grants, dissatisfaction with the position led to a threat by Western Australia to secede. The response was the creation of the Commonwealth Grants Commission "with the objective of evolving some principles that would take the determination of special grants out of the arena of political controversy" (Prest, 1965). The notable accountant-educator-administrator, Sir Alexander Fitzgerald, played a key role in developing a system for assessing the financial needs of claimant states by comparison with the non-claimant states after making due allowance for economy in expenditure and effort in raising revenue. For half a century this accounting for needs played a pivotal role in the distribution to the states of tax revenue collected by the Commonwealth.

INTERNAL AUDIT

It was probably about the 1920s before internal audit began to develop as a separate function in Commonwealth departments. In July 1964 all departments were instructed to examine the adequacy of staff and the work done by internal audit. In due course standards were developed which embraced elements of

"financial and compliance" and "economy and efficiency." This work paved
the way for performance auditing and value for money auditing ideas to be
advocated in the following years (Joint Committee of Public Accounts, 1981).
At this stage the author is unaware of any similar documentation pertaining to
internal audit within the six state and two territory administrations.

PERFORMANCE AUDITING

There has been an active debate on the need for specific public sector audit
standards. There has been support by some public sector executives for the view
that auditing standards should be set by the profession (Glynn, 1988, p. 11).
Others see the need for separate standards. As the Commonwealth Auditor
General stated, the Australian Audit Office Standards also include material relating specifically to public accountability and the independence of the Auditor
General. They also set standards for performance auditing (Gibson, 1988–89,
p. 11).

No one issue has raised so many queries about the jurisdiction or authority
of government auditors as the question of performance auditing. The Commonwealth Auditor General originally found authority in Section 54 of the act to
conduct project audits (Glynn, 1987–88, p. 23). The act was amended in 1979
following the Royal Commission on Australian Government Administration.
The amended act was concerned with the efficiency of achieving operational
objectives while the review of effectiveness of programs remained with the
Prime Minister's Department. The Commonwealth Auditor General has identified the limits to his authority to conduct this type of audit.

Departments and agencies are subject to efficiency and performance audits under the
Audit Act. However, in companies the Auditor-General cannot perform an efficiency or
performance audit under section 48 of the *Audit Act* unless specifically requested by a
Minister. The Government has extended the same limitation to government business
enterprises. The Australian National Audit Office (ANAO) has received no requests to
perform such audits of government companies or government business enterprises. As a
result, Government and Parliament do not have the type of independent assurance that
government companies and business enterprises operate in an efficient, effective, and
economical manner that would be provided by an efficiency audit. (Taylor, 1991, p. 9)

The Victorian Auditor General took the view that the existing Audit Act gave
him the power to produce reports on efficiency and effectiveness. The Solicitor
General provided an opinion to Premier Cain rejecting the Auditor General's
view and this was used by the Premier in the Parliament to support a suggestion
to review the Auditor General's role. This was clearly an indirect attempt to
curb the inquisitiveness of the Auditor General (Kirby, 1989). Moves for new
legislation in Victoria have not borne fruit, but the Auditor General has pushed
on with much efficiency auditing work much to the chagrin of an embarrassed

government (Glynn, 1987–88, p. 29). South Australia, with a new Audit Act has made some limited advances and Western Australia has a legislative framework that should lead to the adoption of performance auditing (Glynn, 1987, p. 31).

Not very much progress has been made in the three other states and two territories. It is somewhat stretching the imagination to rely on the assertion that legislation established last century envisaged a role for the Auditor General which would emerge in the last two decades of the 20th century (Monaghan commentary on Glynn, 1987, pp. 27–28).

FINANCIAL MANAGEMENT IMPROVEMENT PROGRAM

In 1984 the Commonwealth, as part of its Financial Management Improvement Program (FMIP), conducted a diagnostic study which demonstrated that 94 per cent of public service managers perceived financial management as spending the allocated amount or not exceeding the legal appropriation limit (Shand, 1988, p. 65). It was clear that fundamental change in attitudes and then in practice would have to be implemented. Shand in 1988 identified the following developments as having taken place.

- The Explanatory Notes prepared for Senate Estimates Committees (which are a budget-related document and publicly available) now contain a greatly increased amount of performance data. We recognise that the development of performance indicators is a lengthy and difficult process. Again we have quite realistic expectations; we certainly do not believe that magical indicators exist which can be plugged directly into the budgetary process and provide a bottom line for the performance measurement of any particular agency. Unfortunately, with one or two notable exceptions, Parliamentarians do not seem to be particularly interested in this information in their equivalent of our Explanatory Notes as 'dynamite waiting to be exploded'. While ours have not reached that stage they do contain some interesting information.

- The new Annual Reporting Guidelines require a significant increase in the amount of performance information reported in departmental and agency annual reports, in particular information on the results of major review or evaluations which have taken place during the year.

- Departments are required to set out as part of the budgetary process the proposed evaluation arrangements for all new policy proposals.

- Departments are required to develop evaluation plans so as to provide a systematic and formalised approach to the undertaking of program evaluation. (Shand, 1988, p. 70).

In 1984 the Commonwealth government issued a Policy Paper of Budget Reform which announced the intention to implement program budgeting. There is not a view that this will be a "quick fix" but rather a long haul.

PROGRAM BUDGETING

The Labor Party gained office in Victoria in 1982 and announced its intention to introduce program budgeting. Considerable progress has been made and in 1988 was summarized thus:

An important inclusion in the 1986–87 Budget Papers was the program structure for each Ministry (program, sub-program and component levels), on the grounds that while the Budget Papers generally provided information only at the program level, it would be helpful to readers in their understanding of program expenditure purposes to know the sub-program and component elements of each program.

Ministers were again responsible in 1986–87 and 1987–88 for the production of their own supplementary program budgeting information, and this information was sought by the Parliamentary Estimates Committees which were established in these years. The Committee which examined 1986–87 Budget estimates was a Legislative Council one, but a Joint House Committee was established to ensure 1987–88 (sic. examine) Budget estimates.

Other supporting information was also being produced by budget sector agencies in their annual reports, the requirements for which were strengthened with the introduction of the Annual Reporting Act 1983 and complementary regulations. The agency annual report was the main vehicle for reporting on performance of agencies over the past year and, given the introduction of PB, has developed an increasing program focus. The regulations were modified in 1987–88 to provide for the inclusion of sub program information for the budget year (previously the regulations applied only to data for the year just ended). (quoted from *FINET,* March 1988 [Victoria])

ACCOUNTING STANDARDS

The community face of public sector accounting is the form of financial reporting. In 1982 the Joint Committee of Public Accounts of the Commonwealth Parliament (JCPA) identified the need for public sector accounting standards. The accounting profession responded within two years by appointing the Public Sector Accounting Standards Board (PSASB) (JCPA, quoted by Gibson, 1988–89, p. 9). The Department of Finance responded in 1983 by issuing guidelines requiring Commonwealth GEBs to adopt Australian Accounting Standards (ibid., p. 10). The PSASB has subsequently pursued an active program of standard setting. It has also been involved in discussions with a view to merging the boards dealing with the private and public sector.

The intention of the accounting profession is that standards issued by the PSASB should be adopted by all government units in the country. Some hold the view that there is a gap between what the standards offer and the public desire for accountability. There is likewise a gap between the standard setters' expectations and the public sector accounting staff capacity. Carpenter, Chairman of PSASB, discussing these issues concluded:

Many accountants in the public sector, including members of the Society, have not in the past had to deal with accounting standards and consequently have limited knowledge of existing or proposed statements of accounting concepts, accounting standards and guidance releases. With wider application of the profession's standards there is a need for a greater emphasis on training and development and more frequent openings of the Society's blue binders to refer to accounting standards and other publications of the accounting profession.

One of the challenges for any standard setting board is to develop standards which are likely to be applied in practice. It seems to me that the environment is now more open to changes in and development of reporting for non-business Government activities than certainly was the case some four or five years ago. (Carpenter, 1991, p. 111)

ANNUAL REPORTING

The quality and timeliness of financial reporting has been significantly improved by the passage of financial reporting legislation in New South Wales and Victoria (Shand, 1989, p. 141). In New South Wales the Annual Reports (Statutory Bodies) Act 1984 and consequent amendments to the Public Finance and Audit Act 1983 were closely aligned to the subsequent Annual Report (Departments) Act 1985 and further amendments to the Public Finance and Audit Act 1983. This legislation sets the general reporting requirement for, and the content of, departmental financial statements and has been supplemented by detailed regulations (viz. Public Finance and Audit Regulation 1984, Public Finance and Audit (Departments) Regulation 1986 and Annual Reports (Departments) Regulation 1986). The requirement for departments to prepare and present their own audited financial statements reinforces the responsibility of individual departments for their own financial management. A summary of the legislative requirements in each of the states and the Commonwealth has been prepared by Carnegie (1990, pp. 62–63).

RATE OF RETURN REPORTING

Perhaps the most interesting development in Australian public sector accounting has been the move in 1982 to adopt rate of return reporting to specified GBEs in Victoria. The Labor Party (a socialist party) had been in opposition for 32 of the preceding 35 years. Its political agenda included the levy of a community dividend from seven major GBEs based on real returns. Thus at a time when the private sector was abandoning its attempts to introduce current cost accounting, the public sector was actively instituting it. These reports were issued commencing with the financial year ended June 1986 and three of the GBEs included a formal Auditor General's opinion on the rate of return statements in the following year (Carpenter, 1990, p. 192).

PUBLIC BODIES

A natural outcome of all of this activity directed at improving financial management and reporting has been a new emphasis on sub-units within the public sector and the management of those units. A variety of organisational and legal forms have been adopted to conduct government activity. A Senate committee investigated companies which are beyond direct government control, created by the Commonwealth. What it found was described thus by the chairman:

In the event, we were able to identify 388 companies: 208 were fully controlled by the Commonwealth and all but 13 of these were subsidiaries of other companies or of statutory authorities. There were 55 associated companies or those in which the Commonwealth's interest was 20%–50%, 58 companies limited by guarantee and 67 incorporated associations. Those are the figures in our report, but even during its printing we learned of three more. (Coates, 1989, p. 205)

Further information from the Auditor General showed the number of such units identified to be an exploding number. A 1990 Senate Standing Committee Report found 449 companies and incorporated associations, while the 1991 Report found 494 companies and incorporated associations (Taylor, 1991, p. 5).

The multiplicity of such entities was highlighted by the activities of the Public Bodies Review Committee of the Victorian Parliament, which estimated there were over 1000 such bodies within the activities of the Victorian Government (Schultz, 1980). The subsequent activities of this Committee have resulted in major changes in the corporate structure of some government activities.

CORPORATIZATION

Separate financial entities encourage the adoption of management structures reflecting those entities. Likewise the financial performance concentrates on the separate entity. There has thus developed what is described as corporatisation with managerial leadership. This development can be seen as reflecting a competitive market role when applied to many of the competitive GBEs. However, a similar approach is being applied in areas including universities, hospitals, and even some social service enterprises.

The managerialist approach and corporatization has brought with it a new interest in the application of accrual accounting. So long as public sector management concentrated on expenditure appropriations and compliance auditing cash based accounting served the purpose. However, such cash-based systems have deficiencies. Many government entities did not have any asset registers. Thus the absence of the need for accounting brought a lack of physical control. The absence of accrual accounting has meant that vast liabilities have neither been assessed or recorded. The failure to accrue revenue and charges has also meant that there was not any economic assessment of the efficiency with which much government activity was undertaken (Walker, 1988).

The pressure for accrual accounting has led to considerable development of accounting in the public sector. Scullion's account of the introduction in NSW provides an ample list of the difficulties centred mainly on asset registers, staffing, information systems and training (Scullion, 1991). The NSW Land Commission was credited with being the first statutory authority in Australia to prepare its accounts in conformity with current professional accounting standards in 1979 (Davis, 1979, p. 433). In particular, the commission was lauded for writing down land holdings to current market value. This precedent must surely be based on entities other than GBEs incorporated as companies. Whatever the truth of the claim by Davis these accounts did mark the beginning of a new era in financial accountability.

All of the developments discussed so far depend on a simple analogy with the ownership and control dichotomy of private enterprise. There is limited evidence to suggest that a more complex model is being more widely recognised. McCrae has developed a three-part model based on public interest, agency and political interest accountability. His concluding paragraph bears quoting.

Perhaps what is required is a change of emphasis. Mechanical concepts of performance efficiency and effectiveness can only go so far in keeping management honest. Unfortunately these concepts have been embraced by many public sector reform agencies as if they will solve all of the problems of producing a ''leaner'' corporate entity type public sector bodies. What must be recognised is that such terms do not represent absolute concepts of performance measurement with universal applicability. They are concepts which only take on meaning in specific situations, and can be used for political as well as economic ends. Unless carefully used, they may be positively detrimental since they encourage managers to bias performance to achieve optimum short-run economic performance at the expense of longer term improvement or principles of public interest. (McCrae, 1991, p. 20).

There is some evidence of an awareness in the bureaucracy of these aspects of accountability. One of the by-products of corporatization and privatization is a fresh recognition of the community service obligations (CSO) of many GBEs. It has sometimes been these obligations which caused the activity to become a government enterprise.

The Bureau of Transport and Communications Economics (BTCE) completed a full study of Telecom (the telephone authority). The BTCE estimated the avoidable costs of CSOs, that is, losses that would be avoided if the services were not provided, to be $230 million in 1987–88 with capital evaluated at a 13.6 per cent real interest rate. The 13.6 per cent rate was the return Telecom earned on assets valued at replacement costs in that year. At a 10 per cent rate, the discount rate traditionally advocated by Treasury, the cost of CSOs was estimated to be $168 million.

To these estimates should be added net costs of:

- up to $5 million for concession to disabled customers and public institutions;

- up to $10 million representing the loss on public telephones not fully taken into account in the model used to derive the above; and

- $47 million for pensioner concessions funded by the Departments of Social Security and Veterans Affairs. (Haddad, 1991, p. 7)

This is a new approach to such obligations and leads to their identification in the annual budget. This provides much more accountability than past practices of submerging these costs within the overall results of individual GBEs.

COMMENTARY

The eighties began with economic recession, aggravated by serious drought. The long rule of Liberal party (free enterprise) government ended and the Labor party formed the Commonwealth and four state governments. Some of these were strongly reformist and saw the reform of government administration as part of the means of facilitating social change. This was a particularly important force in the Commonwealth and in Victoria. Although there was quick recovery from the drought, the decade would have sluggish economic activity and end with unemployment set to be the worst since the great depression of the thirties. The accord between the unions and government held down wages and hence inflation. It also excluded fiscal policy as an economic management tool. In a country dedicated to tariff protection of manufacturing industry for nearly a century, a union-based party became converted to lead the world in creating the tariff-bare "level playing field." That shut down industries and created unemployment. Reliance on monetary policy in an internationalized economy and the free flow of imports led to extraordinarily high real interest rates to continue the flow of capital to pay for the flood of imports. The consequences of these interest rates on government debt was to commit larger proportions of state government budgets to service debt. Thus a group of avowed socialist governments suddenly became converts to the idea of selling off or privatizing GBEs to reduce debt. The level of unemployment and a sluggish economy at the same time put pressure on budgetary management. The inability to raise taxes, when in truth the accord with the unions promised tax reductions, created the need for improved efficiency and performance. Thus the economic events of the eighties had an impact which led Labor party governments to undertake the changes described above and in many respects behave more as though they were the free enterprise, private ownership advocates.

CONCLUSION

Earlier it was observed that appropriations and compliance auditing dominated financial management of the public sector in Australia for at least a century and a half. Major change has occurred in the last decade at a rate which if it continues will result in emphasis and purpose of financial management in the public sector. These changes have deliberately sought to increase control and ensure tighter financial control over public sector entities. Ironically these advances have come out of a decade which has seen the collapse of more than 16 major private sector entrepreneurs and many companies in distress due to the failure of financial management during a decade of easy credit in part due to deregulation of financial institutions.

REFERENCES

Arndt, H. W., "The Financial Year," *Australian Quarterly,* vol. 35, no. 2 (June, 1963): pp. 51–56, reprinted in Parker, R. H. (ed.), *Accounting in Australia, Historical Essays* (New York: Garland, 1989).

Australia, *Reports of the Ad Hoc Committee of Enquiry into the Commercial Accounts of the Post Office* (Canberra: Govt. Printer, 1961).

Australian Encyclopaedia, Chisholm, A. H. (editor-in-chief) (Sydney: Angus & Robertson, 1958).

Burke, David, *Road Through the Wilderness* (Sydney: New South Wales University Press, 1991).

Carnegie, G. D., *Timing and Frequency of Financial Reporting,* Discussion Paper No. 15 (Melbourne: AARF, 1990).

Carpenter, G. J., "Rate of Return Reporting in Australia," *Public Finance and Accounting Finance* (1988), reprinted in Guthrie, James, Parker, Lee, and Shand, David, *The Public Sector, Contemporary Readings in Accounting and Auditing* (Sydney: Harcourt Brace Jovanovich, 1990).

Carpenter, G. J., "Accounting Standards—Public Expectations," in International Accountants in Government Convention, *Speakers Papers* (Gold Coast, Australia: 1991): pp. 106–112.

Coates, J., "Government owned Companies and Subsidiaries—Issues in Accounting, Auditing and Accountability," from Twilight Seminar on Government Companies: Their Accounting, Auditing and Accountability (1989), reprinted in Guthrie, James, Parker, Lee, and Shand, David, *The Public Sector, Contemporary Readings in Accounting and Auditing* (Sydney: Harcourt Brace Jovanovich, 1990).

Cooper, Jeni, "Consultants Cost Greiner $100m," *Australian* (22 September 1989): p. 2.

Davis, Ian, "Accounting Changes by Commission," *Australian Financial Review* (22 March 1979).

Davis, Ian, "Adoption of Commercial Accounting Standards by the NSW Government's Land Commission," *Australian Accountant* (August, 1979): pp. 433–441.

Gibson, Robert W., "Classification in the Budget," in Australian Society of Accountants, *Prize Winning Papers* (Melbourne: Australian Society of Accountants, 1964): pp. 57–80.

Gibson, Robert, "The Public Sector Accounting Standards Board and the Joint Committee of Public Accounts," *Accounting History Newsletter,* no. 17 (Summer 1988–89): pp. 9–11.

Glynn, John J., *The Development of Performance Auditing in Australia,* Research Lecture in Government Accounting, with commentary by J. V. Monaghan, Australian Society of Accountants, Canberra, 1987.

Glynn, John, "The Jurisdiction of the Commonwealth and States Auditor-General," *Accounting History Newsletter,* no. 15 (Summer 1987–88): pp. 23–33.

Glynn, John, "The Development of Public Sector Audit Standards in Australia," *Accounting History Newsletter,* no. 16 (Winter 1988): pp. 9–13.

Haddad, M., *Community Service Obligations,* paper presented at International Accountants in Government Convention, Gold Coast, Australia, 1991.

Hamburger, P., "Efficiency Auditing by the Australian Audit Office: Reform and Reaction Under Three Auditors—General," *Accounting Auditing and Accountability Journal* (1989): pp. 3–21.

Joint Committee of Public Accounts, *Internal Audit in the Australian Public Service—A Discussion Paper,* Report 184, Australian Government Publishing Service, 1981, Parliamentary Paper No. 1/1981, pp. 9–10 and 29–32. Reprinted in *Accounting History Newsletter,* No. 17 (Summer 1988–89): pp. 12–16.

Kirby, James, "Backing for Vic Auditor-General in Dispute with Govt.," *Australian Financial Review* (4 May 1989).

Kohler, Alan, "Accountants Lusting after re-Formed Govt. Figures," *Australian Financial Review* (17 March 1982): p. 60.

McCrae, Michael, "The Financial Accountability Structures of Australian Public Enterprise—A Descriptive Model," *Occasional Paper No. 120* (Faculty of Commerce, Deakin University, 1991).

New South Wales, "Origin and Development of the Audit of the Accounts of the State," Appendix I, *Office Manual,* NSW Auditor General's Office, 1963, pp. 214–241. Reprinted in Parker, R. H. (ed.), *Accounting in Australia, Historical Essays* (New York: Garland, 1989): pp. 273–300.

Parker, Robert H., "Bookkeeping Barter and Current Cash Equivalents in Early New South Wales," *Abacus* (December, 1982): pp. 139–151, reprinted in Parker, R. H. (ed.), *Accounting in Australia, Historical Essays* (New York: Garland, 1989), and in Parker, R. H., *Papers on Accounting History* (New York: Garland, 1984).

Parker, R. H., *Accounting in Australia, Historical Essays* (New York: Garland, 1989).

Prest, Wilfred, "AAF and the Commonwealth Grants Commission," in Chambers, R. J., Goldberg, L., and Mathews, R. L. (eds.), *The Accounting Frontier* (Melbourne: Cheshire, 1965), reprinted in Parker, R. H. (ed.), *Accounting in Australia, Historical Essays* (New York: Garland, 1989).

Schultz, Julianne, "Victoria Gets Watchdog for 1000 Public Bodies," *Australian Financial Review* (1 May 1980).

Scullion, R., "Accrual Accounting," in International Accountants in Government Convention, *Speakers Papers* (Gold Coast, Australia: 1991): pp. 27–30.

Shand, D. A., "Financial Management Improvement in Government—Where Are We At?" ASA (Vic.) State Congress, *Proceedings* (October, 1988), reprinted in Guthrie, J., Parker, Lee, and Shand, D., *The Public Sector, Contemporary Readings in Accounting and Auditing* (Sydney: Harcourt Brace Jovanovich, 1990): pp. 62–77.

Shand, D. A., "Public Sector Accounting Standards—Progress on Implementation in Australia," ASA (Queensland) State Congress, *Proceedings* (1989), reprinted in Guthrie, J., Parker, Lee, and Shand, D., *The Public Sector, Contemporary Read-*

ings in Accounting and Auditing (Sydney: Harcourt Brace Jovanovich, 1990): pp. 139–154.

Sykes, Trevor, *Two Centuries of Panic: A History of Corporate Collapse in Australia* (Allen & Unwin, 1988).

Taylor, John C., AO, *Accountability under Commercialisation,* paper presented at International Accountants in Government Convention, Gold Coast, Australia, 1991.

[Victoria], "Program Budgeting in Victoria," *Accounting History Newsletter,* no. 16 (Winter 1988): pp. 6–8, reprinted from *FINET* (March, 1988).

Walker, R. G., "Accrual Accounting—Necessary but Not Sufficient," *Report of Proceedings of the Accrual Accounting Seminar* (Sydney: NSW Government Printer, 1988), reprinted in Guthrie, James, Parker, Lee, and Shand, David, *The Public Sector, Contemporary Readings in Accounting and Auditing* (Sydney: Harcourt Brace Jovanovich, 1990): pp. 155–162.

Walker, Bob, "NSW Budget Format Has Changed—But What About the Guarantees?" *New Accountant* (17 October 1991): p. 16 (Walker, 1991a).

Walker, Bob, "The Problem With Public Sector Systems," *New Accountant* (14 November 1991): p. 9 (Walker, 1991b).

12

Notice on the Meat Supply in Burgos, 1536–1537: Ledger of the Town Meat Purveyor

Esteban Hernández-Esteve

INTRODUCTION

This paper is a summary of much more extensive research, expressly undertaken for this Sixth World Congress of Accounting Historians in Kyoto, which has been published in Spanish by the Research Department of the Bank of Spain and should be consulted for further details on the subject, as well as for references and notes. (Esteban Hernández-Esteve: *Noticias del abastecimiento de carne en la ciudad de Burgos (1536–1537). Libro Mayor del obligado de las carnicerías,* Banco de España, Servicio de Estudios, Estudios de Historia Económica, no. 23, Madrid, 1992.)

The purpose of this research is to study the meat supply in Burgos in the business year from 24 June 1536 to 24 June 1537. It is mainly based on a manuscript previously unknown: the *libro de Caxa* or Ledger of the meat purveyor of Burgos, i.e., the person who had agreed to service the town's meat supply during that period. I found this manuscript and other documents used in this investigation in the General Archives of Simancas or in the Municipal Archives of Burgos.

The Ledger of the Burgos meat purveyor is a notable contribution to the Castilian account books that are currently known. In fact, leaving aside the accounting records of Diego Ordóñez of 1518, presented by Carlos Alvarez García and on which I made some comments from the accounting history standpoint, this is chronologically the first account book unmistakably kept according to the double entry system that we know of. On the other hand, this new contribution to the Spanish accounting records of the first half of the 16th century is also to be welcomed for its contents. The account books of that period chiefly deal with banking operations, commercial transactions, or public affairs. This new document, which shows how books were kept in a meat business, will undoubtedly increase our knowledge on the accounting systems used in that period, specifically on the chart of accounts in which operations were recorded in that trade.

Moreover, besides the accounting history aspect, the analysis of the data appearing in the Ledger of the Burgos meat purveyor from St. John's day of 1536 to the same day of 1537 is also of some importance from the economic history aspect. It will allow us to get acquainted with the mechanics of meat supply in a town like Burgos, which had approximately 12,000 to 13,000 inhabitants in 1530, and will provide information on many other particulars, such as livestock-supplying markets and purchase prices; livestock driving and maintenance costs; form of financing; meat consumption in Burgos in all the weeks of the year, broken down by mutton and beef; selling prices by type of meat; use of slaughtered animal by-products; costs of supply service and profit or loss obtained; name of persons involved, etc. All of it is of the utmost interest because, apart from the capital, Madrid, the supply of Spanish towns in the early modern age has been scarcely studied.

Therefore, the investigation has a twofold purpose. In the first place, we shall study the meat supply in Burgos in the mentioned business year within the stated partial areas and objectives. In the second place, we shall analyze the document from the accounting history viewpoint in order to study not only the formal features of the book and its entries but also the type of accounts which were used and how, the recording procedures followed and their results. Particular emphasis shall be put on the special features observed in the light of the current accounting systems and of the early double entry bookkeeping methods used in Castile. The accounting methods used by the Burgos meat purveyor will also be assessed, assessment that will obviously not be referred to current requirements but to the needs that apparently had to be met by that accounting system.

To fulfil these purposes, after this Introduction in which the subject of the investigation and its sources, purposes, and methodology have been described, this presentation will be divided into three sections. Thus, the second section will study the meat supply in Burgos in the period mentioned, paying special attention to service conditions, livestock purchases, financing, and meat sales, as well as organization and operation of the meat business. The third section will examine the accounting history aspect, starting with formal features, before describing the type of accounts used, how they were handled and the accounting procedures followed. Finally, the fourth section, or conclusions, will summarize the main results of the research.

MEAT SUPPLY IN BURGOS

Service Conditions

As it occurred in Madrid, and possibly in most of the Castilian towns of that period, in Burgos the meat supply was entrusted, on an exclusive basis and for a given period, to a lessee or contractor who undertook to comply with previously agreed conditions and selling prices. The person or persons in charge of that service in Burgos in the period mentioned did not seem to make much profit on it, unless a higher selling price than the one prevailing in the region was agreed. For that reason, the town council had difficulty in finding somebody willing to accept that service and had to request emperor Charles V to authorize the collection of a *sisa* or tax on the wine sold in the town. The purpose of that tax was to raise 2,000 ducats, i.e. 750,000 maravedis, to finance the meat purveyor in order to make the operation more attractive and to find a person willing to take charge of the meat supply at a selling price that would not be too costly to consumers. Charles V conferred this power to the town council by a warrant issued on 17 February 1536, after duly studying the case and hearing the opinion of his Council.

As predicted in the document sent to the emperor by the Burgos town council, the second quarter of 1536 must have been particularly hard in this respect, since the difficulties undergone with respect to the meat supply are repeatedly stressed in the Council meetings. In fact, the usual problems were increased this time by an additional difficulty that worsened the situation: the infectious disease which affected a flock of rams purchased in Tarifa that died without any apparent reason. Once the disease was detected, the town council decided to suspend immediately the slaughter and sale of these rams and to find as quickly as possible a new meat purveyor willing to take charge of this service for one year as from St. John's day, i.e., 24 June, which was the usual term for these types of contracts. Finally, after various attempts, the Council discussed and approved on Thursday, 18 May 1536, the offer presented by Gregorio Guerra, denizen of the town, to assume the meat supply and management of the butchery business in Burgos. The contract provided, among other conditions, that the offerer undertook to supply to the town beef and mutton of good quality, from St. John's day of 1536 to the same day of 1537, at the price of 22 maravedis per quarter of mutton and 16 maravedis per quarter of beef.

The remaining conditions would be the same as in previous years in which the service had been awarded to Ortega Martínez and his partners.

At the same time, Gregorio Guerra claimed the right to farm the *alcabala* or sales tax on meat on the basis of a fixed price for the time he wished within the term for which the arrangement with the Crown was concluded. This price would be the same as the one at which this rent (tax) was awarded to the town at the time.

On the other hand, the council would assign him the Entrambasaguas meadow and the town's common for the exclusive use of the livestock that would supply meat to the town. He could also use the slaughterhouse and other butchery's premises and facilities for which he would pay a rent.

The unit of weight used in the sale of meat was the quarter, as mentioned in Gregorio Guerra's offer. This quarter was the fourth part of the *arrelde,* as specified in several entries of the ledger under review. It seems that the *arrelde* used in Burgos to weigh meat was, as established by King Alfonso X the Wise on 7 March 1261, the tenth part of a quintal or *centipodium,* i.e., one hundred pounds. Thus, the quarter or fourth part of an *arrelde* would be two and-a-half pounds, i.e., forty ounces. The Castilian pound had sixteen ounces. As the pound weighed approximately 460.093 grams, and the ounce 28.75581 grams, translated into the decimal metric system, the quarter weighed 1.1502325 kilograms.

Livestock Purchases

As soon as the agreement with the town council was signed, Gregorio Guerra undertook to purchase the livestock required to supply meat to the town. These purchases were made in stages, in various markets, sometimes very distant from Burgos, and at different prices according to the market, to the time of purchase and also probably to the weight of the animals, which is never mentioned. The purchases were made through a fixed agent, Bartolomé de Cevico, to whom Gregorio Guerra paid a salary for his services, and through other persons on several occasions. In some cases, the meat purveyor travelled himself to buy cattle.

In total, 1,026 head of cattle were purchased for a total price of 2,795,281 maravedis. The average price per animal was 2,724.40 maravedis. This price included the *alcabala,* or sales tax, and the *sisa* (another tax on sales), if any, as well as in some cases transport, maintenance, and salary expenses of the persons who where in charge of purchasing the animals and driving them to Burgos, if they were bought in other places. Table 12.1 shows the distribution of cattle purchases by month, as well as the average purchase price.

The main supplying markets were Segovia and Benavente, well above the other places, because they provided around 40 per cent of the cattle purchased, followed by Cervera, Villadiego, Sasamón, and Melgar, near Burgos; Saldaña and León; Medellín, Alba, Medina de Rioseco, El Espinar, Reinosa and Herrera. These places supplied in total 89 per cent of the cattle purchased in the year in which Gregorio Guerra was the town meat purveyor. The remainder was purchased by small batches or loose animals in the Burgos market itself or in unspecified places, possibly the Burgos market in many cases. The best average prices were obtained in the markets of Villadiego, Sasamón, and Melgar, as well as in Medina de Rioseco. The highest prices were paid in Medellín, El Espinar, and Segovia.

Table 12.1
Purchases and Unit Prices of Cattle, 1536–1537

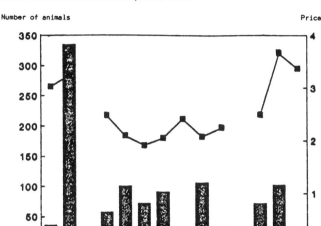

As regards sheep, in the mentioned year, 11,911 rams were purchased for a total cost of 3,594,805 maravedis, at an average price per animal of 301.80 maravedis. As for cattle, the price also includes the sales tax and the purchasing and transport expenses, when they are known. Table 12.2 shows the monthly purchases and the average monthly prices.

The first and most important batches of rams were bought in Burgos as soon as the meat supply agreement was signed. Some of these flocks were purchased from prominent traders of the town. Others were purchased from the town council, probably absorbing the surplus of the former meat supply period. Among these last purchases was the Tarifa flock of rams that caused so much concern. The prices obtained in these purchases made in the town itself were among the lowest of the period, although it would be too hazardous to make assumptions in this respect, since the weight of the animals is not known and it depended, among others, on the period of the year, pastures available, etc. However, at the end of August or beginning of September, when the possibilities of the town and its surroundings were exhausted, it was necessary to send an agent to Medina de Rioseco where rams were purchased twice in the period. Also, without discarding the possibility of purchases in the region or in less distant places, an expedition was sent as far as Extremadura where large flocks of rams were bought not only in the region proper, in Mérida and Badajoz, but also on the way, in El Espinar, Peñaranda, and Puente del Arzobispo. In many cases, the Ledger does not specify the places where the rams were bought, especially when they were purchased in Burgos where Gregorio Guerra used to buy himself. At any rate, other places are

Table 12.2
Purchases and Unit Prices of Rams, 1536–1537

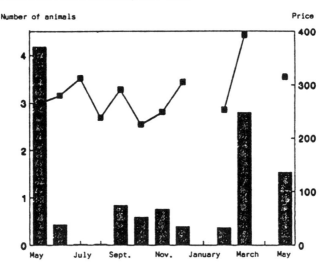

mentioned, such as Campos, Monasterio de Rodilla, Villadiego, Santesteban, Castrillo and Saldaña, Palenzuela, etc. Still, Burgos was by far the most important market for the purchase of rams, although this does not mean that all the animals bought in that town came from its surroundings.

When the livestock arrived in Burgos, it was led to the "meat meadows" where it was entrusted to the care of the shepherds hired by Gregorio Guerra for that purpose. It seems that several persons were in charge of that task, if we judge by the amounts paid every week by Gregorio Guerra for their food allowances or *misiones,* as they were called, that, in some cases or in all of them, probably also covered salaries.

Financing

As mentioned above, in the year in which Gregorio Guerra was in charge of the meat supply in Burgos, 1,026 head of cattle and 11,911 rams were purchased for a total cost of 6,390,086 maravedis. This amount included taxes and duties (*alcabala, sisas, achaques, penas,* etc.), as well as all other direct purchasing and transport expenses which could be identified and attributed to specific items such as maintenance and lodging expenses of purchasing agents, shepherds and pack animals, shepherds' salaries, or even tolls, etc. This considerable amount of 6,390,086 maravedis was gradually raised and payments were made in stages over the business year, so that most of the purchases were obviously financed with the proceeds of the sale as slaughtered animals. However, a strong initial financing was required and was provided by a distinguished Burgos merchant,

Table 12.3
Cumulative Financing Requirements

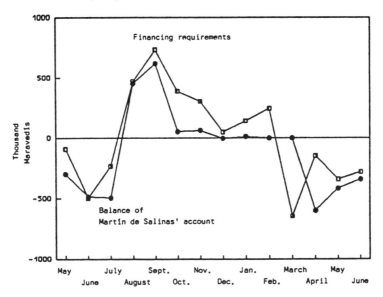

Martín de Salinas, who was prior of the Burgos Merchants' University and Consulate, since the lending fund authorized by Charles V had apparently not yet been constituted. The capacity in which Martín de Salinas assumed this role is not known but the fact is that he not only financed directly the operations but also acted as coordinator and even provided refinancing when it appeared to be necessary. It does not seem that he obtained any profit from that work but there is no evidence that he suffered any damage either, apart from the work and efforts displayed, because refinancing costs were paid for by the account of the town meat purveyor.

In a few cases, Gregorio Guerra also appealed to other financing sources without resorting to Martín de Salinas' services or even mediation, but this occurred very sporadically. In some occasions, especially at the beginning of the business year, the large purchases of livestock were settled through the deferred payment of all or part of the amount of the operation in one or more instalments. Other times, purchases were paid with cash and, if they were very large, the purchasing agents received the funds required before setting off or even after arriving at their destination. In almost all these cases, Martín de Salinas was also involved in one way or another.

The important role played by Martín de Salinas in the financing of the Burgos meat supply is evidenced by Table 12.3, which compares the cumulative financing requirements of the meat business by month (negative amounts) and the balance of Martín de Salinas' account in the purveyor's ledger.

At any rate, rotating around the central financing figure of Martín de Salinas, Gregorio Guerra used a wide range of resources and methods to finance the meat supply in Burgos in the year in which it was under his responsibility.

The main financing resource used by Gregorio Guerra was the deferred payment of livestock purchases, chiefly through bills or orders for payment drawn on Martín de Salinas or through simple payments at maturity made directly to livestock sellers. In other cases, financing was obtained through advances made by Martín de Salinas to provide funds to the livestock purchasing agents. Loans by bankers or individuals were used as well and were also reimbursed through bills drawn on Martín de Salinas.

As far as it can be seen, drafts were largely used in the financing and payment procedures followed in all the processes. They were also used to repay the amounts advanced by Martín de Salinas.

All these money orders were used taking advantage of the possibilities offered by the four fairs that constituted the general payment circuit of Castile, i.e., the May and October fairs of Medina del Campo, the August fair of Medina de Rioseco, and the Lent fair of Villalón.

Recourse was also made to financing provided by the buyers of slaughtered animal byproducts through supply agreements, with the advance payment of a given amount.

It is especially interesting to analyze the refinancing channels used by Martín de Salinas. There is a continued and substantial appeal—always above 400,000 maravedis—to financing provided by bills drawn on Flanders and sold to various money deliverers. These bills were drawn on an employee working for Salinas in Bruges who would retake on Castile the money disbursed, plus the expenses of the operation, if any, by issuing and selling new bills.

In this way, it was possible to raise money during five or six months while bills were coming and going. When these repayment bills were paid in Castile, new financing was raised by drawing and selling new bills and the process started all over again. The commission paid for finding money deliverers and for mediation services was 0.7 per thousand in the cases in which it has been possible to ascertain the amount.

In other cases, Martín de Salinas obtained refinancing or prefinancing through direct loans granted by a Burgos *cambio* or bank. In all the cases in which lending was sought either by Martín de Salinas, in his capacity of financer or intermediary, or directly by Gregorio Guerra or his treasurer, Francisco de Porres, this fact was by no means concealed in the Ledger entries. An interest rate called *contado* and ranging between 12 and 20 per thousand of the principal was paid on these loans during the lending period that was, in some cases, slightly over one month.

The collection and payment of bills in the payment periods of the fairs also implied in many cases the collection and payment of *contados*. The contados disbursed by Martín de Salinas when paying the bills drawn on him to cover the deferred payment of livestock purchases amounted to 6 per thousand, while those received when collecting the repayment bills covering his advances reached 12 per thousand.

In one case only, the expression *contado* is used in the sense—that seems to be the most customary one in that period or at least the best known up to now—of penalty or discount for raising cash money upon presentation of a bill or money order before the end of the payment period.

Finally, it may be interesting to observe that the terminology used for the drawing, purchasing and selling of domestic bills or money orders was very similar to that used for bills of exchange. Thus, it was quite common, when purchasing from a money taker a money order drawn on a given fair, to say that so many maravedis or ducats had been delivered to be paid to so-and-so in such a fair or at such a date. This similar terminology shows that the clear parallelism between domestic bills and bills of exchange as financing instruments was recognized, regardless of their function as means of transfer and placement of funds in other towns or countries to be collected in a different currency.

Meat Sales

This section is in no way intended to describe all the meat consumption of Burgos, which was not limited to mutton and beef, but also included game and poultry. On the other hand, pork was also sold outside the town meat purveyor's circuit, as mentioned in Guerra's Ledger. Therefore, this section will deal with the mutton and beef sales made in the town purveyor's shops from 24 June 1536 to 7 June 1537, the date on which the last entries are recorded in the Ledger under review, which is suddenly interrupted on that day. These sales are specified in the Ledger, week after week, during the period mentioned. At any rate, this information should be interpreted with great care when trying to attribute a meaning to these figures, avoiding the temptation to believe that they reflect faithfully the mutton and beef consumption of the inhabitants of Burgos. As it still occurs nowadays, it is possible that merchants from neighboring villages would come regularly to Burgos to buy meat in order to resell it in their own towns. Therefore, it would be risky to draw per capita consumer indexes from the figures available.

Among the data provided by the Ledger under study, we shall first examine the average weights of slaughtered animals. The average carcass weight of oxen and cows sold throughout the business year follows a very regular pattern, although large weight differences appear as a whole: the maximum average weight by animal, reached in May 1537, is 243 kilograms; the minimum average weight, reached at the beginning of January of the same year, is precisely half this figure, i.e., 122 kilograms. In general, the downward trend goes from the beginning of the season to the end of the year and may be attributed to the difficulty of feeding the livestock adequately due to the gradual exhaustion of the grazing land made available by the town council as summer and autumn came. Afterwards, the new purchases of livestock in January, February, April, and May originated a significant increase in the animals' average weight that reached its highest values in May and June 1537. On the other hand, as it was customary at that time for religious reasons, no meat was sold and, therefore, no animals were butchered, during the six Lent weeks. No meat was sold on Fridays either, as it was a fast day. Moreover, no animals were slaughtered during the week from 6 to 10 May 1537, although it does not seem that this was due to religious reasons but to the lack of stock.

With respect to rams, the average carcass weight, i.e., without head, hoofs, viscera, and skin, follows a very similar pattern, also with huge differences. There is a considerable increase in average weights as a result of the purchases made in February, March and May 1537. The maximum average weight, 15.6 kilograms, was reached precisely in mid-May 1537, while the minimum average weight, 6.8 kilograms, was recorded at the end of January of the same year and did not even reach half of the maximum average weight.

Meat sales followed a pattern similar to that of the average weight of the animals, although the decrease was even greater as winter came. The minimum sale of meat was recorded in the week from 26 to 30 November 1536. Subsequently, these figures slightly increased as a result of beef sales, since mutton sales remained steady. In 1537, the upward trend in beef consumption was confirmed. However, it experienced strong irregularities after Lent, probably due to cattle supply problems, as seems to be evidenced by the fact that the town butcher's shops remained without cattle stocks throughout March and April. The month of April was closed with a stock of six head of cattle.

As mentioned, mutton consumption did not recover like beef from 20 November 1536, and not even at the beginning of 1537, although it had experienced the same strong decline as beef over the season. However, at the end of Lent, there was an almost explosive increase that led to the highest figures of all the meat campaign in April and May 1537. During these weeks, mutton consumption was well above beef consumption that had always been greater up to that moment. The whole process is evidenced in Table 12.4.

Although the decrease in the weight of slaughtered animals as the year elapsed seems obvious for the mentioned reasons, the decline in sales cannot be understood, as the price established did not change at all over the business year. However, the price set in the purveyance agreement could possibly be the amount to be paid to the town meat purveyor by bankers or table-keepers who would subsequently sell the meat to consumers at a different price, according to its quality and to the part of the animal. At any rate, the proportion of bones and scarcely usable material in animals that had lost weight would determine a higher average price for meat proper.

During the 50 weeks accounted for in the Burgos meat purveyor's Ledger, 297,978 kilograms of meat were sold, considering that a quarter of meat weighted 1.1502325 kilograms; the actual sales would be slightly higher because the weight of the meat sold is obtained from the net amounts of sales, i.e., after

Table 12.4
Mutton and Beef Sales (in kilograms)

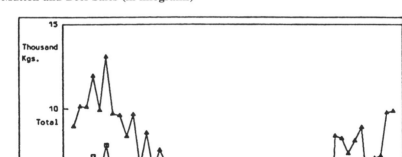

discounting payments to bankers for cutting and food allowances. Of these 297,978 kilograms, 168,705 kilograms, i.e., around 60 per cent of the total, corresponded to beef and 129,273 kilograms to mutton. Beef was one-fourth cheaper than mutton.

The 968 head of cattle slaughtered in the weeks recorded in the Ledger gave to the meat puveyor a net sales revenue of 2,353,667 maravedis, after discounting the amount received by table-keepers for cutting and food allowances. On the other hand, the 11,338 rams butchered and sold in the period produced a net amount of 2,470,533 maravedis. In total, the meat sold yielded 4,824,200 maravedis, as a whole.

As they did with meat, bankers paid to Francisco Porres on each Friday the sale proceeds of the offal of oxen, cows and rams slaughtered from the previous Saturday to Thursday. A single account, called ''Offal of oxen, cows and rams sold,'' was kept for this purpose. For this reason, it is not possible to know the amount obtained from the sale of the offal of each type of animal. The amount obtained in total for offal during the whole campaign was 267,974 maravedis.

Apart from meat and offal or viscera, the town meat puveyor also sold the by-products of the animals slaughtered, i.e., hides, skins, fat, sinews, gall, bladders, horns, wool and fleece.

In total, the proceeds of the sales of meat, offal and by-products amounted to 6,489,414 maravedis, broken down in Table 12.5.

Table 12.5
Proceeds of Sales of Meat, Offal, and By-Products

	maravedis
Beef	2,353,667
Mutton	2,470,533
Offal	267,974
Ram skins	398,007
Wool	75,303
Ox and cow hides	587,938
Fat	326,028
Ox and cow sinews	937
Gall and bladders	2,625
Ram horns	680
Sale of 1 live ox	537
Sale of 18 live rams	5,185
Total	6,489,414

Some Features of the Operation and Organization of the Meat Service

In the previous section, we have touched in passing on a number of subjects regarding the operation and organization of the meat service in Burgos. We must return now to some of them, at the same time as we describe a few other features, in order to deal with this subject systematically.

Gregorio Guerra carried out his task with the permanent assistance of two important employees: a main livestock purchasing agent, Bartolomé de Cevico, to whom he paid a salary of 10,500 maravedis for the year in question, and a treasurer or cashier, Francisco de Porres (Bartolomé's father-in-law), who was paid a salary of 11,000 maravedis for the same period. Gregorio Guerra also paid a high salary to Juan de Sepúlveda, weigher of the king's scale, who was in charge of weighing the meat sold by bankers.

Moreover, Guerra employed a variable number of cattlemen and shepherds for the transport and care of the animals purchased. The total salaries and food allowances paid to these shepherds amounted to 1,000 to 2,500 maravedis per week. This means that their total number could range from 8 to 20 persons. During the Lent period, the meat purveyor remained practically without any shepherd, as it seems to appear from the fact that no salaries and food allowances were paid from 10 February to 7 April. Anyway, this would be quite understandable considering that great care was taken to reduce stocks drastically during that period in which butchers' shops were closed. The few shepherds and cattlemen who were still hired were assigned the task of buying and driving new animals since large herds of cattle, specially sheep, were purchased in the Lent period, in view of the season starting on Easter Saturday.

Apart from Bartolomé de Cevico, Gregorio Guerra employed other livestock purchasing agents and he also effected some purchases himself. In some cases, they had to travel hundreds of kilometers from Burgos for this purpose. To finance these purchases, Gregorio Guerra relied in the first place on Martín de Salinas, an important Burgos merchant.

In accordance with demand, the animals were killed at the slaughterhouse by bankers or table-keepers who were also employed by Gregorio Guerra. There were ten bankers who earned a salary of 600 maravedis per month, apart from receiving cutting and food allowances whose amount is known only in a few cases. From the information available, it can be deduced that, as a whole, table-keepers received, for rams as well as for oxen and cows slaughtered, more than 2,500 maravedis per week, i.e., 250 maravedis per person. If these allowances are added to the salary earned per week, i.e., 150 maravedis, the total amount received was quite high.

Besides these earnings, table-keepers could possibly obtain an additional amount fron the retail sale of meat, for their own account, or their banks or tables, at different prices according to the quality of the meat, as it is not likely that a quarter of mutton would always be sold at 22 maravedis and a quarter of beef at 16 maravedis, whatever their type or quality might be. The same would apply to offal. The viscera, offal and other by-products were also sold by the meat purveyor in various ways and through different channels.

The animals slaughtered and sold by butchers were weighed by Juan de Sepúlveda, weigher of the king's scale, to whom Gregorio Guerra also paid a salary. Up to the date on which entries are interrupted, a total amount of 8,000 maravedis had been paid under that item.

The cost of cattle and sheep purchases appearing in the accounts called ''Rams purchased'' and ''Oxen and cows purchased'' amounted to 6,342,091 maravedis, excluding transport, lodging, salaries, etc., that were added in our study, whenever it was possible to identify these expenses and charge them to a specific item to obtain average prices.

Apart from that, expenses incurred in the meat service and recorded in the account ''Butchery business costs'' amounted to a total of 283,538 maravedis.

Another expense that was not recorded in that account was the sales tax or *alcabala*. In the period under study, the meat service implied the farming of the tax on meat sales. Thus, the meat purveyor received the tax collected on meat sold in 1536 before 24 June, as well as the tax on pork sales. On the other hand, he had to pay the yearly amount of the *alcabala* that the town had agreed with the Crown for the period. Up to the date of the last entries made in the Ledger, the net amounts paid by Gregorio Guerra under this item were 436,925 maravedis for the *alcabala* of 1536 and 123,724 maravedis for the first third of 1537.

Other expenses or losses incurred by the meat puveyor are recorded in the account ''Animals purchased'' which included the purchases and sales of beasts of burden for the meat service and was kept according to the periodic system of accounting for stock with a single account. The total loss recorded in these operations reached 1,898 maravedis.

After correcting a few accounting errors and adjusting accounts on the basis of the above-mentioned data, and without forgetting that entries were interrupted before the end of the business year, a balance sheet may be drawn from the Ledger in order to try to ascertain the results of the meat service. Thus, even though these conclusions are seriously limited by the fact that operations were not completed, we can say that, in the period under review, the meat service suffered substantial losses that are calculated to have reached 317,744 maravedis, as specified in the balance sheet of Table 12.6. However, according to the mentioned limitations, these figures can only be considered as a guide.

ANALYSIS OF LEDGERS FROM THE ACCOUNTING HISTORY ASPECT

Formal Analysis of Books and Entries

Apart from the Ledger of the meat purveyor, one folio of the *Libro Manual,* or Journal, has also been found in the General Archives of Simancas. It contains twelve entries corresponding to 11 to 15 May 1537, i.e., the last period of the business year. Although this evidence is rather scant, it provides additional information on the accounting system used by Gregorio Guerra in the bookkeeping of the meat business and shows that, at least from the formal standpoint, records were kept according to the *"debe y ha de haber"* or *"libro de Caxa con su Manual"* method, as double entry bookkeeping was called in Castile at that time.

Both the Journal and the Ledger are the size of the Castilian folio. The journal is not ruled, although its contents are presented in three columns: two lateral columns and a central one which is approximately twice as wide as each of the lateral ones. The left column shows the number of the Ledger's folios on which the accounts corresponding to the entry are recorded. As it was customary in that period, the numbers of the account folios are written in the form of fractions with a horizontal line between the numerator and the denominator. The numerator is the folio of the debit account and the denominator is the folio of the credit account.

The central column contains the body of the entry which starts with the name of the debit account followed by the formula *"debe por"* (owes for) which introduces the credit account. The amount of the entry comes next with a detailed and meticulous explanation of the operation involved. All of it is in accordance with the generally accepted practices of that time.

The right column showed the amounts of the operations recorded in the entries. These amounts were recorded in the form called "Castilian counting system" which consisted in numerical entries based on cursive Roman numerals, although they were already combined with an incipient relative valuation determined by the place occupied by the figures in the amount.

The Castilian counting system that was similar, with a few variations, to the

Table 12.6
Meat Service Losses

maravedis

ASSETS

Cash (Francisco de Porres)	87,548
Gregorio Guerra, adjusted account	120.639
Adjusted non-personal accounts	17,506
Adjusted debtors accounts	516,573
Stock-in-trade	322,790
By-products not accounted for	77,228
Total assets	1,142,284

==========

LIABILITIES

Martín de Salinas (financing account)	346,090
Creditors accounts	1,085,134
Non personal accounts	20,000
Total liabilities	1,451,224

==========

PROFIT OR LOSS

Total assets	1,142,284
Total liabilities	-1,451,224
Difference between assets and liabilities . .	- 308,940
Error in Ledger's accounts	- 8,804
Total loss	- 317,744

==========

methods followed in other European countries, was used in account books until the beginning of the 17th century, at least in the amount columns, although it was progressively replaced by Arabic numerals in the text or elsewhere in the books. During all the period in which the Castilian "*debe y ha de haber*" (debit and credit) system was used, the amounts were not only recorded in their column but also inevitably repeated in the text of the entry. In the books under review, the amounts appearing in the text are almost always recorded in the Castilian counting system. As these records are very early account books dating from the beginning of the second third of the 16th century, Arabic numerals are vey scarcely used, generally to indicate the page of the Ledger's folios, their reference number, the year of the date, the number of animals or products involved in the operation, etc. Even prices and the number of days spent in travel or required to perform the operations are usually recorded in the Castilian counting system.

None of the pious references or religious invocations that were so common in account books in that period appears at the beginning of our books, which only mention the year in the centre of the folio, between two crosses with a longer arm on the opposite side of the figure. In the Journal, the day and month of the first entry of the folio appear next and apply to all the entries recorded on that date. The beginning of each entry is shown, as usual, with a cross.

Entries had to be recorded in strictly chronological order, so that it would be impossible to introduce new entries at a later date, and this is how they appear in our journal. Likewise, the Journal and Ledger had to be bound in order to prevent adding new folios or replacing the original ones. Moreover, any intercalations, crossings-out, erasures, blanks, etc., were banished from generally accepted accounting practices. Errors had to be corrected through the relevant *contra* entries so as to ensure the most complete reliability of all entries. All these practices were observed in principle in the books under study.

As was usual, the folios of the Journal are not numbered and the amounts are not summed up at the end of the columns, since these data seemed of no importance to accountants in that period. However, our particular accountant wanted to evidence that entries had been posted from the journal to the corresponding accounts of the Ledger, as was the custom. To do so, he marked a point on the left of the folio's reference number.

The Ledger is also kept in full agreement with the rules and practices of the debit and credit or double entry bookkeeping method. Accounts are presented in the Venetian way, i.e., in bilateral form on two facing pages, with the debit entries on the left one and the credit entries on the right one, as is still done nowadays. The two pages actually belong to two different folios, but for accounting purposes the folio is composed of these two facing pages which constitute the account. As opposed to the Journal, the accounting folios of the Ledger are numbered with a figure or Arabic numeral and the number is written in the right upper angle of the Credit page.

On some folios, the three columns of each page are separated by a soft line. The first and largest column, which occupies two-thirds of the folio breadth, shows the body of the text; next, a very narrow column shows the number of the folios on which balancing accounts are recorded; and the third column shows the amounts.

The heading of the account appears only on the Debit side, at the beginning of the first entry, followed by the formula "*debe*" (owes) which introduces all the entries of that side.

When the account is opened, although no credit entry is recorded at that moment, the formula "*Ha de haber*" (must have) is written down on the Credit side. This formula is not completed if no credit entry is recorded, and it also introduces all the entries recorded on that side.

The heading of the account stands out, leaving less margin on the left than the rest of the text of this first entry and of the other entries which are recorded on that page.

In the case of accounts showing physical amounts of products, this margin is precisely used to keep the account of the units of such products.

The Ledger's folios start directly with the year, written in the center, the same as in the Journal's folios, without any pious formula or reference either.

As in the Journal, entries are recorded in strictly chronological order—although in the Ledger this order is obviously followed independently on both sides of each account—without leaving any blanks between entries, to avoid intercalations.

The *contra* account appears at the end of the entry's text and is introduced by the formula "*por cuenta de*" (for account of), according to the current practice of that period.

The amounts of the entries are shown in the relevant column in the Castilian counting system, the same as in the Journal. All of them are repeated in the body of the entry, generally also in the Castilian counting system.

No compound entry, i.e., no entry composed of more than one debit or credit account, has been found in the whole Ledger. Therefore, the relation between entries is always a single debit account to a single credit account. All entries, without exception, consist of both debit and credit, in complete accordance with the very essence of double entry.

In general, there is one folio for each account, unless the account is extensive enough to occupy more than one folio. However, in a few cases in which it was known in advance that there would scarcely be any movement in given accounts, two or three accounts are recorded on a single folio, as it was usually recommended in that period.

When the space assigned to an account in a folio was used up, the balance or difference between Debit and Credit was struck and shown on the side of the lower amount, with an explanation of that kind: "balance of this account which is carried forward to. . . ."

Then, the Debit and Credit, which should match after the former operation, are summed up. Following the accepted practice, these amounts were not carried forward, as opposed to the balance.

In spite of the fact that the rules of the debit and credit system that prohibited intercalations, crossings out and erasures were generally observed by the accountant of the butchery business, and in a few occasions, some heterodox practices do appear. In other cases, errors were not duly corrected, giving rise to non-reconciled figures.

Accounts and Their Uses

The accounts used in the bookkeeping of the Burgos butchers' shops can be seen, suitably grouped to facilitate analysis, in the balance sheet of Table 12.7. However, it should be noted that the Ledger is not closed and accounts are not adjusted, since entries are suddenly interrupted before the end of the business year. This balance sheet also includes cancelled accounts in order to offer a general outlook of the chart of accounts used.

There is a difference of 8,804 maravedis between Assets and Liabilities whose reason could not be ascertained, as several folios of the Ledger are missing.

In total, according to the balance sheet presented, sixty-seven accounts were used in the accounting of the meat purveyor: thirty-seven under Assets and thirty under Liabilities. Only forty-seven of these accounts remained outstanding on 11 June 1537, specifically twenty-eight under Assets and nineteen under Liabilities.

Among the sixty-seven accounts used in total in the business year, fifty were personal accounts, thirty of which were debit accounts, and twenty credit accounts. Of the seventeen remaining accounts, only two were non-personal asset accounts, one obligation to pay, three profit and loss, and eleven belonged to the group that we have called operating accounts. The twenty accounts that had already been cancelled at the end of the records were all personal accounts.

No capital or fixed assets accounts appear in this bookkeeping. This is not surprising considering that the business (activity) recorded was a service rendered. Moreover, premises, facilities and tools were provided by the town council that probably also intervened, in one way or another, by granting or mediating to obtain financing resources. In fact, the account of a financer, Martín de Salinas, was used as capital account.

Apart from that, the chart of accounts is rather complete and it is, at any rate, devised in accordance with the aims pursued. Therefore, also from the standpoint of the contents and use of the accounts concerned, it can be stated that the system is to be considered as double entry bookkeeping. The operating accounts are particularly interesting as they provide varied and extensive information which also includes headings and contents of accounts that were totally unknown so far in the history of Spanish accounting in the 16th century. It is unfortunate that the interruption of the records before the completion of all the operations undertaken in the business year deprives us of the possibility of getting acquainted with the adjusting and closing processes and with the preparation and presentation of the Profit and Loss Account and Balance Sheet.

Let us examine now the various groups of accounts, stressing their most outstanding features.

As it was rather usual in that period, there was no cash account as such, since

Table 12.7
Bookkeeping Accounts of the Burgos Butchers' Shops

ASSETS

CASH ACCOUNT
Francisco de Porres   87,548

PURVEYOR'S ACCOUNT
Gregorio Guerra   131,639

NON PERSONAL ASSETS
Scales and weights purchased   7,774
Animals purchased   11,630

DEBTORS ON SALE OF PRODUCTS
Gil de la Calle, tanner, and
    Pablo de la Calle, his son   173,907
Miguel de Porres   56,250
Pedro de Gámez and Juan de Torres, candlemakers   10,093
Antón Campantón and Juan de Hitero, denizens of Castrojeriz .   59,636
Juan de Poza and Gil de la Calle   5,351
Pedro de Torres   107
Juan de Frías, shoemaker   29,470
Francisco de Medina, shoemaker   729
Lucas de Verviesca and Gregorio Sarmiento and
    Pedro de Quintanilla, tanners   32,595
Diego de Achiaga   2,625
Andrés Sillero de Vega   937
Juan de Villacienzo   680
Gil de la Calle, tanner . . . .   -
Juan de Lenzes, shoemaker . . . .   -

DEBTORS FOR OTHER REASONS
Bartolomé de Cevico   9,967
The town of Burgos   1,536
Alonso de Castañares, denizen of Gamonal   1,530
Juan de Mena, transient in Bruges   5,283
Francisco Revellón, resident in Vega   2,625
Francisco de Oña   2,250
Juan de Sepúlveda, weigher of the king's scale   8,000
Diego Orenzo . . . .   -
Lorenzo de Lerma . . . .   -
Gerónimo Pardo . . . .   -
Alonso de Sasamón, the younger . . . .   -
Alonso de Sasamón, the elder . . . .   -
Hernando de Vivar, table-keeper . . . .   -
Pedro Peinado, table-keeper . . . .   -

Table 12.7 (continued)

```
OPERATING ACCOUNTS (PURCHASE AND STOCK ACCOUNTS)
Oxen and cows purchased  . . . . . . . . . . . . . . . . . . .    2,781,873
Rams purchased  . . . . . . . . . . . . . . . . . . . . . . .    3,560,218

PROFIT AND LOSS ACCOUNTS
"Alcabala" on meat  . . . . . . . . . . . . . . . . . . . . .      436,925
"Alcabala" of 1537  . . . . . . . . . . . . . . . . . . . . .      123,724
Butchery business costs  . . . . . . . . . . . . . . . . . .       283,538

            TOTAL ASSETS  . . . . . . . . . . . . . . . . . .    7,828,440
        ============================================================
```

LIABILITIES

```
FINANCING ACCOUNT
Martín de Salinas  . . . . . . . . . . . . . . . . . . . . . .      346,090

CREDITORS ON LOANS AND BILLS OF EXCHANGE
Iñigo del Hospital . . . . . . . . . . . . . . . . . . . . . .      265,206
Pedro de la Torre Vitoria  . . . . . . . . . . . . . . . . . .      215,390
Heirs of Gerónimo de Castro  . . . . . . . . . . . . . . . . .      225,540
Rodrigo de Zamora, Segovia "cambio"  . . . . . . . . . . . . .           —
Juan de Paredes  . . . . . . . . . . . . . . . . . . . . . . .           —
Juan de Llantadilla  . . . . . . . . . . . . . . . . . . . . .           —

CREDITORS ON LIVESTOCK PURCHASES
Juan Sánchez de Palenzuela . . . . . . . . . . . . . . . . . .       43,080
Juan de Ribera, the youger, denizen of Villacastín . . . . . .      192,115
Rodrigo de Brijuela, denizen of Castrojeriz  . . . . . . . . .       57,904
Pedro Ibáñez, town councillor of Segovia . . . . . . . . . . .       85,450
Juan de Castro of Moxica . . . . . . . . . . . . . . . . . . .           —
Diego López Gallo  . . . . . . . . . . . . . . . . . . . . . .           —
Bachelor Gallo . . . . . . . . . . . . . . . . . . . . . . . .           —
Hernando de Fromesta . . . . . . . . . . . . . . . . . . . . .           —
Bartolomé Márquez  . . . . . . . . . . . . . . . . . . . . . .           —
Juan Guisado, denizen of Badajoz . . . . . . . . . . . . . . .           —
María Doca and her son Luis Vázquez, denizens of El Espinar  .           —

CREDITORS FOR OTHER REASONS
Juan Rodríguez, wineskinmaker  . . . . . . . . . . . . . . . .          449
Pedro de Mena, tax farmer of the
   toll-bar of Burgos  . . . . . . . . . . . . . . . . . . . .           —
```

Table 12.7 (continued)

```
OBLIGATIONS TO PAY
Rent for butchery's premises and slaughterhouse  . . . . . . .        20,000

OPERATING ACCOUNTS (SALES ACCOUNTS)
Oxen and cows sold . . . . . . . . . . . . . . . . . . . . .      2,354,204
Rams sold  . . . . . . . . . . . . . . . . . . . . . . . . .      2,551,021
Offal of oxen, cows and rams sold  . . . . . . . . . . . . .        267,974
Skins of rams sold . . . . . . . . . . . . . . . . . . . . .        398,007
Horns of rams sold . . . . . . . . . . . . . . . . . . . . .            680
Hides of oxen and cows sold  . . . . . . . . . . . . . . . .        612,928
Fat sold . . . . . . . . . . . . . . . . . . . . . . . . . .        326,028
Sinews of oxen and cows sold . . . . . . . . . . . . . . . .            937
Gall and bladders sold . . . . . . . . . . . . . . . . . . .          2,625

                    TOTAL LIABILITIES   . . . . . . . . . . . .    7,965,628
           ==============================================================


    Total Assets  . . . . . . . . .     7,828,440
    ("The town of Burgos")  . . . .   +   121,002
                                                        7,949,442 maravedis

    Total Liabilities   . . . . . .     7,965,628
    ("Hides...")  . . . . . . . . .   -    24,990
                                                        7,940,638 maravedis

                            Balance . . . . . .          8,804 maravedis
                    =============================================
```

it was personified in the cashier or treasurer. Thus, the account of Francisco de Porres worked as an authentic cash account. Debits meant cash receipts, credits meant cash expenses and the debit balance was the existing cash.

Gregorio Guerra obtained funds from Francisco de Porres to make himself some of the payments of which he was regularly in charge, such as the cash payment of salaries and food allowances to shepherds or other less frequent large payments. He also collected some amounts directly or effected payments without any previous provisions of funds but, in general, collections and payments were made by Francisco de Porres, who was paid a salary to fulfil this duty. Accordingly, at the end of the entries, the debit balance of the account of Gregorio Guerra, lessee of the meat service, includes many of the expenses made for account of this service pending to be debited to the "Butchery business costs" account. As a result, the lessee's account was not a typical personal account with respect to the meaning of its balance but it was so with respect to the debit and credit mechanics.

In the accounting of the Burgos meat service, there were only two authentic non-personal asset accounts. One of them "Scales and weights purchased" recorded only debits, with the relevant credit as a counterpart to the account of Francisco de Porres for the cash purchase of various batches of weights for the butchery business. Therefore, the way in which the account was kept is not exactly known, although in view of what occurs with the other asset account "Animals purchased," there are reasons to believe that, if the case arose, the periodic system of accounting for stock with a single account would have been used.

On the Debit side of the "Animals purchased" account, six items are recorded covering the purchase of six animals for the use of butchery business. Purchases are accounted for at the cost price. Of these six animals, three were sold later and the relevant entries were recorded on the Credit side at the selling price, following the rules of the periodic inventory system with a single stock account. As a whole, sales were made at a loss, so the debit balance of the account shows the cost price of the existing animals, plus the loss experienced on the animals sold.

In spite of the fact that payment orders and bills of exchange are very frequently used in meat operations, in the bookkeeping under review, no bill account appears among asset accounts. No one conceived such a need because accounts were personified in the *"debe y ha de haber"* system at that time. Thus, when a payment order or bill was purchased, it was debited to the account of the taker of the money and seller of the bill and credited as balancing entry to the cash account or, in our case, to the account of the treasurer, Francisco de Porres, for the amount delivered. When the amount of the bill was collected, it was debited to the cash account or the account of the treasurer who received the money and was credited to the account of the seller of the bill who had appeared, in the meanwhile, as debtor in the records, since he was taker of the money he had received for the sale of the bill.

Conversely, when a bill was sold, as it occurred in the records under review with the bills drawn on Flanders, it was debited to the cash account or, if need be, to the account of the drawer of the bill and taker of the money for account of the meat purveyor, i.e., to the account of Martín de Salinas. The bill was credited to the account of the deliverer of the money and buyer of the bill who appeared as creditor in the records until the bill was paid in Flanders by the drawee, i.e., by Salinas' employee, to the holder. At that moment, the account of the deliverer of the money was debited and the account of the drawee was credited.

Debtors' accounts have been divided in two groups: debtors on the sale of products and debtors for other reasons. The first group includes all the persons who owed money to the meat purveyor for the purchase of slaughtered animals by-products: skins, hides, fat, etc. The second group includes miscellaneous debtors, such as Bartolomé de Cevico, who owed money to butchers on unsettled surpluses of funds provided for livestock purchases, or the town of Burgos on funds due to Gregorio Guerra for the *alcabalas* of the previous business year that were still unpaid.

Among these debtors appears Juan de Sepúlveda, weigher of the king's scale, whose account was not a typical personal account, since the debit balance corresponded to the amounts that had been paid cash to him as salary for his work. Actually, this account was a transitory expenditure account in which the amount of the salary was recorded as it was paid in full. At that moment, it is assumed that the balance would be posted to the "Butchery business costs" account.

The other debtors' accounts are debited and credited following the usual rules: the amounts that increase the debit are recorded on the debit side and the amounts that reduce it are entered on the credit side. The debit balance is the amount due at any moment to the books' owner.

The creditors' accounts under Liabilities are kept symmetrically: the amounts that reduce creditors' credit, i.e., the debts of the books' owner, are debited and the items that increase creditors' credit are credited. The credit balance is the amount owed by the books' owner to the account's holder. In this section, we have distinguished three groups of creditors: creditors on loans and moneys taken in exchange, creditors on livestock purchases and creditors for other reasons. Their headings are self-explanatory with regard to the content of the group's accounts. However, it is necessary to explain the fact that among creditors for other reasons is included the account of "Juan Rodríguez, wineskin-maker"—who was a regular buyer of ram skins—whose provision of funds upon striking the balance sheet exceeded the amount of the skins withdrawn. The other account included in this group, and already settled when the balance sheet was struck, is that of "Pedro de Mena, tax farmer of the toll-bar of Burgos" on whose Credit side was credited the amount of this tax that was debited to the "Butchery business costs" account, and the amount paid was subsequently debited on the debit side when payment was actually effected.

The account of the financer, Martín de Salinas, has been included in a separate group precisely to stress this fact, although the account is kept exactly the same as that of any other creditor.

In the balance sheet, liabilities include an "Obligation to pay" account, that of "Rent for butchery's premises and slaughterhouse." At the beginning, the amount due by Gregorio Guerra to the Burgos town council for the rent of the butchery shops and facilities during the whole business year was credited to this account, debiting in balance the "Butchery business costs" account. However, as provided in the purveyance agreement, the money spent in new puchases as well as maintenance and repair expenses of butcher shops and slaughterhouse had to be deducted from the above-mentioned amount. In fact, these amounts are debit entries, the same as the amounts paid to the town council on account of the total. The credit balance is the total outstanding debt of the meat purveyor to be paid to the town council under this item at any moment.

Finally we shall analyze the debit and credit groups that we have called operating accounts, as well as the group of profit and loss accounts included on the debit side.

Operating accounts include all the accounts that are related, on the one hand, to the animals purchased to supply meat to Burgos in accordance with the purveyance agreement signed by Gregorio Guerra and, on the other hand, to the products obtained from the sale of slaughtered animals, i.e., meat and viscera, as well as by-products such as skins, fat, horns, etc.

These are the most important and specific accounts of these books because they are the essence and *raison d'être* of the accounting under review, since they reflect directly all the developments of the activity recorded. Moreover, they are of special interest as they are the first example known of this type of account in the meat business. In fact, the few double entry, or even single entry, account books of the 16th or previous centuries that have been studied in the history of Spanish accounting basically show the activities of merchants and bankers. None of them refers to such an activity as the purchase and slaughter of livestock and the subsequent sale of meat and by-products. This is why the name and concept of the operating accounts used in this accounting have a meaning unknown so far. Moreover, the operation of butcher shops, with the purchase of live and differentiated raw material (oxen and cows, on the one hand, and rams, on the other) and the sale of also very differentiated products (meat and viscera, as well as various by-products, such as hides, skins, fat, and horns) raised a serious and new accounting problem.

Even without knowing the accounts' adjusting and closing processes due to the fact that entries were interrupted, this accounting problem can be deemed to have been adequately solved by creating two groups of operating accounts: one to record the purchase of animals and the other to record the sale of the products obtained after slaughtering these same animals. This solution gives rise to what is currently known as a periodic inventory system, with separate accounts for purchases and sales, i.e., the creation of a purchasing account or group of accounts on the debit side to which the amount of purchases is debited at cost price, and a selling account or group of accounts on the credit side to which the amount of sales is credited at selling price. In this system, accounts work separately, and at the end of the business year, they are adjusted in order to calculate the profit or the loss by reducing stocks sold from the purchasing group of accounts at cost price, and by comparing them subsequently with sales. This allows the accounts to establish, on the one hand, the remaining stock and, on the other hand, the profit made on sales. In our Ledger, this adjustment was not made, since entries were interrupted before the end of the business year. Therefore, we do not know how the meat business accountant devised and implemented the adjusting process whose analysis would have undoubtedly been highly interesting. In the simple state in which they are separately presented, the debit balance of purchasing accounts shows only the total cost of purchases and the credit balance of selling accounts the total proceeds of sales. In fact, purchasing accounts are usually only debited during the business year and can be credited exclusively through cancellations or, if need be, discounts obtained *a posteriori*. At the end of the business year, the accounts are credited as a result of adjusting entries. Likewise, selling accounts are ordinarily only credited during the business year and debits are made in case of cancellations or discounts granted after the operations are recorded. At the end of the business year, selling accounts can be debited as a result of adjusting entries.

At any rate, it is highly interesting to see that, to cover different needs, two different inventory systems were so early applied in the same bookkeeping to purchases and sales: the periodic inventory system with a single account and the periodic inventory system with separate accounts for purchases and sales, the latter being a suitable solution to record inputs which experience changes during the production process and give rise to multiple outputs. In fact, in this case, the single account system, which is excellent as an early accounting formula for purely commercial processes in which goods are bought and sold without experiencing changes or giving rise to other products as a result of the process, would have hardly met accounting requirements. The fact that the meat business accountant realised that and offered us such an early example of the separate accounts system reveals a notable understanding of the accounting logic and mechanisms.

In the Ledger of the Burgos meat purveyor, the group of profit and loss accounts include three accounts on the debit side. A general profit and loss account to which profit or loss made on the meat service could have been carried is probably missing. However, the accounts were not adjusted and, therefore, this general account was not opened. It should be remembered in passing that the meat service suffered heavy losses. On the other hand, one of the three accounts included in the group, ''Butchery business costs,'' was more a profit and loss account than an expenditure account.

Of these three profit and loss accounts, two are used to record the *alcabala* or meat sales tax: one for the *alcabala* of 1536 an the other for 1537. Both work in a similar way. The method followed is to debit the amounts paid by

Gregorio Guerra for this tax and to credit the amounts he collected, as farmer of this tax, either because they covered a period in which he was not in charge of the meat business but had already been appointed tax farmer of the *alcabala* on meat sales, or because of the sales of meat other than mutton or beef made by other people. The debit balance showed the amount of the tax borne by the meat purveyor and it is assumed that, when accounts were adjusted, it had to be transferred to the "Butchery business costs" account, i.e., the third account included in this group of nominal accounts, or to a new account, to be created, that would show the final general results of the meat business. The account of the *alcabala* of 1536 includes three credit entries corresponding to three fixed price agreements established with pork sellers that do no refer only to the mentioned year but to the business year comprised between 24 June 1536 and the same day of 1537. The accrual principle is, therefore, not applied in this case.

As mentioned above, the "Butchery business costs" account is more a profit and loss account than an expenditure account, since it is used to record both expenditure and profit made on small operations. The items recorded in this account were quite heterogeneous, as they included financial expenses and receipts, salaries of Guerra's employees, rent of premises and facilities, lacks of money, errors, taxes, etc. They worked according to the typical mechanics of this type of account: they were debited with expenses and losses and credited with profits. The debit balance reflects total expenses or losses, in the absence of a general profit and loss account, and the credit balance shows profits. However, the accounts were not adjusted and closed and, at any rate, several expenditure items that were provisionally recorded in other accounts were pending to be transferred to this account. For all these reasons, the balance of this account when entries were interrupted did in no way reflect the result of the meat service operations. Among other less important items, the results of the adjustment of operating accounts, in particular, were missing.

CONCLUSION

The previous sections have described the main results provided by the analysis of the Ledger of the Burgos meat service in the business year that started on 24 June 1536 and had to end on the same day of 1537. This was the basic source of information of the research carried out whose detailed development appears in the volume of the same title published in Spanish by the Research Department of the Bank of Spain.

As stated in the Introduction, from the economic history viewpoint, the analysis undertaken has enabled us to get acquainted with interesting details on the conditions of the meat supply service in Burgos in the mentioned period. The records have specifically provided information on livestock purchases made for this purpose, financing instruments and forms, sales of mutton and beef during the business year and amount obtained from the sale of by-products, as well as on the most outstanding features of the organization and operation of the meat service, including the assessment of final results.

From the accounting history standpoint, it has been ascertained that the Ledger studied is the first Castilian account book proper known so far that was kept according to the double entry system, as regards the formal requirements of that period, as well as the extension of the chart of accounts used and the accounting procedure followed. It was interesting to see how accountants recorded operations in a meat business and how they were able to solve the problems raised by the existence of an operating process in which inputs were transformed and gave rise to a multiple and diversified output.

REFERENCES

Manuscripts

General Archives of Simancas

Section "Casa y Sitios Reales," bundle 36, No 2.
Section "Consejos Reales," bundle 192, No 2.
Section "Contaduría Mayor de Cuentas, 2ª época," bundle 1004.

Municipal Archives of Burgos

Historical Section, No 4269.
Libro del Conçejo de la çibdad de Burgos, año 1536.

Printed Sources

Alvarez Garcia, Carlos: "La revolución de las comunidades en Medina del Campo," in Eufemio Lorenzo Sanz (editor): *Historia de Medina del Campo y su tierra,* (Valladolid: 1986) vol. I.
Alvarez Garcia, Carlos: "Diego Ordoñez, hombre de negocios y clérigo. Restos de su archivo privado (1497–1520)," in *Revista Española de Financiación y Contabilidad,* vol. XVII, no. 55 (January–April, 1988).
Anes, Gonzalo: "Los pósitos en la España del siglo XVIII," in *Moneda y Crédito,* no. 105 (1968): p. 39–69.
Anes, Gonzalo; "Los pósitos en el siglo XVIII; las fluctuaciones de los precios del trigo, de la cebada y del aceite en España (1788–1808)," in *Economía e Ilustración* (Barcelona: 1969).
Argente del Castillo Ocaña, Carmen: *La ganadería medieval andaluza. Siglos XIII–XVI.* (Reinos de Jaén y Córdoba) (Jaén: 1991).
Basas Fernandez, Manuel: *El Consulado de Burgos en el siglo XVI* (Madrid: 1963).
Basas Fernandez, Manuel: "Banqueros burgaleses en el siglo XVI," in *Boletín de la Institución Fernán González* (1964).
Benassar, Bartolomé: "L'alimentation d'une capitale espagnole au XVIe siècle: Valla-

dolid,'' in Jean-Jacques Hémardinquer (editor): *Pour une histoire de l'alimenta-tion* (Paris: Colin, 1970).

Boletín de Estadística: No. 481 (January–February, 1990).

Bonachia Hernando, J. A.: *El concejo de Burgos en al Baja Edad Media (1345–1426),* (Valladolid: 1978).

Casado Alonso, Hilario: *Señores, mercaderes y campesinos. La comarca de Burgos a fines de la Edad Media* (Valladolid: Junta de Castilla y León, 1987).

Castro, Concepción de: ''La política ilustrada y el abastecimiento de Madrid,'' in: Gonzalo Anes, Luis Angel Rojo, and Pedro Tedde (editors), *Historia económica y pensamiento social* (Madrid: 1983): Alianza Editorial, Banco de España, p. 205–236.

Castro, Concepción de: *El pan de Madrid. El abasto de las ciudades españolas del Antiguo Régimen* (Madrid: Alianza Editorial, 1987).

De Roover, Raymond: ''Aux origines d'une technique intellectuelle: La formation et l'expansion de la Comptabilité à partie double,'' in *Annales d'Histoire Economique et Sociale* (1937) vol. IX.

De Roover, Raymond: Review of the work of Federigo Melis: *Storia della Ragioneria,* Bologna, 1950, in *Journal of Economic History,* vol. 14 (1954).

De Roover, Raymond: ''The Development of Accounting prior to Luca Pacioli according to the Account Books of Medieval Merchants,'' in *Studies in the History of Accounting,* compiled by A. C. Littleton and Basil S. Yamey, London, 1956, and reprinted in *Business, Banking, and Economic Thought in Late Medieval and Early Modern Europe. Selected Studies of Raymond de Roover,* work compiled by Julius Kirshner (Chicago: 1974).

Direccion General del Instituto Geografico y Estadistico: *Equivalencias entre las pesas y medidas usadas antiguamente en las diversas provincias de España y las legales del sistema métrico-decimal* (Madrid: 1886).

Dominguez Ortiz, Antonio: ''El abasto de pan a Madrid por los pueblos circunvecinos,'' in *I Jornadas de Estudios sobre la provincia de Madrid* (Madrid: 1979).

Espadas Burgos, Manuel, and Mª Ascensión Burgos: ''Abastecimiento de Madrid en el siglo XVI,'' in *Madrid en el siglo XVI* (Madrid: Instituto de Estudios Madrileños, 1961).

Estepa, Carlos, Teófilo F. Ruiz, Juan A. Bonachia, and Hilario Casado: *Burgos en la Edad Media* (Valladolid: Junta de Castilla y León, 1984).

Garcia Cavallero, Joseph: *Breve cotejo y valance de las Pesas, y medidas de varias Nacionales, Reynos, y Provincias, comparadas, y reducidas à las que corren en estos Reynos de Castilla* (Madrid: 1731).

Garcia Isidro, M.: *Historia de los pósitos españoles* (Madrid: 1929).

Garcia Monerris, Mª Carmen, and José Luis Peset: ''Los Gremios menores y el abastecimiento de Madrid durante la Ilustración,'' in *Moneda y Crédito,* no. 140 (1977).

Garcia Sainz de Baranda, Julián: *La ciudad de Burgos y su concejo en la Edad Media.* I. *La ciudad.* II. *El concejo* (Burgos: 1967).

Gomez Iglesias, A.: ''El alcalde de la Panadería y la mudanza del Peso Real,'' in *Revista de la Biblioteca, Archivo y Museo* (1944).

Gonzalez, Nazario: *Burgos, la ciudad marginal de Castilla. Estudio de geografía urbana* (Burgos: 1958).

Gonzalez Diez, E.: *El concejo burgalés (884–1369). Marco histórico institucional* (Burgos: 1983–1984).

Gonzalez Ferrando, José María: "Los 'libros de cuentas' de la familia Ruiz, mercaderes-banqueros de Median del Campo (1551–1606)," in *Actas del Primer Congreso sobre Archivos Económicos de Entidades Privadas, 3.4 de junio 1982* (Madrid: Banco de España, 1983).

Gonzalez Ferrando, José María: "De las tres formas de llevar 'cuenta y razón' según el licenciado Diego del Castillo, natural de Molina," in *Revista Española de Financiación y Contabilidad,* vol. XVII, no. 55 (January–April, 1988).

Gonzalez Jimenez, M.: *El Concejo de Carmona a fines de la Edad Media (1464–1523)* (Seville: 1973).

Guerrero Navarrete, Yolanda: *Organización y gobierno en Burgos durante el reinado de Enrique IV de Castilla, 1453–1476* (Madrid: 1986).

Gutierrez Nieto, J. I.: "Los Libros de Actas del depósito de Madrid y las crisis cerealistas de mediados del siglo XVII (1645–1652)," in *I Jornadas de Estudios sobre la áprovincia de Madrid* (Madrid: 1979).

Hernández-Esteve, Esteban: *Contribución al estudio de la historiografía contable en España,* Servicio de Estudios del Banco de España, Estudios de Historia Económica, no. 3 (Madrid: 1981).

Hernández-Esteve, Esteban: "Législation Castillane du Bas Moyen Age et du début de la Renaissance relative à la comptabilité et aux livres de comptes des marchands." Paper presented to the *Journées Internationales d'Histoire du Droit,* Valladolid, 1–3 June 1981. There is a Spanish version entitled "Legislación castellana de la baja Edad Media y comienzos del Renacimiento sobre la contabilidad y libros de cuentas de los mercaderes," in *Hacienda Pública Española,* no. 95 (1985).

Hernández-Esteve, Esteban: "Accounts of Fernán López del Campo, first 'Factor General' of Philip II, for the kingdoms of Spain (1556–1560). Contribution to the Study of the History of Accounting and Public Finance in Spain in the 16th Century." Paper presented to the *Fifth Annual Congress of the European Accounting Association,* Arhus, 5–7 April 1982. There is a Spanish version entitled: "Las cuentas de Fernán López del Campo, primer factor General de Felipe II para los reinos de España (1556–1560). Contribución al estudio de la historia de la contabilidad y de la Hacienda Pública en la España del siglo XVI," in *Hacienda Pública Española,* no. 87 (1984).

Hernández-Esteve, Esteban: "A Municipal Purchase of Corn. Bread Ledger and Journal of the Town Council of Medina de Rioseco (1540)." Work presented to the *Fourth International Congress of Accounting Historians,* Pisa, 1984, and published in the Proceedings of the Congress. The Spanish version was published under the title: "Una operación municipal de compra de cereales. Libros de Caja y Manual de compra del pan del Ayuntamiento de Medina de Rioseco (1540)," in *Moneda y Crédito,* no. 181 (June 1987).

Hernández-Esteve, Esteban: "A Spanish Treatise of 1706 on Double-Entry Bookkeping: 'Norte Mercantil y Crisol de Cuentas' by Gabriel de Souza Brito," in *Accounting and Business Research,* no. 60 (Autumn 1985).

Hernández-Esteve, Esteban: "Comentario histórico-contable sobre los libros de cuentas de Diego Ordoñez," in *Revista Española de Financiación y Contabilidad,* vol. XVII, no. 55 (January–April 1988).

Hernández-Esteve, Esteban: "Apuntes para una historia de la contabilidad bancaria en

España," in *Revista Española de Financiación y Contabilidad*, vol. XVIII, no. 58 (January–March 1989).

Hernández-Esteve, Esteban: "El negocio de los mercaderes de oro y plata de Sevilla a mediados del siglo XVI. Noticia de algunos libros de cuentas de la casa de la Contratación," in *Contaduría. Universidad de Antioquía*, Nos. 17–18 (September, 1990–March, 1991). This work was originally a paper presented to the *I Seminario de Historia de la Contabilidad*, organized by the Accounting Department of the University of Seville, on 28–29 May 1990.

Hernández-Esteve, Esteban: Organizational, Operational, Administrative and Accounting Aspects of the Project of "Erarios Públicos." Contribution to the Study of Public Banking in Spain in the Late Middle Ages and Early Modern Times. Paper presented to the "Convegno Internazionale Banchi Pubblici, Banchi Privati e Monti di Pietá nell' Europa Preindustriale. Amministrazione, Tecniche Operative e Ruoli Economici," Genoa, 1–6 October 1990. Published in the Proceedings of the Congress.

Informe de la imperial ciudad de Toledo el Real, y Supremo consejo de Castilla, sobre igualación de Pesos, y Medidas en todos los Reynos, y Señorios de S. Mag. según las leyes (Madrid: 1758).

Iñiguez, F.: "La Casa Real de la Panadería," in *Revista de la Biblioteca, Archivo y Museo* (1948).

Melis, Federigo: *Storia della Ragioneria* (Bologna: 1950).

Metz, Jacob de: *Sendero mercantil* (Amsterdam: 1967).

Michelena Paliargues, Pascal: "Perspectivas de la ganadería ovina y caprina," in *El Campo. Boletín de Información Agraria*, no. 118 (October–December 1990).

Palacio Atard, Vicente: "Problemas de abastecimiento en Madrid a finales del siglo XVIII," in *Villes de l'Europe méditerranéenne et de l'Europe occidentale, Annales de la Faculté des Lettres et Sciences Humaines*, Nos. 9–10 (1969): p. 279–288.

Palacio Atard, Vicente: "Algo más sobre el abastecimiento de Madrid en el siglo XVIII," in *Anales Madrileños*, vol. V (1970).

Pardos Martinez, Julio Antonio: "La renta de alcabala vieja, portazgo y barra . . . del concejo de Burgos durante el siglo XV (1429–1503)," in *Historia de la Hacienda Española (Epocas antigua y medieval). Homenaje a García de Valdeavellano*, (Madrid: Instituto de Estudios Fiscales, 1982).

Perez Aparicio, M. Aparicio: "El Trigo y el pan en Valencia (1700–1713)," in *Cuadernos de Historia*, vol. 5 (1975).

Perez de Castro, F.: "El abasto de pan en la corte madrileña en 1630," in *Revista de la Biblioteca, Archivo y Museo* (1946).

Prieto Bances, Ramón: "El abasto de Oviedo en el siglo XIV y sus problemas," in *Homenaje a Don Ramón Carande* (Madrid: Sociedad de Estudios y Publicaciones, 1963): vol. II.

Ramsey, Peter: "Some Tudor Merchants' Accounts," in A. C. Littleton and B. S. Yamey (editors): *Studies in the History of Accounting* (London: 1956): p. 185.

Ringrose, David R.: *Madrid y la economía española, 1560–1850* (Madrid: Alianza Editorial, 1985).

Rodriguez Gonzalez, Ricardo: Los libros de cuentas del mercader Simón Ruiz. Análisis de una década (1551–1560), Doctoral thesis directed by Prof. Dr. Rafael Ramos

Cerveró, Universidad de Valladolid, Facultad de Ciencias Económicas y Empresariales, Valladolid (December, 1990).

Ruiz, T. F.: *Sociedad y poder real en Castilla* (Barcelona: 1981).

Ruiz Martin, Felipe: "Las ferias de Castilla," in Eufemio Lorenzo Sanz (editor), *Historia de Medina del Campo y su tierra* (Valladolid: 1986): vol. II.

Salva, A.: *Historia de la ciudad de Burgos* (Burgos: 1914).

Salvador de Solorzano, Bartolomé: *Libro de Caxa y Manual de cuentas de Mercaderes, y otras personas, con la declaracion dellos* (Madrid: 1590).

Serrano, Luciano: *Los Reyes Católicos y la ciudad de Burgos (1451–1492)* (Madrid: 1943).

Souza Brito, Gabriel de: *Norte mercantil y crisol de quentas*, 2nd edition (Amsterdam: 1770).

Tovar, V.: *El pósito de la villa de Madrid. Historia de su construcción durante los siglos XVII y XVIII* (Madrid: 1982).

Vazquez de Prada, Valentín: "Die kastilischen Messen im 16. Jahrhundert," in the collective work *Brcke zwischen den Völkern. Zur Geschichte der Frankfurter Messe,* published by Rainer Koch, vol. I: *Frankfurt im Messenetz Europas,* compiled by Hans Pohl with the cooperation of Monika Pohle (Frankfurt am Main: 1991).

Yun Casalilla, B.: *Crisis de subsistencias y conflictividad social en Córdoba a principios del siglo XVI* (Cordova: 1980).

Zabalo Zabalegui, F. Javier: *El Registro de Comptos de Navarra de 1280* (Pamplona: 1972).

13

The Development of Walter Mahlberg's Inflation Accounting and Valuation Theories in the Light of Contemporary Critiques by Schmalenbach and Schmidt

F. L. Clarke, O. F. Graves, and G. W. Dean

Walter Mahlberg's 1921 *Bilanztechnik und Bewertung bei schwankender Währung* (Accounting technique and valuation during periods of changing prices) was the first monograph-length treatise on price-level-adjusted accounting. It was recognized only recently as one of the most powerful influences on Henry Sweeney, the earliest English-language writer on the topic. Both Mahlberg's price-level-adjustment technique and his valuation theory have been described and debated previously in the English-language accounting literature (Sweeney, 1928; Graves, 1987, 1991; Clarke and Dean, 1989; Dean and Clarke, 1989). Those discussions focussed primarily on the 1923 (third and final) edition of Mahlberg's *Bilanztechnik*. They did not attempt to reconstruct the development of his ideas. Yet, in 1922 and 1923 *Bilanztechnik und Bewertung bei schwankender Währung* underwent two revisions in rapid succession during those hyper-inflationary years of the great post-World War I German inflation. These revisions were followed in 1925 by a further treatise on the topic, *Die Tageswert in der Bilanz* (Current value accounting). That requires clarification of the relationship between the 1921, 1922, and 1923 editions of *Bilanztechnik* and *Die Tageswert in der Bilanz*.

Mahlberg's revisions of *Bilanztechnik* followed a review of the 1921 edition by Eugen Schmalenbach (1922, review). There, Schmalenbach disavows Mahlberg's claims that certain of his ideas sprang from Schmalenbach's path-breaking work on indexation procedures. It also criticized Mahlberg's inflation-accounting model. Recent translations of Mahlberg's major works provide the opportunity to speculate, *inter alia,* on whether the conventional wisdom that Mahlberg was the "developer of *Goldmarkbilanz*" (e.g., Schmidt, 1924, p. 120), adequately captures his views on indexation accounting. They also facilitate assessment of whether Mahlberg's "scheduled" or "programmed" values, or his "neutralized" values,[1] have much in common with Schmidt's "current costs."

Further they facilitate informed conjecture on what may have influenced the developments of Mahlberg's ideas over the period; first in his 1920 article, "*Wirtschaftsrelativität*" (Economic relativity) containing one of the first references in the German literature to the "rubbery" nature of accounting data during the post-World War I period of inflation. Revisions to *Bilanztechnik* were followed in 1925 by *Die Tageswert in der Bilanz.* The latter was an attempt by Mahlberg to clarify, respond to, reject some and take account of, Schmidt's criticisms of his gold-mark accounting and Schmalenbach's dynamic accounting.

Schmidt was the leading current-value apologist of the German *Betriebswirtschaftslehre,* and a constant critic of indexation solutions. This was a turbulent time in Germany—socially, politically and economically (see Graves, Dean and Clarke, 1989; and Table 13.1). And a period when the German *Betriebswirtschaftslehre* (business economics movement) was actively seeking panaceas for the ills of the hyperinflation. As a result the possibly unusual views of Mahlberg were subjected to criticism by members of the *Betriebswirtschaftslehre,* particularly its leaders, Schmalenbach and Schmidt.

This analysis assesses both Mahlberg's four monographs seriatim and his critics' views. The antecedents of those monographs provide insight to the economic and political setting from which the monographs emerged.

ANTECEDENTS OF THE FOUR MONOGRAPHS

Table 13.1 captures the mood of the period by providing a broad overview of the movements in some main monetary indicators in Germany 1914–1923.[2]

Ex ante: April 1921[3] First Ed., *Bilanztechnik und Bewertung bei schwankender Währung*

Publication in January 1921[4] of the first edition of *Bilanztechnik* had been preceded by the inflationary pressures on the economy and the general impoverishment of the populace associated with the Allies-imposed war reparations of the Treaty of Versailles. These were coupled to the flow-on for Germany from the world wide economic malaise in the early 1920s. The post-1914 wartime price controls were in the process of being lifted—with price decontrols on products from the iron and steel industry having occurred in 1919.

However, that was not the universal experience in respect to the prices of goods and services. Food prices were a typical exception, "bread and bread grains were not decontrolled until 1922" (Holtfrerich, 1986, p. 92; see pp. 87–

Table 13.1
Movements of the German Wholesale Price Index, 1914–1923. (1913 = 1) (W = Wholesale Price Index)

Month	1914 W	1915 W	1916 W	1917 W	1918 W
January	0.96	1.26	1.50	1.56	2.04
February	0.96	1.33	1.51	1.58	1.98
March	0.96	1.39	1.48	1.59	1.98
April	0.95	1.42	1.49	1.63	2.04
May	0.97	1.39	1.51	1.63	2.03
June	0.99	1.39	1.52	1.65	2.09
July	0.99	1.50	1.61	1.72	2.08
August	1.09	1.46	1.59	2.03	2.35
September	1.11	1.45	1.54	1.99	2.30
October	1.18	1.47	1.53	2.01	2.34
November	1.23	1.47	1.51	2.03	2.34
December	1.25	1.48	1.51	2.03	2.45
Annual Average	1.05	1.42	1.52	1.79	2.17

Month	1919 W	1920 W	1921 W	1922 W	1923 W
January	2.62	12.56	14.39	36.65	2783
February	2.70	16.85	13.76	41.03	5585
March	2.74	17.09	13.38	54.33	4888
April	2.86	15.67	13.26	63.55	5212
May	2.97	15.08	13.08	64.58	8170
June	3.08	13.82	13.66	70.30	19385
July	3.39	13.67	14.28	100.59	74787
August	4.22	14.50	19.17	192.0	944041 in mil.
September	4.93	14.98	20.67	287.0	23.9 in bn.
October	5.62	14.66	24.60	566.0	7.1
November	6.78	15.09	34.16	1154	725.7
December	8.03	14.40	34.87	1475	1261.6
Annual Average	4.15	14.86	19.11	341.82	

Source: Statisches Reichsamt: Zahlen zur Geldentwertung in Deutschland 1914 bis 1923 (Berlin, 1925).

88, esp. Table 24, for information on other wartime price controls and their duration). Inflation was out of control, but economic activity was (despite superficial appearances) depressed.

An obviously closely related consequence of that were expressions of general concern over the appropriate accounting measures for determining assessible taxable income or profit. At the beginning of the Weimar Republic fundamental changes to the tax system had been instituted (*Erzbergersche Steuerreform*). There was an attempt to deviate from the Prussian income tax system in which capital gains were exempt from taxation, to something akin to the Haig-Simon (-*Schanz*) income-concept-based taxation system. Taxation issues thus formed a major part of the debate occurring in technical and trade newspapers during 1920 and 1921 (for translations and commentary see Dean, Clarke and Graves, 1990). Mahlberg's "*Wirtschaftsrelativität*" was an early contribution to that debate. But as Schneider's (1992) review of Dean, Clarke and Graves (1990, p. 95) notes: "Nevertheless this [Weimar Republic's] attempt failed because of inflation [hyper] and was soon abandoned."

In this setting of uncertain economic conditions, unreliable income measures, questionable statements of financial position and volatile taxation regimes, ascertaining relevant costing data for determining (and justifying) appropriate prices and appropriate tax strategies were critical policy issues for businessmen and for accountants. Schoenfeld (1992, p. 637) has recently noted that: "during that time period [1921–1923] cost, by and large, did determine prices due to the war-induced shortages and the prevailing attitude, which determined purchasing power behavior under hyper-inflationary conditions." According to Mahlberg (1921, p. vi) the most notable early contributor to that debate was the appropriately named Geldmacher (1920), who had commented on *accounting problems* created by periods of large fluctuations in the value of *money*:

The weighty inheritance of the war, the constantly falling buying power of the Reich Mark is bearing down on our German trading enterprises like a mill-stone. . . . Annual profits are growing, as evidenced by many balance sheets! Mere tricks with figures! . . . Commercial profit and loss accounting is sabotaged and has gone wrong in this day and age. . . . Especially since November 1919 many business people have been complaining almost ceaselessly that the money they are getting their hands on through the sale of their goods and products is often far less than what they have to invest . . . in immediately replacing the goods sold . . . [then, in the context of the 3,000 marks *reported* profits of a piano dealer, he decries] had the dealer not sold his ten pianos, he would not have made *any* profit, but he would now own ten pianos of the same quality [and valued at 100,000 marks], instead of only one [valued at 10,000 marks]. (1920, p. 364)

Bilanztechnik und Bewertung bei schwankender Währung appeared after a period of stable prices in Germany from about January 1920 to March 1921 (see Table 13.1). Some thought price rises had plateaued. But the primary concerns since the end of the war, that conventional accounting failed to incorporate the effects of factor input price rises, spawned the publication of numerous articles in newspapers, trade journals and monographs (see Clarke and Dean, 1986, for details). Dean, Clarke and Graves (1990) produced translations of a small part of that 1920 debate appearing in the technical and trade newsletters. Specifically the debate disclosed anxiety about the "rubbery" nature of conventional profit numbers and the concomitant need for replacement cost data to supplant historical cost information as the "proper" basis for taxation and pricing policy deliberations. Schmalenbach (1922, p. 1) captures the mood appositely:

The indefensibility of balance sheet laws and regulations during periods of inflation has been expounded in the press and technical journals since early 1920. The business community, too, has become increasingly aware of the impossibility of the situation, and a succession of chambers of commerce has demanded an end to the problem. (Reproduced in translation, Graves, Dean and Clarke, 1989, p. 26.)

As a leading member of the *Betriebswirtschaftslehre*, Schmalenbach had first discussed this problem as it applied to internal costing purposes, in a series of articles in 1908. In 1919 his monograph-length treatise, *Dynamische Bilanz* appeared. Although not primarily concerned with the effects of inflation, it contained a section on the need to make adjustments to conventional accounts, particularly for cost and profit determination purposes. And in 1921 Fritz Schmidt's "*organic, substanzerhaltung*" principles appeared in a monograph, *Die organische Bilanz in Rahmen der Wirtschaft* (The organic balance sheet in the framework of the economy). By the end of 1921 the primary German thinkers on these issues—Mahlberg, Schmalenbach, and Schmidt—were injecting the debate with their ideas. As the state of the economy changed, as inflation changed in intensity, impact and importance, it appears their respective ideas also responded in kind.

Ex ante: April 1922 Second Ed., *Bilanztechnik und Bewertung bei schwankender Währung*

Commodity price rises during June and July 1921 presaged a resurgence in the rate of increase in prices in general (Table 13.1) and a deterioration in other monetary indicators. Extensive deliberations occurred throughout 1921 between business and the government. Business and government leaders feared that the social, political and economic systems were nearing breakdown.[5] Business leaders focused on microeconomic factors: the impact recording fictitious profits had on taxation levies; the inadequacy of existing pricing policies; and that excessive dividend payments could result in reductions of enterprises' capitals. Government concern was at a macro-level. The high (albeit fictitious) profits of German industry were acting as a misleading signal to France and the other Allied countries that Germany possessed an adequate capacity to pay its war reparations. Witness to this is the claim by Schmalenbach that Poincaré defended his administration's policies in the French National Assembly (19 January 1922) based, inter alia, on the following:

The enormous dividends paid by German companies proved that things were going well, very well for the Germans, much better in fact than for other countries. Its factories were operating at full capacity, its economic power increases daily, while the State is going to ruin [because of insufficient taxes and unproductive expenditures], the people are getting rich. (Reproduced in translation, Graves, Dean and Clarke, 1989, p. 28.)

Schmalenbach noted that a similar claim was contained in the famous 15 April 1922 letter of the Reparations Commission to the German Chancellor. But he further noted that those claims were wide of the mark and were caused by false profit (*Scheingewinne*) signals emanating from the existing historical cost-based accounting system.

Possibly these issues motivated the formation of a subcommittee of the Reich Economic Advisory Council in May 1921 to draft suitable accounting reforms via a private members' bill. Political haggling intervened and the bill stalled. Into the breach stepped the October 1921 Congress for the Society of Economic Development in Frankfurt am Main, to become known as the *Indexkommission*. According to Schmalenbach's (1922) own account the

conference [was set up] specifically to address the problem of fictitious profits in balance sheets, income calculations and cost calculations, and financing arrangements. . . . [It was] extraordinarily well attended by Reich and government officials, representatives from industry, members from trade associations, chambers of commerce, academic specialists and private businessmen. (Reproduced in translation, Graves, Dean and Clarke, 1989, p. 26).

An Indexation Committee was formed by the *Indexkommission*. It comprised leading members of the *Betriebswirtschaftslehre*, including Schmidt and Mahlberg, and had Schmalenbach as its chairman. The Committee sought to establish:

1. Which of the known index number series was the most suitable for balance sheet purposes?

2. Which of the suggested methods of computation was to be selected for balance sheet conversion? and

3. What were the practical consequences of these changes for accounting and revenue laws?

Graves (1987, p. 48) suggests:

[that i]t was Mahlberg whose voice prevailed: the committee elected to endorse Mahlberg's method of restating accounting values in terms of their pre-war gold-mark value, albeit by the more practicable means of indexation. The task of drafting the report fell ex-officio to Schmalenbach.

The principal conclusions of the report were:

(1) A proper elimination of balance sheet distortions during inflation is only possible if one deflates the value of money to a common measure; (2) Specifically taking the effect outside Germany into account, deflation to the pre-war mark is preferable to other values; and (3) A wholesale index which contains to the greatest extent possible the prices of finished goods as well as the prices of raw materials and which is published monthly and on a timely basis appears sufficient for purposes of balance sheet replacement. (Schmalenbach, 1922, p. 4; reproduced in translation Graves, Dean and Clarke, 1989, p. 27)

Schmalenbach's review of the first edition appeared prior to the 2nd edition of *Bilanztechnik* appearing in April 1922. It was critical in many respects. It reflected many of the arguments catalogued in his seminal price-level adjustment article, "*Geldwertausgleich in der bilanzmäßigen Erfolgerechnung*" (Monetary stabilization in profit-and-loss accounting) published a few months earlier in October 1921. There, Schmalenbach had rescaled beginning-of-the-year balances to year-end price levels and ignored all price and price-level movements during the year. Accordingly, asset and equity data homogeneity could be inferred to be Schmalenbach's primary goal. Income data comparability is a fortuitous corollary.

Ex ante: 1923 Third Ed., *Bilanztechnik und Bewertung bei schwankender Währung*

There may be some conjecture as to the major antecedents of the first two editions. But, there can be little dispute that the hyperinflation, which dominated the thoughts of all in Germany during the latter part of 1922 and during 1923, almost surely influenced recommendations contained in the third edition. Support for this proposition might be inferred from the attendant circumstances.

First, the May 1921 London Ultimatum on Germany's final War Reparations obligations disrupted the presumed price plateau. An unexpected demand for increased repayments in the Ultimatum sent the financial markets into panic, providing the catalyst for the increase in the rate of inflation during the latter part of 1921. In fact, it possibly was the seed of the eventual hyperinflation, which is generally agreed by historians to have begun in June 1922 (Dean and Clarke, 1990, p. 20). Second, although not required by legislation immediately after its recommendation by the *Indexkommission*, proposals for the implementation of stabilization procedures from business, political, and academic quarters were intensifying throughout 1922 and 1923. By October 1922 the mark was no longer regarded as a reliable store of value or a serviceable unit of account. Accordingly, businessmen had begun to transact in other currencies, particularly the US dollar and Dutch guilder. Although informal stabilization of wages had occurred since 1921—every two months during 1921, every month in 1922 and then biweekly in the early part of 1923—in July 1923 the indexation of wages was formally introduced. The congruence of these events has led some historians to claim de facto stabilization existed prior to the official November 1923 monetary reforms (e.g., Kindelberger and Holtfrerich).

Schmidt on Mahlberg and Schmalenbach's Goldmarkbilanz

As well as Schmalenbach, Schmidt, the other leading member of the *Betriebswirtschaftslehre,* was a constant critic of *Goldmarkbilanz* proposals. His ambivalence was a product of the times. During 1920–1923 the volatility of Germany's economy in general, and of its monetary system in particular, spawned considerable diversity ansd short-term allegiances to successively price and price-level adjusting mechanisms. In contrast to many in the *Betriebswirtschaftslehre,* Schmidt was loyal to his proposal of stabilization based on recording physical assets at their current replacement value. And whilst acknowledging that *Goldmarkbilanz* was an improvement on historical cost accounting he constantly lampooned indexing the defects of historical cost accounting (e.g., Schmidt, 1924, p. 197).

Economic Pragmatism and Arithmetical Orthodoxy

To sum up the backdrop to Mahlberg's three editions of *Bilanztechnik, Betriebswirtschaftslehre* responses to the post-World War I price and price-level problems were of two generic types: economic pragmatism and arithmetical orthodoxy. Initially, given the obvious need to replace worn out or destroyed capital, economic pragmatism dictated that firms utilized replacement cost data for costing and pricing purposes. This need spilled over into the external reporting domain, possibly by accident more than by design. Schmalenbach (1919), Mahlberg (1920), and primarily Schmidt (1921) were the primary transporters of this idea into financial accounting. This economic pragmatism phase was displaced by arithmetical orthodoxy. First, by the forward-indexed CPP-type adjustments when the level of prices started to increase dramatically early in 1921 (see proposals by Schmalenbach, 1921, and Mahlberg, 1921). Then, as this rate of increase changed to hyperinflation in 1922–23, the indexation proposals reversed to backward (*Goldmarkbilanz*) techniques—best illustrated by Schmalenbach (1922) and the second and third editions of Mahlberg (1922 and 1923). The focus of this latter reform phase however, shifted from pricing and budgeting to balance sheet reforms. Fictitious profits and excessive tax were now the primary focus. Balance sheet indexation had three visible impacts. It promoted the importance of achieving arithmetical homogeneity in balance sheet data; it evoked increased interest in the balance sheet per se; and it emphasised the need for fairness in tax treatments.

Ex ante: 1925 *Die Tageswert in der Bilanz*

The introduction of the monetary reform measures on 15 November 1923 introduced a new currency, the *Rentenmark,* secured by real assets comprising

German industrial property and agricultural real estate. On the 20 November 1923 the paper mark, which remained Germany's sole legal tender money, was stabilized on the basis of 4.2 trillion marks per US dollar. By the end of December 1923 stabilization regulations relating to accounting and taxation were in force. And in August 1924, a tremendous load was lifted from the German economy when the war reparations were rescheduled under the Dawes plan. Clarke, and Dean and Clarke (1990, p. 29) note that the immediacy of the successful effects of these changes has proven difficult for historians to explain:

Guttmann and Meehan suggest that: "The public's confidence was created by the conviction that the *Rentenmark* was backed by land and industrial property, and this in the public's mind was accepted as a *Sachwert,* as stable value."

[Whilst] Beusch claimed the success was due to: [T]he return to the accounting basis of the peacetime [i.e. pre-war] gold currency. Since the new currency was identical with the former national gold currency as a unit of account, and the government took all manner of steps to ensure its value remained stable, the German people felt itself liberated from the oppressive burden of *astronomical* figures and with *astonishing rapidity* found its way back to reckoning in the old unit of account. The "miracle of the rentenmark" lay in appreciating the *psychological* importance of enabling this return to take place. With a "rye mark" this magic property would have been missed. (As cited in Holtfrerich, 1986, p. 317, *emphasis added*)

By 1925, stabilization of the currency and accounting data had been replaced as the major concerns of businessmen, politicians and members of the *Betriebswirtschaftslehre*. Periods of relative stability evoked suggestions that indexation accounting proposals were no longer necessary. Protagonists of historical and replacement cost proposals came to the fore. But it is important to note that in these so-called "stable" periods, the general price level was still vacillating, and that changes in specific asset prices were moving faster, slower, and sometimes even in the opposite direction to the general price level. In short the price and price-level problem had not disappeared. Price and price-level changes remained a serious threat, albeit more subtle, to both the economy and to the systems of financial calculation.

Schmidt's constant criticisms of Mahlberg's (and Schmalenbach's) *Goldmarkbilanz* proposal had motivated Mahlberg to put the record straight. In the 1925 monograph he sought to counter Schmidt's criticisms by demonstrating that the gold-mark accounting and replacement cost accounting methods yielded similar results. What he did not appear to grasp was that, whereas the results may well be similar mathematically, the essential essence of the numbers, their referents, would be as dissimilar as ever. The congruence of the mathematical outcomes had the potential to give incorrect signals regarding the serviceability of the accounting data.

DEVELOPMENTS IN MAHLBERG'S WORKS

Against that background Mahlberg's specification of accounting techniques emerged with a deliberate focus on rectifying the underlying unreliability at the time of the accounting for the affairs of German companies.

Restatement Technique

1921 Edition of Bilanztechnik

The three editions of Mahlberg's *Bilanztechnik* pursued the problem of the "rubbery" nature of accounting data during periods of inflation first expressed in his 1920 paper, "*Wirtschaftsrelativität.*" In this edition several stabilization techniques were described. The (1921) preferred stabilization proposal was partial and exploratory. It entailed rescaling opening balance sheet data relating only to real, physical items (*Realwerte*), such as Plant, Buildings and Merchandise. Monetary items (*Geldwerte*) and Capital were not scaled. The restatement procedure was based on movements in the price of gold (*Gold agio*). In contrast, the closing balance sheet data for like items were established using "scheduled" or "programmed values" (*etatsmässiger* or *planmässiger Wert*). Mahlberg regarded any resulting increase in paper mark wealth as profit. The principal ideas were summarized in his 1921 monograph (pp. 19–20; see also Figures 13.1 and 13.2).

Restatement was effected by deflating depreciated German marks in balance sheets by the amount of the premium contained in the current price of gold, over the price of gold in 1914, the last year in which German marks were redeemable in gold. Mahlberg maintained that gold enjoyed a fundamental relationship to all other goods that endured over time and at all price levels; a reasonable proposition whilst the currency is backed by a gold standard. This line of reasoning provides one of the links between Mahlberg's views on indexation and his views on valuation. The other was an assumption that during periods of inflation "every firm, willy-nilly, was engaged in a grandiose monetary speculation" (Graves, 1987, p. 25; based on Mahlberg, 1921, p. 35). Thus Mahlberg maintained that the proper management of monetary assets and liabilities would determine whether a firm survived, much more so than how operationally efficient the firm had been. In this respect he was slightly at odds with Schmalenbach whose "dynamic" accounting system stressed the need for measures of operating efficiency to permit timely corrective actions to be taken when they were needed.[6]

1922 Edition of Bilanztechnik

Appearing after the seminal 1921 indexation article by Schmalenbach, Mahlberg's second edition claimed that some of his ideas sprang from the works of his mentor, Schmalenbach. Schmalenbach had reviewed Mahlberg's first edition in the early part of 1922, disavowing the claim that their respective ideas sprang from the "same well." The view that their ideas had a common source seemingly prevails in the Anglo-American literature. Tweedie and Whittington (1984, p. 19) note:

Mahlberg was a pupil of Schmalenbach, and *both preferred the stabilization of historical costs* as a method of dealing with inflation rather than the alternative of replacement cost, although Mahlberg preferred the gold-Mark as the constant unit of measurement, whereas Schmalenbach preferred a unit based upon a general price index, such as was later used in the CPP proposals of the 1970s. (*emphasis added*)

That assessment contradicts the history on several points. It misses the import of the fluidity in authors' views over the crisis years of the 1920s. Second, it fails to recognize that Mahlberg had a preference for "programmed" or "scheduled" values both before and after the hyperinflation, as an alternative to historical cost valuation (further details appear under *Valuation*). Third, it does not seem to take into account Mahlberg's desire to report "neutralized" values in the balance sheet.

Schmalenbach's 1921 stabilization method entailed a forward restatement of the historical cost data for both real and monetary items. Although there is no preferred measuring unit advocated in his 1921 article, numerous possibilities are canvassed, including: retail or wholesale price indices, foreign currency exchange rates, the price of gold and numerous other indexes. His forward-indexing procedure produced the same profit result as the *Goldmarkbilanz* solution, subsequently used by larger concerns during the 1922–1923 hyperinflation, and ultimately recommended by both Mahlberg and Schmalenbach in 1922.

But it should be noted that their change followed the deliberations of the Indexation Committee of the *Indexkommission*. Graves (1987) contrasts the mechanics of both Mahlberg (1921) and Schmalenbach (1921); generally, Schmalenbach's 1921 method entailed:

• Opening balance sheet acquisition values (both real and monetary items) being restated to their equivalent ending paper mark value. *General* index numbers were used;

• Differences between the adjusted opening and closing capital amounts, being regarded as *Profit*;

• Part of the value (wealth) change between the opening and closing balance sheets being regarded as a business profit. Whereas Mahlberg saw it as only a *value adjustment* entry resulting from the *value fluctuation in capital*. Profit variations arising from Mahlberg's and Schmalenbach's methods were due to their different treatment of monetary items;

• Gains and losses on the opening balances of monetary items (Cash, Debtors and Creditors) being included in the Profit and Loss Account.

Figure 13.1
Gold-Mark Restatement of the Inventory Account

Inventory Account

Beginning balance, 100 kg	100	Sales (dr. accounts receivable)	200
Purchases (cr. accounts payable)	200	Ending balance restated, 20 kg (dr. balance sheet)	20
		Loss (dr. profit-and-loss)	80
	300		300

Source: Mahlberg, 1923, p. 103.

The differences are not only explicit, they are indicative of what Schmalenbach had perceived to be significant differences underlying their methods.

1923 Edition of Bilanztechnik

Appearing at the zenith of the hyperinflation, it is not surprising that the *Goldmarkbilanz* indexation method was now strongly advocated by Mahlberg. Clarke and Dean (1989, p. 299) suggest that some officially prescribed form of stabilized accounting was inevitable from as early as 1922 following the Committee of the *Indexkommission*'s advocacy of *Goldmarkbilanz* in late 1921. Detailed illustration and analysis of Mahlberg's preferred backward restatement technique is detailed in Graves (1987, pp. 38–45). For this purpose an illustration (pp. 40–41) from that discussion is instructive:

To illustrate Mahlberg's methodology, if the inventory account contains a beginning balance of M100 representing the cost in gold of 100 kg. of a good and shows at the end of the ensuing accounting period (1) the sale of the 100 kg. for M200 (dr. accounts receivable, cr. inventory) and (2) the purchase of 20 kg. of the same good for the M200 received (dr. inventory, cr. accounts payable) representing a price-level change of 1000%, the M200 ending balance would be restated to M20 "gold" (M200/1000% = M20) resulting in a loss of M80 instead of a paper-mark profit of M100 (sales of M200 less cost of goods sold M100).

The calculation of the M80 loss is shown in T-account form in Figure 13.1.

Mahlberg also demonstrated a gold-mark method by which the nominal values in the accounts might be preserved if one were reluctant to alter the original paper (mark) data. According to this method, Mahlberg introduced restatement accounts that adjoined or offset the various nominal value accounts and effectively restated them by the amount of any monetary gain or loss (real or quasi)

Figure 13.2
Gold-Mark Restatement of the Inventory Account Using an Inventory
Restatement Account

Inventory Account

Beginning balance, 100 kg	100	Sales (dr. accounts receivable)	200
Purchases (cr. accounts payable)	200	Ending balance, 20 kg (dr. balance sheet)	200
Profit (cr. profit-and-loss)	100		
	400		400

Inventory Restatement Account

Cr. balance sheet	180	Dr. profit-and-loss	180

Source: Mahlberg, 1923, p. 108.

that related to them. If the paper-mark data reflecting the activity in the inventory described above, were left intact, for example, the M200 ending inventory would require a M180 valuation entry (dr. inventory restatement, cr. balance sheet) representing the reduction of its paper-mark value to gold (M200/1000% = M20; M200 − M20 = M180). In addition, the M100 paper profit closed to the profit-and-loss account would require an offsetting entry of M180 (dr. profit-and-loss, cr. inventory restatement) to reflect the 80 mark net "loss" Mahlberg would recognize on the account (the M100 gross profit less the M180 restatement difference). The use of a restatement account to achieve the gold-mark results of Figure 13.1 is shown in Figure 13.2.

Valuation—"Scheduled or Programmed" Values
and "Neutralized" Values

Mahlberg's valuation prescriptions have been described "as an anomaly in the development of inflation accounting."[7] However, undeniably there is an intertwining between Mahlberg's restatement mechanism and his valuation concepts. It has been shown that Mahlberg's preference was for a backward restatement in terms of 1914 gold-mark values. Those same gold values influenced his thinking on valuation, especially his "programmed" or "scheduled" value concept. As noted Mahlberg maintained that gold enjoyed a fundamental relationship to all other goods that endured over time and at all price-levels. Graves (1989, p. 24) describes it thus:

Phenomena such as variations in production and consumption, political upheaval, and an uneven progression of general price-level change might temporarily disturb individual value relationships between gold and other goods (giving rise to specific price-level changes), but once economic, political or monetary stability returned, the original underlying value relationships inevitably re-established themselves.

The fundamentally stable long-term relationship between gold and other commodities and the fact that firms engage in a grandiose monetary speculation in periods of inflation were the foundations of his fundamentals of valuation which are succinctly stated (Mahlberg, 1921; reproduced in translation by Clarke, Graves and Dean, 1993):

In valuing assets and equities the continued existence of the enterprise is assumed. The measure of value is gold, based on the *gold agio*. The profit and loss calculation then yields: (1) nominal results; (2) the loss from the decline in the value of the mark; (3) the gains from the same; (4) the overall operating profits for the year, which for most enterprises will probably be negative. The overall results balance indicates that portion of the loss for the year attributable to inflation. The latter may continue or abate during the next year or in the ensuing years. The valuation process is a speculative one in as much as a judgement must be made regarding future price developments. The current [paper-mark] value of an individual asset can (a) have risen at the same rate as the price of gold, (b) have risen at a faster rate, (c) have risen at a slower rate. The accountant must make a judgement as to whether and by how much such specific price-level premiums or discounts will change in the relevant future. . . .

Monetary assets such as cash, bills of exchange, and accounts receivable are to be restated straightforwardly by using the inflation factor.

Items held for resale are to be valued as described above. Speculative items—items that do not belong to the base stock—are to be valued at their current paper-mark value restated in gold marks. . . . Base stocks, on the other hand, are to be entered at their scheduled values, that is net of an extra write down for specific price-level premiums (or if applicable write up for specific price-level discounts), so that they are valued at a paper-mark amount that corresponds to the increase in the value of gold.

Fixed assets are to be entered at their simple gold value. Relative deviations in their current paper-mark value should be eliminated so that valuation is at a scheduled value. . . . Fixed assets should be valued, accordingly, at the price expected to be in effect when they are replaced.

Mahlberg's ''programmed or scheduled'' values were not commonly promoted in the German *Betriebswirtschaftslehre*. Relying on the two assumptions referred to (viz., the fundamentally stable long-term relationship between gold and other commodities and the fact that firms engage in a grandiose monetary speculation in periods of inflation), ''Mahlberg argued that on any balance sheet date two types of inflationary gains and losses lay in a firm's future and affected valuation in the balance sheet as of the current date. These gains and losses related to the nature of assets and included both avoidable and unavoidable gains and losses. Avoidable referring to gains and losses associated with monetary items and non-monetary items deemed *not essential* to the operations of the firm'' (Graves, 1989, p. 25). Thus Mahlberg perceived that the results (including *all* gains and losses) were best measured when the gold-mark equivalent of the current paper-mark ''scheduled value'' of these items was entered in the balance sheet.

In the 1925 monograph, Mahlberg reiterates that historical cost accounting fails (i) as it does not measure gains and losses on monetary gains and losses,[8] and (ii) since depreciation is problematical because there is a failure to match current depreciation with current revenues—something inimical to allowing insight into the efficiency of an enterprise's operations.

Whilst Mahlberg had advocated gold-mark accounting during the hyperinflation, he was now returning to his preferred accounting method. He described it as being premised on ''neutralization'' of values in the balance sheet. By this was meant that ''balance sheet items are pasteurized, that is removed from the living world of price movements'' (Mahlberg, 1925; reproduced in translation by Clarke, Graves and Dean, 1993). Illustration of this notion followed with the example: ''land on which a factory is located enters the balance sheet at the historical cost and remains unchanged at this value (according to traditional accounting practice), that is 'neutralized', in all future balance sheets without regard for price changes. Section 261 of the Commercial Code even permits the retention of neutralization when the value of an item has fallen. . . . [Also cited was the basis of valuing base stock—i.e., stock necessary for the conduct of the business.] A base stock is to be entered at the same value, year after year, that is neutralized'' (Mahlberg, 1925; reproduced in translation by Clarke, Graves and Dean, 1993).

His preferred method comprised: a base stock method of accounting for inventories necessary for the conduct of the business; current value accounting for speculative inventory—that is, inventory held above the base stock (recognising gains and losses thereon periodically); a method of current value-based depreciation accounting being recorded in a ''*Fabrikationskonto*'' (Manufacturing account)[9]; and measuring monetary gains and losses by means of changes in a general index. In the respect of equipment Mahlberg advocates a dual system of depreciation—for reporting (''*Jahresrechnung*'' or annual accounts) purposes depreciation based on historical, ''neutralized'' values are favored. But for pricing purposes depreciation charges based on current replacement costs were to be recorded in the ''*Fabrikationskonto*.'' In both cases the approach was rationalized in terms of trying to reflect the outcomes of the speculative objectives of business. The question of articulation received little attention, an aspect of Mahlberg's work of which Schmidt was critical.

It is interesting to consider Mahlberg's examples combining current and historical cost depreciation of fixed assets at this point. Assume the replacement cost of a depreciable asset, which is being depreciated at 10%, rises from 1,000,000DM to 1,400,000DM:

| Dr | *Fabrikationskonto* | 100,000 | |
| Cr | Accumulated Depreciation | | 100,000 |

| Dr | *Fabrikationskonto* | 40,000 | |
| Cr | Profit and Loss | | 40,000 |

The effect is to charge the *Fabrikationskonto* for the full 140,000DM current value depreciation, but to offset the 40,000DM extra charge in the *Fabrikationskonto* (which is closed to the P&L) with a "gain on price change" so that only the net charge of 100,000DM affects the annual accounts.

If the current value of the equipment were to decline to 600,000DM, then:

| Dr | *Fabrikationskonto* | 60,000 | |
| Cr | Accumulated Depreciation | | 60,000 |

| Dr | *Fabrikationskonto* | 40,000 | |
| Cr | Profit and Loss | | 40,000 |

The net effect of Mahlberg's preferred depreciation mechanism was to have the cost of goods manufactured charged with the current cost depreciation to set the mark-up base for pricing; to have the profit and loss account eventually reflect only historical cost depreciation, and report only historical cost depreciation in the balance sheet. It seems to have been more a method designed to justify cost-plus pricing than a scheme of prudent financial reporting. Despite Schmidt's questioning, Mahlberg's preferred method actually did little other than to retain historical cost.

Graves (1989, pp. 27–28) provides this summary: "Schmidt suggested that Mahlberg's idea of adjusting to a good's 'scheduled value' before restatement to gold opened the way to arbitrariness. He also questioned the certainty of the future losses Mahlberg foresaw and thus the wisdom of recognizing them immediately (1924, pp. 65–68). Schmalenbach on the other hand, questioned the use of the price of gold as a measure of general price-level change (1922, p. 36)." On these issues Mahlberg was critical of Schmalenbach's reluctance to adopt "scheduled" values, but regarded Schmidt's current value model more favorably because of the similarity in outcomes it produced relative to his preferred method.

CONCLUSION

Mahlberg's major research activity spanned a short period of economic, social and political turbulence previously unknown in Germany. The German *Betriebswirtschaftslehre* struggled in this environment to modify existing accounting and managerial methods to aid businessmen and governments seeking solutions to problems that had surfaced.

Two main types of *Betriebswirtschaftslehre* responses were identified—following World War I economic pragmatism dominated; it was displaced by arithmetical orthodoxy with the onset of the hyperinflation. Hyperinflation began with the forward-indexed CPP-type adjustments when the level of prices started to dramatically increase in the middle 1921. Then, as hyperinflation emerged in 1922–23, the indexation proposals reversed to backward (*Goldmarkbilanz*) techniques. Evidence confirms Mahlberg as the "developer of *Goldmarkbilanz*." Focus of the latter reform phase had shifted from pricing and budgeting to balance sheet reforms. Elimination of fictitious profits and excessive tax were now the primary focus of reformers.

Mahlberg's works throughout the four-year period covered both mirror these changes—especially his restatement techniques—as well as depict an individuality and willingness to explore unusual solutions—as evident in his proposals based on programmed or scheduled values.

These initial assessments of Mahlberg's works provide a further research setting for those attempting to explore the influences on the transportation of the main *Betriebswirtschaftslehre* stabilization concepts into the Anglo-American literature, principally by the American, Henry Sweeney. At present it is still uncertain as to which of the three leading German *Betriebswirtschaftslehre* should be accorded the mantle as having had the greatest impact. What is certain is that all three had a large, albeit in some cases subliminal, influence on the development of mechanisms to account for price and price-level changes in the United States and other countries.

NOTES

1. Mahlberg's "scheduled" or "programmed" values and "neutralized" values concepts are explained later in the Valuation section.

2. Table 13.1 was reproduced in Clarke and Dean (1990, p. 17) as part of their attempt to understand how the ideas of the *Betriebswirtschaftslehre* developed during this period of economic, social, and business turmoil.

3. Dates of editions are as stated in the preface.

4. The date that the preface was written.

5. Holtfrerich (1986, p. 334) suggests that it was more the concern for social and political stability that led politicians to search for appropriate monetary stabilization measures.

6. It should be noted at this point that Mahlberg also claims "operating efficiency . . . is the most important purpose double-entry book-keeping serves" (1921, p. 3). This is not surprising, as Mahlberg was a pupil of Schmalenbach.

7. O. Finley Graves, "Walter Mahlberg's Valuation Theory," *Abacus*, March, 1989, pp. 22–30. This work forms the basis of this subsection.

8. With respect to Schmidt's current cost accounting system, Mahlberg had earlier noted in *Goldkreditverkehr und Goldmarkbuchführung* (April, 1923) that "[all attempts

at current value accounting] starting from a peacetime value and a quantity of material assets—fail due to the existence of monetary items, that is, debtors, cash, bills of exchange, creditors, bonds, mortgages, etc., for which is required a third neutral standard in order to measure the influence of devaluation. Apart from that, it is not sufficient to establish the capital value of a firm only with the money value which has been derived from the special index of the individual firm. If one wants to compare the value of one firm with that of another, and this is the ultimate purpose of a balance sheet, then the special index proves to be completely useless since it is directed towards merchandise prices, fixed asset values and other costs of a special firm in a single industry.''

9. In the *"Fabrikationskonto"* all manufacturing costs, including depreciation based on current costs, were matched against sales revenues, with the balance being closed to the profit and loss account.

REFERENCES

Clarke, F. L., *The Tangled Web of Price Variation Accounting* (New York: Garland Publishing Inc., 1982).

Clarke, F. L., and Dean, G. W., "Schmidt's *Betriebswirtschaft* Theory," Abacus (September, 1986); pp. 65–102.

———. "Conjectures on the Influence of the 1920s *Betriebswirtschaftslehre* on Sweeney's *Stabilized Accounting*," *Accounting and Business Research* (Autumn 1989); pp. 291–304.

———. *Contributions of Limperg and Schmidt to the Replacement Cost Debate in the 1920s* (New York: Garland Publishing Inc., 1990).

Clarke, F. L., Graves, O. F., and Dean, G. W., *The Development of Walter Mahlberg's Inflation Accounting and Valuation Theories* (Forthcoming, 1996).

Dean, G. W., Clarke, F. L., and Graves, O. F., *Replacement Costs and Accounting Reform in Post World War I Germany* (New York: Garland Publishing Inc., 1990).

Geldmacher, E., *Bilanzsorgen* (Industrie-und Handelszeitung, 1920).

Graves, O. F., "Accounting for Inflation: Henry Sweeney and The German Gold-Mark Model," *The Accounting Historians Journal* (Spring 1987): pp. 33–51.

———. "Walter Mahlberg's Valuation Theory: An Anomaly in the Development of Inflation Accounting," *Abacus,* March 1989, pp. 7–25.

———, "Fritz Schmidt, Henry Sweeney and Stabilised Accounting," *Accounting and Business Research* (Spring 1991): pp. 119–24.

Graves, O. F., Dean, G. W., and Clarke, F. L., *Schmalenbach's Dynamic Accounting and Price-Level Adjustments: An Economic Consequences Explanation* (New York: Garland Publishing, Inc., 1989).

Holtfrerich, C. L., *The German Inflation 1914–23* (Berlin: de Gruyter, 1986).

Mahlberg, W., *"Wirtschaftsrelativität,"* Zeitschrift für Handelswissenschaft und Handelspraxis (1920–21): pp. 133–36, 182–86, and 195–97.

———. *Bilanztechnik und Bewertung bei schwankender Währung* (Leipzig: G. A. Gloeckner, 1921); 2nd ed. 1922; 3rd ed. 1923.

———. *Goldkreditverkehr und Goldmarkbuchführung* (Berlin: Julius Springer, 1923).

———. *Die Tageswert in der Bilanz* (Leipzig: G. A. Gloeckner, 1925).

———. Schmalenbach, E., *"Die Abschreibung,"* Zeitschrift für handelswissenschaftliche Forschung (1908/9): pp. 81–89.

———. *Grundlagen dynamische Bilanzlehre* (Berlin: Spaeth und Linde: 1919).

————. *"Geldwertausgleich in der bilanzmäßigen Erfolgerechnung," Zeitschrift für handelswissenschaftliche Forschung* (October, 1921): pp. 401–17.

————. "Review of *Bilanztechnik und Bewertung bei schwankender Währung," Zeitschrift für handelswissenschaftliche Forschung (1922)*.

Schmidt, F., *Die organische Bilanz in Rahmen der Wirtschaft.* (Leipzig: G. A. Gloeckner, 1921); 2nd ed., *Die organische Tageswertbilanz* (1922); 3rd ed. (1929).

————. *Bilanzwert, Bilanzgewinn und Bilanzumwertung* (Berlin: Spaeth und Linde: 1924).

Schneider, von D., "Book Review: *Replacement Costs and Accounting Reform in Post-World War I Germany," Accounting Historians Journal* (1992).

Schoenfeld, H. M., "Book Review: *Replacement Costs and Accounting Reform in Post-World War I Germany," Accounting Review* (July, 1992): pp. 636–37.

Sweeney, H. W., "German Inflation Accounting," *Journal of Accountancy* (February, 1928): pp. 104–116.

Sweeney, H. W., *Stabilized Accounting* (New York: Harper and Brothers, 1936; reproduced by Arno Press, 1976); Reprint (New York: Holt, Rinehardt and Winston, 1964).

Tweedie, D., & Whittington, G., *The Debate on Inflation Accounting* (Cambridge: Cambridge University Press, 1984).

Index

About the Editors and Contributors

ATSUO TSUJI is Professor Emeritus at Osaka City University and the former President of the Accounting History Association of Japan.

PAUL GARNER is Professor Emeritus and the former Dean of the Graduate School of Business at the University of Alabama.

F. L. CLARKE is the Dean of Commerce, University of Newcastle.

G. W. DEAN is a member of the Department of Accounting, University of Sydney.

ROBERT GIBSON is the Associate Dean, Faculty of Commerce, Deakin University.

CLAUDIA GORMLY teaches at the University of Sydney.

O. F. GRAVES teaches in the School of Accounting, University of Mississippi.

ESTEBAN HERNÁNDEZ-ESTEVE is Doctor of Science and Economics at the University of Cologne and Deputy Director General of the Bank of Spain.

YASUHIKO KATAOKA is a member of the Faculty of Economics at Daito Bunka University.

MAKOTO KAWADA is the General Manager, Teijin Seiki, and Lecturer, Osaka City University.

C. S. McWATTERS teaches at the University of Calgary.

CHRISTOPHER J. NAPIER is a member of the Department of Accounting and Finance, London School of Economics and Political Science.

GARY JOHN PREVITS is a Professor of Accountancy, Weatherhead School of Management, Case Western Reserve University.

SHIGETO SASAKI teaches at Senshu University.

MARCELL SCHWEITZER is a member of Eberhard-Karls-Universitat, Tubingen.

TSUNEHIRO TSUMORI is a Professor of Business Accounting, Kyushu University.

MURRAY WELLS teaches at the University of Sydney.

XU ZHENG-DAN is an Accountant and Professor, Shanghai University of Finance and Economics.